THE NEXT
WAR ZONE

THE NEXT WAR ZONE

CONFRONTING THE GLOBAL THREAT OF CYBERTERRORISM

JAMES F. DUNNIGAN

CITADEL PRESS
Kensington Publishing Corp.
www.kensingtonbooks.com

CITADEL PRESS BOOKS are published by

Kensington Publishing Corp.
850 Third Avenue
New York, NY 10022

Copyright © 2002 by James F. Dunnigan

All Kensington titles, imprints, and distributed lines are available at special quantity discounts for bulk purchases for sales promotions, premiums, fund-raising, educational, or institutional use. Special book excerpts or customized printings can also be created to fit specific needs. For details, write or phone the office of the Kensington special sales manager: Kensington Publishing Corp., 850 Third Avenue, New York, NY 10022, attn: Special Sales Department, phone 1-800-221-2647.

CITADEL PRESS and the Citadel logo are Reg. U.S. Pat & TM Off.

First printing: September 2002

10 9 8 7 6 5 4 3 2 1

Printed in the United States of America

Library of Congress Control Number: 2002104311

Designed by Leonard Telesca

ISBN: 0-8065-2413-8

To Emily Mulcahy, who was much too
sensible to get involved in any of this.

CONTENTS

FOREWORD

This book is written for a general audience, although there's a lot of history and a few technical angles here that the geek community will find interesting. One of the major challenges in writing all this was keeping the language in plain English. It's impossible to avoid a lot of technical terms when talking about PCs and the Internet. For this reason there is a small glossary at the beginning of each chapter, and all the glossary terms are repeated at the end of the book. While much effort has been made to write all this in English, not Geekish, this has been complicated by the fact that the technology of the Internet is a lot easier to explain in Geekish. But such brevity would be comprehensible to only about 10 percent of the population. So if you don't think you fully understand some technical angle described here, don't worry about it. You're close enough.

The unavoidable technical language is a reminder that the Internet, and PCs (as they are now designed) will never become "appliances." Eventually, all this computing and communications technology will be as simple and hassle free as appliances, but at that point they won't quite be "personal computers" anymore. Then again, a lot of the so-called appliances are not as easy to use as their manufacturers would have us believe. A lot of this has to do with the ongoing microprocessor (the tiny computers on a chip that make PCs work) revolution. Little computers are in most appliances these days, not to mention being a key part of game consoles, cell phones, and automobiles. Some manufacturers have been able to make their computer-controlled products so simple to use that we don't realize (or care) that they are run by a microprocessor. But rapidly moving technology always has what we in the business like to call, "the bleeding edge." The demand for the latest and greatest always brings forth products that have a lot of rough edges. PCs, and especially the Internet, fall into this category. And this isn't going to change anytime soon. The underlying technology of the Internet is not only very complex, it's also murky. No one really knows all that's going on with the thousands of programs that make the Internet work. It's like a game where many of the rules are unknown. Whoever discovers a new wrinkle can do good, or go for the headlines and attempt a monumental bit of mischief.

We've gotten past the point where the main victims of Internet skull-duggery are the major players. The banks, big corporations, and large Web sites have the money and talent to protect themselves. The most likely victims are now the rest of us, and this book is an attempt to give us folks a fighting chance.

Jim Dunnigan

jfdunnigan@aol.com (and about a dozen other e-mail addresses, some going back over twenty years—and some of them still work . . .)

ACKNOWLEDGMENTS

Walter Zacharius came up with the idea, and Bob Shuman kept after me so that it got done on schedule. I would also like to thank several people for helping me gather, or review information for this book. Unfortunately, none of them wanted to see their names in print in association with the subject of cyberwar. They did like the book, though, they just didn't want to deal with the vengeful script kiddies.

CHAPTER 1

Cyberwar and You

Technical Terms You Might Not Recognize in This Chapter

A complete glossary, including the terms defined below, can be found at the back of the book.

Bulletin Board System (BBS) is a computer program that allows users to connect to the BBS via their modems (today this is done via the Internet) and read and write messages from and to all the people using that BBS. The Internet version of a BBS is Usenet, which has thousands of separate forums (for different topics).

Cyberwarrior is any military or government Internet specialist who knows how to make attacks using communications networks (like the Internet) and defend friendly networks from such attacks. Since World War II, this sort of thing has been called "electronic warfare." When the Internet is involved, civilian volunteers are often brought in for this work as well.

DDOS Attack—distributed denial of service attack, using several computers to send massive amounts of data to a Web site. Web sites can only handle a limited number of users at once. Normally, this is not a problem, but if you purposely try and grab all of a Web site's capacity, as in a DDOS attack, no one else can use the Web site.

Server—A computer from which Web sites operate. A server is often just a PC, like the one you use at home, but with special software and a very fast connection directly to the Internet. Basically, any PC can be turned into a server with the right software and a direct connection (which is quite expensive—several hundred bucks a month and up) to the Internet.

1

SysAdmin is short for system administrator. This is the person responsible for keeping a Web site, LAN (local area network in an office), or server going. It's a tricky job, as there are a lot of things that can go wrong, and the software that runs the server, Web site, or LAN must be constantly updated to keep everything running, and to keep the system secure from intruders. There are never enough good sysadmins available, and this produces a lot of Web sites that are very vulnerable to hacker attack.

Zombie is a program hackers slip into poorly protected computers (either a server running a Web site or a PC with a cable modem or DSL connection). There are dozens of different zombie programs, but what they all have in common is the ability to communicate with the hacker who put them there and seize some control over the computer they are planted in. Antivirus programs can spot, and remove, zombie programs.

We are at war. No, this is not about Afghanistan and the war on terror. There is a war being waged via the Internet. And many of you have probably already been victims of the skirmishes that go on every day. It's called cyberwar, and it's got the generals and politicians worried. Because this is the kind of war that can come right into any home connected to the Internet, hundreds of millions of Internet users have something to fret about as well.

Cyberwar is using electronic networks, and information, as a weapon. Or, to be more precise, as part of a weapon system. This form of cyberwar has been around as long as warplanes have used electronic warfare to get past enemy interceptors and missiles. Most of the time we think of cyberwar as something that just takes place on the Internet, but that's not always the case, especially when the military is involved. A fairly recent example can be found in the Afghanistan War of late 2001. Cyberwar (hacking into banks and pro-Taliban servers) was also mixed with Information War (using information and news as a weapon). Very twenty-first century. But, as will be described further on, Information War has been around for thousands of years, and cyberwar for over a century. What's really different is that future cyberwar is likely to visit the personal computer you have at home.

Good News, Bad News

Cyberwar isn't a totally dismal situation. There is some good news. But first the bad news. Yes, there is a lot of hacking going on. Many of you have gotten nasty worms and viruses with your e-mail, which in some cases has damaged your PC. Big Web sites get hit as well, as do parts of the Internet infrastructure. The result is that, at times, you cannot go where you want to go on the Web. Worse yet, pundits like me get in front of a TV camera and go on about even more dire events. Yes, it is, in theory, possible to do massive amounts of damage to the Internet and the computers, businesses, government agencies, and military units also connected to the Internet. But at the same time it is really, really easy to avoid becoming a victim. At the end of the last chapter in this book, the path to (relative) safety is described.

The most vulnerable people on the Internet are those with fast, always-on connections (cable modem and DSL). These PCs are hacker magnets. That's because these PCs are plentiful, generally unprotected, and just the sort of computers cyberwarriors and hackers in general like to take over. The big Web sites and major corporate networks have protected themselves because they have the money and incentive to do so. For example, since September 11, 2001, it's been noted that a lot of hackers from the Middle East have been trying to get into American power-plant Web sites, without much success. The power plants have well-protected Internet operations, and are equipped to detect attackers, often revealing where they are from. But the millions of home users with these fast connections have no way to protect themselves to the same degree. These PCs are the ideal places for cyberwarriors to launch attacks from. If the Middle Eastern hackers can't get into nuclear power plants, they can always put zombies in thousands of home PCs and launch DDOS attacks on military, commercial, and government Web sites and shut them down for days. Actually, a really massive attack might shut down major parts of the Internet for even longer periods, as the remedies for truly large-scale attacks have not been tried under "combat conditions" yet. The "home PC zombies" are a major weakness in the Internet and the most likely battlefield for the foreseeable future. Hostile cyberwarriors can use those exposed home PCs for all sorts of mischief. There are a lot of other weaknesses out there, but none as stark as this one.

But before you go pull the plug on your home PC, there is a bit of good news.

The Internet is a vast and constantly changing beast and, fortunately, you can't make a major attack on it without a map. Today, no one admits to having such a map. This is not to say that such maps don't exist. They probably do, but they are considered military secrets. Unlike military maps, the Internet versions are more like skywriting, they are constantly being distorted by the winds of change that propel the Internet.

With millions of major sites, over two billion Web pages, and millions of programmers, sysadmins, and contributors constantly altering the Internet's content, anyone's map would be a strictly temporary document. Several nations admit to having thousands of soldiers and civilians working on such cyberwar projects, but it's an ongoing effort because you need that many people just to keep the map somewhat up to date. Without accurate knowledge of what is out there, cyberwar weapons are much less effective.

Because of the secrecy surrounding military mapping of the Internet, no one knows how far anyone has gotten in creating and maintaining such a map. It is known that if you put a new server on the Internet, within hours several different anonymous organizations will be probing it. And if you dress up that new server to look like it has some military or government function, expect to get some more serious visits within a few days.

No one is sure if this prompt attention paid to new servers is the result of some military operation, but we do know that keeping track of militarily valuable targets is a standard operating procedure. Who is doing all this probing? There are several likely suspects. The U.S., China, Taiwan, and Japan, to name a few, have announced the formation of cyberwar units. However, there are also millions of people who dabble in scanning the Net, and hacking into sites that seem interesting and vulnerable. This is now considered a hobby, despite the dubious legality of some of this activity. If you equip the new server with good intrusion detection and monitoring tools, you can find out who is sniffing your site. Some of the scanners will be traced back to known cyberwarrior bases in foreign countries, but most will be from all over. They might be script kiddies (teenagers with easy-to-use hacking tools), marketing companies, or hobbyists. There are a lot of people poking around on the Net, for a lot of different reasons.

The script kiddies just want to use your server or PC for their own amusement. The marketers want to get to know and exploit you. There are also fairly harmless hobbyists poking around who are simply curious to know more about the Net and are generally just inquisitive. But in the case of a war, cyberwarriors want to use your PC as part of the battlefield. Constantly scanning the Internet for new developments is part of the ancient military scouting tradition, and it is a useful one. Here, cyberwarriors use many poorly guarded servers and always-on PCs for storing cyberweapons and other tools. If your PC or server meets their criteria, you go on a list (and are then scanned periodically), or put to use right away. Cyberwarriors have to constantly test their tools and weapons, as well as train their troops; your PC could be part of some cyber–boot camp or training exercise. You'd probably never know it. One of the most critical skills a cyberwarrior has to learn is stealth. Surprise and getting away undetected are valuable weapons.

Bringing the War Home

Yes, the next war is going to take place in a new battlefield: your own home. Cyberwarfare is the battle for control of the Internet and the large chunk of our economy that now depends on this network of computers. This includes the computers you use at home. There have already been skirmishes. Those computer viruses and worms you hear about are just a few of the weapons that can be used to shut down computers, destroy data, and damage the nation's power plants, factories, fuel supplies, communications systems, and even parts of the armed forces. Most of the weapons unleashed so far have been used by amateurs. Government cyberwar units constantly develop even more damaging tools, and plan to use them on a huge scale. You won't see these super viruses and monster worms until there is a cyberwar because, once unleashed, the victims can develop an antidote. But when first released, these military-grade Web weapons will do enormous damage. Taiwan has boasted that it has an arsenal of a thousand military-grade computer viruses. In 2001, just three viruses caused over 60 percent of the cyberwar Internet attacks reported that year. Terrorist organizations are known to be investigating this angle for their attacks. Note that the first cyberwar weapon to infect a large number of computers (the Brain virus) was developed in Pakistan in the 1980s. Pakistan still has a large population of skilled programmers and Internet experts. Most of these fellows are just out to make a good living. But some back Islamic radicalism and organizations like the Taliban and Al Qaeda. Now you can understand why the U.S. government maintains several separate internets, completely independent of the one we all use. This expensive operation is justified because it provides more protection to military internet users.

Why would your home computer become part of the cyberbattlefield? Because one of the most common tactics is to secretly place zombie programs on as many computers as possible. Once the signal is sent, these zombies use your computer to send out the weapons that will overwhelm government, business, and even some military computers connected to the Internet. The zombies are less likely to be detected on home computers. At any given time, thousands of personal PCs will harbor zombies. Military-grade zombie programs are not harmless to their hosts; they will probably destroy personal data on their host PC after they have done their dirty work on the Net.

The civilian bad-guy hackers are doing this for kicks, the military cyberwarriors are doing it to help win a war; to inflict maximum damage on another nation's economy and armed forces. There are so many zombies around in peacetime because the civilian hackers are always trying to outdo one another in the cleverness of their actions. Things like how many PCs have they planted zombies on (some hackers brag of over a thousand zombies deployed on PCs they have secretly broken into). One of them may be yours. While home PCs are easy to use for storing zombies, there's more prestige in planting zombies in well-protected military or commercial sites. Despite the fact that the zombies are more likely to be discovered and cleaned out if stored in professionally run sites, there are dark-side hotshots who want to show off. Same with writing computer viruses. But hackers are really attracted to things they can do with simple tools like Web browsers or e-mail programs. For example, one nasty, and simple, bit of software was created by a hacker to show that e-mail provider hotmail.com's security could be penetrated with three lines of code. Taking up the challenge, another hacker came back with a routine that did it in one line of code. This particular hack allowed the perpetrator to take over anyone else's e-mail account. Note that hotmail.com is a Microsoft operation. More on that angle later.

But there's more. Despite the obvious danger, more government and business functions are being controlled via the Internet. It's cheaper and more efficient to pay traffic tickets, check public records, and the like, on the Net despite the fact that it makes America the most vulnerable nation when it comes to Net warfare. And as often is pointed out, it would take a cyber–Pearl Harbor to wake most people up. Of all countries, however, the United States benefits the most from use of the Internet, and, fortunately, it has the largest number of skilled Net operators. But in the first cyberwar, this won't be enough to stop an attack on America, and no one knows how much damage will be suffered.

Let's Just Do It

The freewheeling, "let's just do it," attitude of the Internet's early days created many of the security problems we have today. Back in the '70s and '80s, when a lot of the fundamental Internet software was designed and created, security was not a major concern. The Internet community was small and everyone knew everyone. Moreover, no one really expected all this "experimental software" to become the stuff running a worldwide network serving several hundred million users. In truth, the whole thing just sort of snuck up on everyone. Who knew?

The freewheeling attitude toward security and quality control was made worse by two other unexpected developments: personal computers and Bulletin Board Systems (BBSs). Both of these phenomena were responsible for creating the huge audience for the Internet once the government made the Internet, then called ARPANET (Advanced Research Projects Agency NETwork), available to the public in the late 1980s. PC software was always seen as, well, sort of amateur. In the beginning, a lot of it was. But PC users didn't care that much. They tolerated the bugs and worked around the problems. The BBSs got millions of people in the e-mail and networking habit before the Internet showed up. So when the easier-to-use World Wide Web software appeared in the early 1990s, the Internet took off like a rocket. It was too late to tighten up the security or reduce the bug count. As the Internet audience approaches half a billion in 2002, we find our past truly coming back to haunt us.

The Internet was built to survive natural disasters and war, even nuclear war. It was not designed to survive assaults from millions of malicious users. Where did all these nasty people come from? The crackers and black-hat hackers (the bad guys) came from the same place as the good guys. From all over. The Internet enabled people of like mind and intentions to, well, network. In the past, there would be small communities of programmers all over the country (and world), largely brainstorming new products and working in isolation. This changed as more software developers got on ARPANET. This ability to connect with like-minded people in far-off places was intoxicating. All of a sudden you were not just one of a few geeks in your neighborhood, but part of a virtual worldwide geek horde. This was heady stuff, but no one anticipated that eventually the bad guys would form their own worldwide organizations as well.

The Bad Guys and What They Do

Once the Internet audience reached a few million (in the 1980s), those who wanted to damage it began to discover one another on the Net. And then they proceeded to do what malicious, asocial creeps usually do: mass vandalism and mindless destruction. While the effects of a virtual community helped speed the building of many good things on the Internet, they also allowed those with destruction in mind to get together and build their weapons more efficiently. For years, it was thought that the first Trojan horses and viruses, spread around on the Net to destroy people's data, were the work of demented loners. Eventually the realization came that even loners like to get together, and the ability to do so anonymously via e-mail and chat rooms had great appeal to most of those interested in Internet vandalism. Creating malicious software became a group effort and more powerful vandalware was the result.

To better understand the destruction that the bad guys can commit on the Internet, you have to understand the vocabulary of Internet warfare:

Trojan horses are programs masquerading as another, legitimate, program. Someone would modify a program that, for example, told you what day of the week it was for any date in the last two hundred years. The modification would add routines that did something cute, or nasty. Before the Internet came along, Trojan horses were an annoying form of vandalism you had to watch out for. There were many variations, but the basic idea behind Trojan horses was to get a program you didn't know about, or want, onto your PC. Trojan horses were first used as pranks, and performed harmless practical jokes (like having bugs crawl across your screen). But during the 1980s, the Trojan horses turned nasty; some destroyed data and programs. Some Trojan horses, once you ran them, would spread by modifying another program with the Trojan horse routines. At about the same time the Trojan horse creators began rapidly spreading their infected software via the BBS systems. Before that, most people were not online; most of the software was exchanged via floppy disk. Once BBSs became popular, distribution became faster, and Trojan horses got onto the (then new) hard drives. Out of all this came the antivirus software industry. Even now, however, most PC users still don't bother with antivirus software.

Viruses are what Trojan horses evolved into. A virus attaches itself to a legitimate program or document (for example, a Microsoft macro virus is embedded in word processing or spreadsheet files). In the 1990s, as Trojan horses began to spread via the Internet with such speed that the catch-all term for them changed and they came to be called "computer viruses." The computer virus was an accurate term, as the medical definition is of an organism (like influenza) that will attach itself to a larger and more complex organism (like you) and use its new host to do nasty things and spread itself again. Not all viruses that prey on humans are harmful; some are actually useful. But we rarely hear of those. For much the same reason, we only hear of the nasty computer viruses.

Worms are viruses that don't attach themselves to other programs. For example, the logic bomb is a program that is hidden on a computer system and activates when certain conditions are met. At that point, the logic bomb goes off and does something. Usually something very bad. Logic bombs are generally inserted by a programmer that has legal access to the computer in question. Managers are always worried that an unhappy (and recently fired) programmer will leave a logic bomb that will go off if the departed programmer is no longer around to tell the logic bomb to keep waiting. When the logic bomb does go off, it does something unhelpful, like deleting payroll records or doing more subtle damage to business records. Those who create the logic bombs often get caught, and, in recent years, more of these wayward lads are being sent to prison.

Zombies (sometimes also called "bots," as in "robots") are a form of Trojan horse. Unlike real Trojan horse programs, zombies are usually controlled (via the Internet) by the person who inserted it rather than being left to operate automatically. Zombies are powerful programs that provide the intruder with a variety of capabilities. The common features are easy access to the invaded computer, the ability to launch attacks from the invaded computer, password-protected chat rooms, and storage for the invader's files (stolen software, pornography, hacking tools). Many other features often show up on the dozens of zombie programs available on the Internet.

Vampires are worms or viruses whose sole purpose is to run so intensively that the infected computer can't do anything else. The results are like what happens when too many programs are run at once on your PC: it becomes very sluggish. A vampire running on a Web server will insure that most people trying to reach Web sites on that server will time out (drop connection due to no reply) because the vampire has slowed the server so much.

Sniffers   are hacker tools that just collect information entering and leaving a computer (usually a server). The information is then sent to whoever planted the sniffer. Sniffers are good for picking up passwords and user IDs.

Buffer Overflow Exploitation   is a technique whereby you send a certain type of data to a Web server and trigger a software flaw (which is common in many Microsoft products) that allows you to sneak in a virus or zombie program and, in effect, get inside the server despite defenses. There are many other types of bugs that can be exploited in this fashion. When these flaws are discovered, the publisher tends to quickly provide a fix. But sometimes it takes awhile, and in the meantime damage can be done. A major fear among cyberwarriors is that the enemy will find one of these flaws first, and that they will keep quiet about it. If no one else stumbles across the flaw, the people who know about it have the makings of a powerful cyberweapon.

There are more hacker tools and weapons, but you get the idea.

Cyberwar

There hasn't been a cyberwar. There have been lots of skirmishes, but nothing approaching what an all-out battle over the Internet would be. What would the first cyberwar be like? Let's be blunt, no one really knows. But based on the cyberweapons that are known to exist, and the ones that are theoretically possible, one can come up with a rough idea.

A successful cyberwar depends upon two things: means and vulnerability. The "means" are the people, tools, and cyberweapons available to the attacker. The vulnerability is the extent to which the enemy economy and military use the Internet and networks in general. We don't know who has what cyberwar capabilities exactly, although China and the U.S. have openly organized cyberwar units, and both nations have lots of skilled Internet experts.

Vulnerability is another matter. The United States is the most exposed to cyberwar attack because, as a nation, we use the Internet more than any other country. That's the bad news. The good news is that if an attacker ever tried to launch a cyberwar by assaulting the U.S., it could backfire. This risk has to be kept in mind when considering what a cyberwar might do. Recall military history. The Pearl Harbor attack in

1941 actually backfired on the Japanese by enraging Americans and unleashing a bloodthirsty response that left Japan in ruins. The lesson of the original Pearl Harbor is, if you're going to hit someone this way, better make it count. If your opponent is bigger than you, and gets back up, you could be in some serious trouble.

There are some cyberwar attacks worth considering. Shutting down the Internet itself is possible, although unlikely, because then additional attacks via the Internet would be impossible. So whatever kind of cyberwar might unfold, the Internet itself would be left alone, or would be the last thing to go. Another scenario would be to take down most of the Internet access in a single country, although an attack like this on just the United States would be a formidable undertaking. Here, however, the United States makes use of several separate internets (the regular Internet, four separate government internets, and internet 2, the experimental, next-generation internet). Taking down the main Internet won't do as much damage to the other internets; while the economy would suffer tremendously, government functions would be less damaged. That is, unless the enemy makes an extraordinary, and successful, effort to penetrate and attack the government internets.

With the Internet still intact, all manner of mayhem could be accomplished. We've already seen worms and viruses destroy enormous quantities of data. This would be done more quickly and on a larger scale in wartime because of the larger number of more destructive viruses and other attacks launched all at once. The destruction could include taking many key military, government, and commercial Web sites down. Other cyberwar weapons could be used, like DDOS attacks and special viruses for destroying routers and other specialized computers that keep the Internet going.

It's important not to lose sight of the fact that just about any Web server or PC connected to the Internet can be hacked into. There are many cases of individuals or small groups of hackers getting into hundreds of servers over a short period of time. These instances are the ones where the hackers are caught. What makes a lot of people nervous is not knowing how many people do this sort of thing without ever being detected. We know this happens because some attacks are discovered long after they took place, and some arrested hackers give details of past undetected attacks. One reason many attacks are not found in peacetime is that the average Web site is more likely to be down from the usual screwups (hardware or software failure or human error) that require a server reboot than from a hacker attack. It also remains the case that the well-protected servers get hacked very rarely, while Web vandalism is much more prevalent for poorly protected servers. But in wartime, there would be no doubt that most computer problems were the result of cyberwar attacks. The damage and disruption would be too widespread and intense to misinterpret.

Beyond Web sites, there are many industrial and communications facilities that depend on computers to keep functioning. Transportation sites include the handful of rail yards that support most of the nation's rail traffic. Truck traffic can be crippled by attacking the computers controlling fuel supplies (refineries, pipelines, storage sites, and distribution systems). Hitting these fuel targets would also hurt air transportation. Commercial aircraft can be hampered by getting into the computers used for the air-traffic control system. The extensive maintenance systems for commercial aircraft are also dependent on Internet-connected computer systems.

The majority of PCs in American businesses are connected to some kind of network, and usually have an Internet connection as well. So the number of potential targets is enormous, as is the degree to which our daily lives would be affected. Many businesses can operate without their computers, but not very well and not for very long.

Non-Internet communications are also quite vulnerable. You may not want to take down the Internet, but shutting down separate financial systems, like the Federal Reserve system, would freeze up the local and international financial operations of many companies. The Federal Reserve is acutely aware of the vulnerability of their money transfer system. After years of planning and preparation to upgrade their network, they decided, at the last minute (in March 2002), to change plans and dump their reliance on Microsoft software. Microsoft operating systems were seen as too vulnerable for something as vital to the national economy as the Federal Reserve network.

For all those operations that are not highly dependent on the Internet, it is possible to interfere with the electrical-power system. The power plants themselves often have some remote-control capabilities, a lot of it via the Internet. Same goes for the power-distribution system, which has a small number of large power transformers that, if used the wrong way, are damaged. It takes months to build replacements for these transformers, and there are only a few spares for the two dozen or so transformers operating in North America. Finally, there are those oh-so-vulnerable space satellites and their computer-controlled ground stations. Interfere with communications to these birds and you take away GPS navigation, weather reporting, spy satellites, and some phone and television networks.

The Major Unknown

No one has ever attempted a major cyberwar attack. No one even knows exactly how vulnerable the key targets described above really are. Remember, the enemy would have to find flaws of which the people running these targets are unaware. The administrators of the target sites have some advantages in that they have full control of their servers. Security systems on these servers tend to be changed or upgraded regularly, making it more difficult for anyone planning a cyberassault. An attacker would see many attacks fail because between the times the attack was planned (based on information gathered weeks or months before) and carried out, too many changes would have been made in the target servers.

The side with the best information about the state of the Internet, especially key, enemy sites, will be the most successful. What the professional cyberwarriors plan on doing is unleashing their cyberwar weapons when it is clear that working the cyberangle will provide an edge. This means that more cyberwar action will be seen in smaller wars, or even when there isn't a declared war. So far, this has been done in the United States especially by taking advantage of wireless networks popular in many less-industrialized nations. The wireless systems can be more easily hacked into and played around with. This worked in the war against Iraq in 1991 and Serbia in 1999. The war on terrorism features a lot of detective work via the Internet, and the war in Afghanistan was over quickly because of the ability of American forces to rapidly create instant, wireless voice and data networks in Afghanistan. Although this was not mentioned at the time, these networks were ready to resist attempts to hack them. Such attacks never came, but the troops were ready.

Other nations find it useful to steal valuable data from the numerous commercial, government, and military sites in America. This is actually cyberspying, and has been going on for several generations. But with the Internet, and the many other networks now in use, electronic spying opportunities are much greater today. Since spies don't want to be detected (so they can return for more secrets later), this espionage also serves as scouting for damaging cyberwar attacks.

For the Internet itself, only the industrialized nations are heavily dependent on it. For that reason, Japan and South Korea are more concerned about a cyberwar attack from North Korea than the other way around. Heavy Internet use just makes it more expensive to attack the nations with large Internet dependence. And this dependence will only grow, as it is clear that heavy use of the Internet provides a major boost to economic growth.

The Most Likely Cyberwars

Nuclear weapons have kept the major nations from going to war with one another for the past half century. That will probably continue. But cyberwar provides an opportunity to fight an anonymous war against another nation. This has been done in the past, largely by quietly supporting opposition or terrorist groups in enemy nations. The key here is hiding your tracks. It is thought that the highly damaging Code Red virus of 2001 came from China. The origin of the virus was traced back to China, but China denied any responsibility. Code Red did much less damage in China because there the operating system of choice is Linux, and Code Red only attacks PCs using Microsoft software. This makes it easier for a nation like China to launch cyberattacks on the United States without fear of the weapons coming back to hurt China's growing Internet infrastructure. China, unlike other nations hostile to America (North Korea, Iraq, and Iran), has a large and growing Internet presence. China has thousands of skilled Internet programmers, and has admitted it is putting together military units for developing and using cyberweapons. So the next time there are tensions between the United States and China, there might be an outbreak of nasty, and hard to trace, cyberwar attacks on the United States. The only problem China faces with this approach is that if its weapons hit other nations as well, and were China found out, the diplomatic backlash would be damaging. Even if attacks were made only against the United States and were not traced back to China, China would still be the chief suspect. It would be a case of China being the only nation with the motive and means. Of course, China could always slip Iraq, Iran, or North Korea a CD full of choice cyberweapons and wait for those nations to take a shot at America. And the Chinese are no doubt aware that America could launch its own anonymous cyberattack on China. You wouldn't be able to hide the effects of such a covert war, nor the scrambling of diplomats to bring the undeclared war to an end. It will happen.

There is also fear that terrorists will try a major attack via the Internet. This has not materialized. Yet. There are a lot of Internet-savvy people in, or sympathetic to, terrorist organizations. Most terrorist groups are known to be enthusiastic users of the Internet. Osama bin

Laden and Al Qaeda have long made use of the Internet (and said so publicly before September 11, 2001). The lack of terrorist attacks via the Internet is actually indicative of the amount of skilled manpower you need to create and execute an original attack. Remember, once a new virus is created and released, or a newly found Net software's vulnerability is exploited, high-profile sites (that would be most attractive to terrorists) usually are the first to adjust their defenses. Pulling off a damaging cyberwar attack requires talent and technology. Without doubt, a terrorist organization will eventually manage to put together such a group and something grim may happen. Will it be sooner rather than later? Note that in late 2001, there was a noticeable increase in scanning and probing of U.S. and European power plants from locations in the Middle East. Someone's apparently trying to get into a nuclear power plant and cyberblitz it.

The current terrorist threat is from Islamic and Arab countries, which tend to have the least developed Internet resources (in terms of Internet use and Internet experts). But if the terrorists have money, there are any number of criminal gangs who will deal with anyone. There's also the possibility that an espionage effort might obtain some of the military-grade computer weapons (especially viruses and other cyberweapons). At the end of the Cold War, both Russia and the United States were surprised at the number of traitors there were on both sides who did it for money.

China is unlikely to provide cyberweapons for Islamic terrorists because China has its own Islamic minority that has been fighting Chinese domination. But since China has cyberweapons that can really only be used against American targets, who knows what might happen in this department.

The Usual Suspects

The people who do perform most of the damage on the Internet are either a small number of criminals, or a large number of troublesome teenagers and antisocial creeps with computers. The cybercriminals are a small bunch, a few thousand people. Most of them specialize in low-tech scams employing lots of spam or misleading Web pages. Big-time Internet criminal scores (taking more than $100,000) tend to be inside jobs. Most of the cybercrime losses are actually in the form of labor costs to get vandalized Web sites back in operation, and lost business while these sites are down. Companies, by the way, are more willing to calculate and announce these losses than they are to publicize large thefts of money.

Even before the arrival of the Internet, it was the practice of large financial institutions to keep such thefts quiet (and eat the loss), rather than risk loss of public confidence. This attitude continues to prove problematic for police and the FBI. In fact, the FBI is pushing for a law that would allow companies to report potentially embarrassing hacks without fear of a Freedom of Information request dragging it out into the open. Again, we see how the Information War angle is closely linked with cyberwar issues.

The most visible Web vandals are the millions of script kiddies and low-level criminals who use the readily available hacking and stealing tools available on the Internet, where this group provides a lot of the background noise. If you are monitoring an intrusion detector on a server (or even your own PC), you'll see a lot of scans and probes. With a little training, you can learn to spot the activities of the pros, and the much more abundant noise and nonsense generated by the amateurs. As a practical matter, the professional hackers will hide behind the wall of noise created by all the script kiddies and other amateurs who are scanning and hacking. There are a lot of thrill seekers who don't do much harm; they spend most of their time sniffing about the Internet without much of a clue as to what they are doing. The professional hackers aren't going to come after your home PC, but the amateurs might. That's not much consolation if one of these wannabe geeks trashes your hard drive, or gums up your Internet connection while they try to use your PC to shut down their high school Web site.

It takes the full- or part-time effort of over ten million people to keep the Internet going. Most of these folks are pretty knowledgeable about how the Internet works, and more than a match for those who are destructive. Except in one area: the black hats and script kiddies have the element of surprise. This makes all the difference. And if the cyberwarriors attack, the good guys will have to absorb that first hit. The Internet, and the people who make it work, have proven very responsive and capable when hit with major assaults. But this capability does not come cheap. The overtime bills, not to mention the wear and tear of all those all-nighters, is very expensive. It's one reason why about half the people who become programmers leave the business within ten years. There are less stressful ways to make a living.

The people who are really going to get hit when (not if) there is a major cyberwar attack are the hundreds of millions of Internet users. Most of them have no technical staff (as do companies and governments) to help repair the damage. Those who take the last chapter of this book to heart will be in better shape, but most Internet users see their PCs and Net connections as appliances. They just want to use it, not make maintaining and understanding it a time-consuming chore. What will probably happen in the wake of a cyberwar, or something like a major terrorist attack on the Internet, is the emergence of disaster recovery companies. There is already a small industry for this sort of thing; they help recover data from a dead hard disk or provide geeks to make house calls and unscramble the damage from a nasty virus or other computer catastrophe. But this is expensive (at least a few hundred dollars, and often a few thousand, per job), and some data is lost for good and much aggravation and angst remains behind.

What Can Be Done?

If home users are the most vulnerable targets in a future cyberwar, what can you do to protect yourself? As will be explained in the final chapter, there are a few things that will eliminate most of your vulnerability. The short version of this is (all necessary details in the last chapter):

1. Turn off the scripting. This what most computer viruses currently use to damage home and business computers. This applies mostly to PCs using Microsoft operating systems, but some 90 percent of PCs do, which is why most viruses are written to attack Microsoft software. But scripting can be exploited by a virus on Macintosh and Unix computers as well.
2. Use an antivirus program. It is something that will reassure you if your PC is acting up and you suspect a virus or other intrusion. Most of the time it's something else, but peace of mind is worth the cost of an antivirus program.
3. Keep your software up to date (with the free updates). Most software publishers make it easy to get these updates over the Internet.
4. And, finally, if you have a fast Internet connection at home (usually cable modem or DSL), get a firewall program. You, my friend, are the main target of any future cyberwar. Yes, I know there are millions of people like you, but for reasons explained later in the

book, your PC is ground zero for the opening attacks in a cyber-war. Get yourself a firewall program and you'll probably be able to sit the war out.

Starting in the next chapter, you will find all the intriguing details.

CHAPTER 2

Where Cyberwar Came From

percent of the speed and storage capability of today's cheapest ($500) PC.

Nodes are one (or more) servers (see Glossary) that serve up the information for a Web site.

Cyberwar is quite ancient, but the word is relatively new. The term is derived from "cybernetics," which began being used early in the twentieth century to describe relationships between people and machines. "Cyber" is the Greek word for "pilot." When computers came along in the late 1940s, cybernetics was a word in vogue, and "cyber" began finding its way into the language as a prefix for anything involving computers. By the 1990s we were hearing newly coined terms like "cybermanagement," "cyberschool," and "cyberwar." But cyberwar is something that's still in the process of being invented. Put simply, cyberwar is the use of all available electronic and computer tools to shut down the enemy's electronics and communications. No holds barred, anything goes. What's new about this area of warfare, however, is the use of computers and other electronic gear. The objective, as it has been for thousands of years, is to disrupt enemy communications. In the past, this meant chasing down enemy messengers or using enemy bugle calls and counterfeit enemy flags to send deceptive signals during a battle.

This is an important point, for the most common methods of waging cyberwar don't involve computers or electronics. Stealing passwords by overhearing someone or riffling through a desk is very common. A lot of this is now called Information War, which you see played out during political campaigns as spin, deception, and outright lying. Information War also plays a major role in how cyberwar is fought because deceptive or disruptive messages have so many electronic mediums (radio, TV, telephone, and the Internet) to operate over.

Throughout human history, communications have always been a key military weapon. With time, the ability to verbally transmit massive amounts of complex information, and later write it, allowed humans to create organizations larger than those found anywhere else among animals. A tribe was roughly equivalent to a herd or pack. But a kingdom was so large that it could not be run by being within sight of all the other members. Managing a large organization required new forms of communications. The ancient empires didn't have telephones or the Internet, of course, but they did have long-range communications. American Indians used smoke signals and Africans used drums. Three thousand years ago, the first empires set up networks of towers that used smoke, fire, flag, or even voice signals to quickly send messages from one tower or hilltop to another. With these systems, a king or emperor would know within a day what was going on anywhere within hundreds of miles. This was a key tool for governing such a large area. If raiders invaded your lands, they had little looting time before imperial troops advanced on them. Simply knowing about communications systems kept many raiders at bay, and the emperors' subjects offered their loyalty, happy for the protection the system provided.

These ancient communications networks were vulnerable, however. A thoughtful invader would send in small units of troops to seize signal towers (or hilltops from which the enemy sent flag or light signals to other towers over long distances). On the Internet, that would be a DDOS attack. If communications could be cut, the invading army would be able to do a lot of damage before the imperial forces were alerted and mobilized. The Mongols, who conquered most of Eurasia in the thirteenth and fourteenth centuries, were particularly interested in destroying enemy communication networks before they attacked. The Mongols themselves used relays of mounted couriers that would work wherever their armies were on the move, but they would use the signal towers as well once they had captured an area. The Mongols also energetically protected their own communications. Protecting your own ability to communicate is still a key strategy for any cyberwarrior. Being able to talk to your own troops while the enemy cannot talk to his has obvious advantages, and always has.

Most histories don't talk about communications systems, but without them, these ancient empires could not have survived. The networks were obviously not high tech, but they were expensive and there weren't too many of them. And they worked. Also at issue was the speed at which information could be disseminated. The ancient emperors were the only ones who could afford the expense of building and staffing hundreds of signal towers to quickly send and receive messages hundreds of miles across the empire. Any potential rivals in the empire had to use slower communications (usually a guy on a fast horse). Information has always been a powerful weapon. And the guy who got the most information fastest was a lot more powerful than those that did not.

Alexander the Cyberwarrior

Some 2500 years ago, the Macedonian conqueror Alexander the Great understood how to communicate agendas with the help of word of mouth. In an ancient public relations context, Alexander wrote his own press releases, as it were, in official letters to his sometimes rebellious subjects back in Greece. Getting letters like this from the king was itself something of a novelty, and as copies were made and posted in the marketplaces throughout Greece, the king was seen as a thoughtful and successful fellow. Alexander also carefully crafted directives for his new Persian subjects, which had the same effect as the letters to Greece. Modern media barons are very aware of the need to create "buzz" to meet consumer expectations, just as in the distant past people without twenty-four-hour media channels eagerly sought news. Back then, travelers knew they could get a free meal if they had information to share. Putting a spin on news isn't a product of the cyberage at all; the technique is over three thousand years old. The ancient Egyptian pharaohs had their version of events permanently painted or carved on huge monuments. Alexander was aware of this technique and it probably influenced his thinking. The pharaohs were thinking long term, for those monumental press releases were often erected years after these wars and battles actually took place. Since there were no investigative reporters back then, and the pharaoh had a monopoly on this mass media, the pharaoh's version lasted for thousands of years. Additionally, the Egyptian people were conditioned, after centuries of this kind of news management, to believe the "official" version of events.

It's only in the last few decades that archaeologists have uncovered the spin in the pharaohs' claims. For example, we now know that the pharaohs would often present a version of events that, in addition to being false, also made that particular pharaoh look better than he deserved. The best example of this occurred in 1287 B.C., when pharaoh Ramses got ambushed by a Hittite army at Kadesh (in Syria) and barely escaped with his life. Ramses came home, said he had won a great victory, and had that version of history painted on walls and carved into monuments. This deceptive version of the battle was accepted until the twentieth century, when archeologists dug up evidence to the contrary.

A thousand years after Ramses, Alexander began his own campaign to get his interpretaton of events accepted as the real thing. The Greek cities that dotted the eastern Mediterranean contained a more educated population than did ancient Egypt. The literacy rate, still only about 15 percent, nevertheless allowed written communications to travel quickly. Greek rulers before Alexander found it useful to post letters reporting on government activity in the center of an urban area. Most Greek cities were democracies, so you had to keep the voters (adult men, who were even more likely to be literate) on your side. The letters were then copied and carried to lesser cities and towns to be read, or spoken to those who could not read. By Egyptian standards, news zipped around the Greek cities at high speed. However, even at this juncture in the history of communications, it was the technique used, and how well you used it, that was most important. When Alexander's father, Philip of Macedon, managed to conquer the Greek cities in 338 B.C., he found himself on the losing end of an Information War. A lot of Greeks didn't like Philip, or the idea of being ruled by this Macedonian. Many of these critics were literate. Philip could never put a favorable spin on all the nasty things Greeks were saying about him (mainly that he wasn't Greek). Eventually Philip was assassinated (in 336 B.C.). His son, Alexander, came into a perilous situation. But early on, Alexander gave people reason to call him "the Great." While Philip stepped on a lot of toes while conquering Greece, Alexander came onto the scene as a young man without a lot of malodorous baggage. Philip favored treachery and mass murder to get his way, while Alexander was less bloody minded and more attentive to his public image. Alexander was also seen as more Greek than Macedonian. Alexander had been educated by eminent Greek scholars and it showed. Moreover, Alexander was, like his father, a very active guy: a hustler with all manner of interesting propositions in one hand, and a sharp sword in the other.

Before any of these hustles could catch up with him, Alexander gathered the army he inherited (and that he could no longer afford to support) and invaded the Persian Empire. Invading a rich neighbor in a desperate attempt to extricate oneself from political problems at home is an ancient gambit. It is also a modern one. Although it didn't work for Saddam Hussein in 1991 (he owed Kuwait billions of dollars and couldn't pay it back), it did work for Alexander the Great. Alexander maintained his position as king of Greece largely through his army of professional soldiers, which he didn't have the money to pay for. Rather than disband most of his army, he marched it into Persia.

The Persian War worked better than the Gulf War because Alexander was a much, much better military commander than Saddam. Alexander won nearly all his battles, unlike Saddam Hussein, who lost most of his. But it also helped that Alexander used some primitive, but effective, public-relations efforts.

Here's what he did: Alexander had a staff of what we would today call public-relations experts; he took them along with him during the war. The ancient publicists then composed letters about the war for the cities back in Greece. In "personal letters from General Alexander at the Front," the Greeks got a version of events that made Alexander look better than he was; at least, they softened the blow when there was bad news (like casualties from victorious battles, or the need for reinforcements). The letters were often accompanied by some of the loot Alexander was plundering from the wealthier Persians. Providing a newsletter of sorts worked. Alexander's campaign against the Persians went on for years, and Greeks continued to support him. There were no rebellions back in Greece while Alexander was in Persia, even though many Greeks were still upset about being ruled by a Macedonian. Alexander also took a team of historians with him on his campaigns as well, which is why today we know so much about what he did and how he did it. Team Alexander was generally pretty accurate and fair in describing the Greek military operations, which not only provides essential material for us to study the wars in our time, but they also demonstrate a valuable step forward in the evolution of fighting with information that is especially recognizable with regard to cyberops.

All successful commanders in antiquity not only parlayed content, they also engineered the network that distributed information. Alexander the Great was known to go after as much information about his opponent as possible. Alexander not only wanted to know the usual stuff, like where the enemy army was, who was in it, and who was leading it, he went after additional details, like the loyalty (to the emperor) of the various provinces he and the emperor's army had to pass through before meeting for combat. Alexander wanted to know what the weather was usually like in the land he was invading and what crops were grown. He was able to make good use of all this information. Anyone attacking, or defending, on the Internet must do the same. The more you know about what you are dealing with, the more successful you will be. During the Persian campaigns, Alexander won the Information War, and it was not a matter of luck.

The Persians had, for centuries, considered the Greeks a nuisance, not a major threat. While Alexander collected massive amounts of information on how the Persians operated, the Persians remained largely ignorant about the capabilities of the Greeks. Big mistake. Like a modern-day information warrior, Alexander noted the vulnerabilities in the Persian information systems. Think of the provincial governors and officials as servers on the Internet. They expected certain kinds of information to come their way at certain times. If you find out what the weaknesses of some of the provincial governors and officials are, you can compromise them. Neutralize or take over enough provinces, and eventually you have control of the system (the Persian Empire). Yes, Alexander had to fight a number of battles, and besiege a number of cities, but winning battles does not defeat something like the Persian Empire. What Alexander did was understand how the system worked, and then developed ways to take it over. While the Persian Empire was, technically, an absolute monarchy, in reality, the many parts of the empire did not speak the same language or have the same loyalty to the emperor. The provincial governors and royal officials were all looking out for themselves. You could say that Alexander was simply a better politician than the Persian emperor. Alexander used his army as just another tool, along with promises of future rewards, blackmail, or whatever else he could come up with. Many other conquerors, like Hannibal, or the British generals during the American Revolutionary War, won most of their battles, but ultimately lost because they were not able to bring down the system they were up against. Empires are, like the Internet, mostly about software, not hardware. Find out how to crash the system and the enemy is left, so to speak, staring at an error message on his computer screen. Alexander understood systems better than his opponents. For example, a large Persian fleet in the eastern Mediterranean threatened Alexander's ability to get supplies and reinforcements from Greece. Alexander could not buy or build a fleet to match the Persian ships, but Alexander did understand that the Persians depended on a small number of fortified ports to keep the fleet running (food for the thousands of sailors, shipyards for repairs, ability to find shelter in harbors to escape storms). Alexander concentrated on taking ports such as these, and the fleet surrendered to him because their needed access had been disrupted. Alexander's diplomacy against the Persian emperor's officials and provincial governors also showed how Alexander used information campaigns against the enemy. The Persian Empire is often thought to have fallen because of Alexander's military campaigns, but that was not the case. Alexander took the empire apart, piece by vital piece. In its place he created a better system. Alexander cracked the system from Afghanistan to Egypt and the entire region was never again the same.

The concept of "cracking a system" is a twentieth-century invention. Doing it is ancient, but being able to explain it is new. This is not as strange as it sounds. The whole idea of probability only evolved in the last few centuries. Alexander the Great, however, was again ahead of the curve with regard to statistical analysis, which was in itself a nineteenth-century development. Alexander, like many successful people of antiquity, had skills (like accurately figuring the odds) that worked, which no one at the time could really explain. He was also a leader. Alexander was from a family that had produced talented individuals over many generations. He had the benefit of good genes: he was smart, athletic, and good looking. His father believed in education during this Golden Age of Greek intellectual development, which, surprisingly, was not universally praised at the time. Alexander, however, was taught by some of the most accomplished scientists and thinkers of the day. He also had to "prove himself worthy" to inherit his father's kingdom, because in Alexander's day there was not the concept of divine right to the crown; Alexander had to compete and prove himself. He did, and ever since, Alexander's accomplishments have been considered outstanding. But it's only been in the twentieth century that we began to understand exactly what he did. Among other things, Alexander built his own powerful information network, and hacked his enemy's net as well.

Alexander was not only admired by people of his time, but those with exceptional skill borrowed Alexander's techniques. The Roman politician Julius Caesar, two centuries later, used Alexander's techniques to take over the Roman Empire. Julius Caesar had a keen understanding of the power of information. His history of the campaigns he led in Gaul (modern-day France, Belgium, and adjacent areas) were so well written that, for centuries, it were considered the definitive account of the creation of a unified France, one that was not wholly Germanic or Celtic. With time, it was understood that the main reason Caesar wrote all those letters back to Rome about the campaign (for inclusion in a book) was to enhance his political standing. Indeed, Caesar, like Alexander, was extremely adept in using and controlling information. Caesar was, in fact, a master of spin, and he parlayed this talent into placing the entire Roman Empire (and the demise of the Roman Republic) under his own control. Like Alexander, Caesar knew how to make himself look good while outmaneuvering his opponents. The exploits of Alexander and Caesar made a lot more sense when, in the twentieth century, the concept of systems analysis was developed. These two ancient hotshots figured out how to hack the systems they lived in. Today, we take it for granted that many people can hack the Internet. And that's all because we also take it for granted that systems exist and have vulnerabilities. But all this stuff about systems and hacking them is nothing new. It's been around for thousands of years.

Khan of the Information Warriors

Perhaps the most spectacular "Information Warrior" of antiquity was Temujin (Genghis Khan) and the Mongol Empire he created. The

Mongols conquered lands from Hungary to China, from Russia to the Middle East. It was accomplished with a decisive use of communications. Temujin collected information (intelligence) with the intent of relaying it to to the commanders who needed it as quickly as possible. He used spies and far-ranging scouts, but what changed the rules for the twelfth century was the effective implementation of long-range communications. The nineteenth-century American pony express was similar, as the Mongols also used riders to carry the mail thousands of miles. The Mongols established remount stations at twenty-five to fifty mile intervals. Travelers possessing a "tablet of authority" (an official pass in the form of a small, wooden panel) could get fresh horses and supplies at these stations. Tooting a horn before they reached the next station told the station contingent to have a new horse and saddle waiting. An individual rider could cover over 200 miles a day, and the use of fresh riders (a few were on call at each station) allowed important letters to cover over 400 miles a day. This system allowed Mongol generals to control troops over an enormous area. Such a system also allowed Temujin to quickly organize a campaign using widely separated forces, as new remount stations could quickly be set up. At the time, most rulers depended on their spies or travelers from neighboring areas to give them warning of an enemy gathering forces for an attack. More established armies used a tower system, or a slower pony express operation, but Temujin could organize a major campaign long before an intended victim could get wind of it. Unleashing armies on an unprepared enemy was yet another Mongol advantage. Normally, it took a local ruler weeks to assemble all of his troops from their farms and towns. When the Mongols hit without warning, the defending troops assembling piecemeal were chopped to bits before they could put together a full-strength army. Thus, Mongol speed multiplied the effect of Mongol armies and this became history's first record of the significant impact of speed. It is the essence of an attack on the Internet: The more speed you have, the less capable the defense is.

Edward the Great Communicator

Shortly after Temujin died, Edward III of England came to the throne. In a period where there was no electronic media, or printing, it was difficult to use modern propaganda techniques (like massive advertising or saturation coverage using print, radio, and TV). Edward managed to run a masterful public relations campaign throughout his reign anyway. His main tool was the proclamation. This was a common medieval device, but usually it was a means of proclaiming new laws and regulations. The proclamations were transmitted to the people via public readings at fairs, town squares, and other public functions. Edward used proclamations simply to report on how he was doing while fighting the Hundred Years' War in France, and in general. The proclamations were purposely written in simple language the common people could understand. Edward reported his successes, his tribulations, and point of contention with the French. This Medieval (fourteenth-century) version of CNN, plus all the loot English soldiers brought back from France, created tremendous enthusiasm for the war. Effective propaganda wasn't Edward's only networking tool. He also had the advantage of a much more effective government; again, it was networking.

This was because the Normans (French-speaking Vikings from France) had conquered England in 1066. The Vikings were an enormously enterprising people, and supported the concept of efficient organization. They took England, which was, like most European kingdoms, a patchwork of Roman, German, and Celtic laws and government practices, and put it all in order. France, in comparison, remained cumbersome and inefficient, and because of its larger size offered more varied governing issues. By 1337, therefore, when Edward II kicked off the Hundred Years' War, he had already ripped out all of England's existing systems and was working in a comparatively streamlined environment in which to do business. He used one system of law throughout the nation, a parliament, an efficient system of taxation, and a paid, professional army. He also had quicker information in his kingdom than the king of France did and better tools to get it. When Edward III went to war across the channel, France had dozens of different legal systems, several parliaments (none as useful as England's), and a hodgepodge of duties and responsibilities among the feudal lords. Edward was able to divide and conquer in France by playing these mighty nobles against one another. Moreover, the English could raise more troops much more quickly than the French (who depended on feudal obligations, not soldiers serving under contract).

Edward III would recognize the Internet for what it is: a very useful tool for communications and command. He would appreciate the cyberwarriors of today, because he was waging their war before the term was invented. Since humans had not yet developed our current tools for systems analysis and rapid transformation of systems, whoever adopted a fundamentally new way of doing things first had a huge advantage. Back then, tradition had much more clout than it does today. Initiative was frowned upon, and many things were done the same way year after year simply because that's how they were always done. As the English hammered the French during the Hundred Years' War decade after decade, some French leaders realized that the game was being played by new rules and the French were not keeping up. Some of these insightful leaders did adopt some of the superior English military techniques (like a professional, paid army), but it wasn't until the fifteenth century that the French kings realized that some serious reform was needed. At that point, the English could no longer do as they pleased in France and the war was over.

Electric Warfare

One reason Europeans (and their colonies the future United States) became major industrial, economic, intellectual, and military powers on the planet is that more of these people adopted the heretical notion that systems should change. In most other parts of the world, change was seen as somehow unseemly and wrong. China was the best example of stagnation because of rigid adherence to tradition and resistance to innovation. Change brought on the Industrial Revolution in the nineteenth century, and the Information Revolution (which the Internet is part of) in the twentieth century. By historical standards, the jump from smoke signals to the Internet was a rapid one. It took less than two centuries, from the beginning of the Industrial Revolution to the Internet Age.

Until the nineteenth century, the signal towers were still the only way to build a long-range communications network. Although signal towers using mirrors or flags were being used in most places by then, enabling more information to be sent over the communications network, information wasn't moving any faster than it had two thousand years earlier. At this point, even businessmen were using these networks. But then the first electronic communications network arrived in the mid-nineteenth century. The telegraph was a major revolution in communications, on the same scale as the Internet. Even the telephone didn't make as big an impact as the telegraph did in the 1840s. In fact, the telephone (1870s) was basically just a more expensive version of the telegraph and, for many decades, only businesses, wealthy individuals, and governments could afford it. But the telegraph was mass communication; cheap enough for everyone to use, at least for emergencies. Government and business made the most use of them, and here's where cyberwar begins to escalate: the telegraph began being used with regard to espionage during wartime. Tapping telegraph lines became part of mission instruction for long-range cavalry patrols hidden behind enemy lines. For the mathematically inclined, devising and breaking secret codes became something of a hobby; and when applied to war in a war zone, the truth was, the ciphers of the nineteenth century weren't all that difficult to crack.

A century ago, the wireless telegraph was invented. You couldn't cut the wires on this one, but it was a lot easier to tap into. It was during the twentieth century that governments became serious about developing secret codes that were a lot harder to break. But not hard enough—the United States and Britain broke the German and Japanese codes during World War II.

Electronic communications networks are now over 150 years old. The first was the telegraph network. This one could only be directly used by skilled operators (called, literally, "telegraph operators") who knew Morse code as well as how to use the equipment. Some four decades later, the first telephone networks began to appear. While anyone could be a user, the requests for connections had to go through operators. Subscribers to local telephone companies called the human operators in order to be connected to other subscribers. At the time, this was considered as amazing as computer networks are today. It was only in 1878 that the first local telephone exchange (in New Haven, Connecticut) was opened, two years after the first practical telephone device was demonstrated.

It took only five years before distant cities began to get connected. At this point, a human operator was still needed in order to connect subscribers from two distant telephones. For example, in 1883, the first long-distance calls took place between New York City and Chicago. This was followed in 1884 with a network linking New York City and Boston. In 1915, the first transcontinental telephone "net" between New York City and San Francisco opened for business. The first transoceanic telephone call was made in 1926, between New York City and London. It was not until the late 1890s that the dial telephone replaced the "ring up the operator and make your call" system. In fact, the last hand-cranked telephone exchange did not go out of service in the United States until 1983. The telephone companies themselves did not become sufficiently automated to allow long-distance calls without using operator assistance (direct dialing) until 1951.

It's only been in the past few decades that all the telephone systems have been computerized. Before that, you had to connect with several people in order to talk with someone far away. Once computers were put in charge, that quickly changed. But it was then discovered that the computer programs could be fooled much more easily than the human operators could. There had always been people trying to pull various cons and deceptions on human operators, of course, but you needed automated systems before the first true hackers could go to work.

At the beginning, hackers didn't use personal computers to attack the phone network; personal computers hadn't been invented yet, and it was difficult to get telephone company access to the computers they did use. Rather, the "phone phreaks" of the 1960s used handheld, battery-powered devices that emitted the various electronic tones that the telephone company used to control the long-distance phone net. Even if some of the phreakers could whistle the tones, anyone could use the various electronic boxes. All one could really do with this phreaking was to make long-distance calls for free. But that was enough to attract a lot of people to phreaking. This battle between telephone companies and phreakers goes on to this day, even though the phone system attackers equipped with personal computers get most of the attention.

The century-old telephone networks then became subject to other forms of cyberwar, mainly in the form of phone taps. These were used legally and illegally to gain an advantage in commercial and military matters. Phones were also used to send misinformation. It was easier to disguise one's voice than one's person. But the telephone network itself was basically secure. Phone users could not get into the software that ran the huge telephone networks.

Where the World Wide Web, and All Our Problems, Came From

The World Wide Web (aka "the Web," "the Internet," and "the Net") was not planned. It came from three different directions, in pretty much an unpredictable fashion. It's a strange tale, and it's true.

First came timesharing computers, which were developed in the early 1960s. This was a natural development of the extremely expensive (by current standards) computers of the day. It was very costly to have any of these multimillion dollar beasts idle for a moment. In the late 1950s, researchers figured out how to make timesharing systems work, and by the early 1960s could run more than one program at once. It didn't take long for programs to appear that allowed the exchange of text messages and even real-time chat among users at different terminals. However, these systems were limited in use to the groups of people using the same computer. No cyberwarfare problems here, and this is where e-mail and instant messages began, although only between people using the same computer.

By the 1960s, the idea of hooking up computers via telephones became more popular. Modems had been around since 1955. The first modems were built to link the United States air-defense system together. But these first modems were large, very expensive, and slow (110 baud). The only people who could really afford this sort of thing were businesses. Not a mass-market item at all. General use would not happen until the technology got a little cheaper. A lot of the research on computer networks was funded by the U.S. government, a project that later became the Internet. During the 1970s, commercial (business to business) networks were developed. Companies like Tymshare, Compuserve, and Telenet appeared and hooked companies up to mainframe computers that provided a wide array of business software and database access. These were all run by professionals; if there was any hanky-panky, it was by insiders. These systems were not nearly as easy to hack into as the Internet. Still no threat of cyberwar.

But in the late 1970s, the game began to get interesting. What was about to happen was totally unexpected. In effect, three different online systems were developing. The obvious ones were the commercial networks (for businesses) and ARPANET (a government-funded experiment to create a robust communications system in case of a nuclear war). But the third angle was completely unexpected: the BBSs (Bulletin Board Systems) run by individuals. All three of these systems eventually fused into what we now call the World Wide Web (the graphic version of the Internet). And all the problems we have with Net security and cyberwar come from how these three different concepts of the online world merged.

In the end, the modern Internet was created piece by piece. For example, in 1962, AT&T released a commercial modem (a few thousand bucks for 300 baud). You needed modems to cheaply connect computers via the telephone system. But modems stayed slow and expensive until the law was changed in 1975, allowing anyone to connect to the phone system without dealing with the telephone company. Before this, the telephone companies made it very difficult, and expensive, to use a modem. As a result of this law, and the introduction of personal computers in the late 1970s, the Hayes company began making cheaper modems in 1977, and they established standards for consumer-grade modems. The modems sold very well, but mostly to businesses that wanted a cheaper connection to the expensive online computer-services companies like Compuserve.

Then, in 1978, the first BBSs (bulletin board systems) were up and running. Created by PC hobbyists mainly to see if it could be done, this simple idea set off another revolution. These systems used PCs to run a BBS program, which allowed other PC users to call into the BBS with telecommunication (telcom) programs to leave, and read, messages (on the bulletin board) as well as send and get files (programs, data, pictures of naked women, whatever). The only other piece of equipment needed was a modem, which enabled the PC to send and receive data over a phone line. When the first Hayes modems came out in the late 1970s, the price quickly came down to under $500. The first of these modems were aimed at personal-computer owners. This goes on to show another example of the huge impact the introduction of PCs had in the late 1970s. The early modems were slow (300 baud, or about thirty to thirty-seven characters a second, versus 56,000 baud in the late 1990s), but they brought people together. Within a few years there were thousands of BBSs in operation, and some of the more popular ones had multiple phone lines and were charging small monthly or annual fees for use. By 1990, there were over 30,000 BBSs, mostly in the United States. The vast majority were run as hobbies by their operators. This was in the spirit that had arisen early among many computer professionals and hobbyists, an attitude of sharing and public service. This attitude would be carried over to the World Wide Web, for that's where most of the BBS operators and users ended up. But through the 1980s and into the early '90s, all the wild stuff later associated with the Web (hacking, user enthusiasm, and new stuff), was played out with the growth of the BBS community. There was one big difference, the BBS world was a lot smaller, and the technology was more complicated than what we see on the Internet today. The Web is mass market, the BBS scene was largely for nerds, or people willing to struggle with the rough end of computer technology.

Even as the BBSs were being invented, however, the commercial data-communications services were creating yet another online community. In 1979, Compuserve, noting that its business network was pretty much idle after the end of the workday, decided to provide access for consumers at night and on weekends. At $12 or $24 an hour (depending on the hour), it wasn't cheap ($20–$40 an hour in today's money), but it did begin creating a worldwide community of those who could not get to where the government was: the Internet. At the time, the Web was still a Department of Defense research project (ARPANET). This project began in 1969 and, by 1971, was up and running with twenty-three host computers ("nodes," that you could call into) at major universities. ARPANET didn't send its first e-mail message until 1972, and it didn't reach a thousand nodes until 1984. During the 1970s and '80s, the commercial networks like Compuserve were much larger. Even the BBS community was larger than the Internet during the 1980s.

Compuserve then began finding out that letting outsiders onto its timesharing system during the evenings had led to the first incidents of what today we would call hacking. Users could write software, test it, and then run it on the Compuserve computers. Being let loose on Compuserve's computers was too tempting, however, for hackers to play nice. The hackers immediately began revealing flaws in Compuserve's security and, before they could become too malevolent, Compuserve blocked access. Nevertheless, it was a warning of things to come.

During the 1980s, commercial services like Compuserve (and a much smaller rival that eventually became AOL) were *the* networks to be on. The year Compuserve came online, the Internet introduced BBS capability (they called them newsgroups). But as active as the newsgroups were, the "forums" on Compuserve were where the action was. A major reason for this was that the commercial networks attracted a better-educated user. And because one had to pay for access, the hackers who often disrupted BBS and Internet discussion groups were usually kept at arm's length. At this point, the Internet was still restricted to universities and the Department of Defense.

This is not to say that a well-educated group would always be angels. There was a high incidence of boisterous arguments ("flames") and highly technical user discussions. By 1989, with only two million online users of the commercial services, including many (perhaps half) who were actually business users enjoying the nonbusiness parts of the commercial services, the total number of people online was only some five million. The majority of online users were not on the commercial systems, or the Internet, during the 1980s. No, most modem owners were on a totally unexpected network, a net of Bulletin Board Systems (BBS). The BBS was a totally unexpected, grassroots use of PCs, modems, and telephone lines.

Over 100,000 BBSs existed at one time or another from 1978 to the present. But by the early 1990s, the BBS community and the commercial services were fighting it out for market share. Although the commercial services were somewhat easier to use than BBSs, that was changing. BBS software was being created by thousands of energetic, and independent, programmers. These were the members of the PC generation who were revolutionizing the software business. By 1990, graphic programs (like Windows or Macintosh) were appearing, making it easer to get online and use all that BBSs had to offer. The big appeal was price and a sense of community. Most BBSs were free, although a very popular one would be difficult to get on during prime time. This gave rise to another hacker's tool: the auto-dialer program.

Created to help get onto a BBS when all the modem lines connecting it were full, the auto-dialer program automatically kept dialing until you got in. Another program that appeared first for BBS users was the offline reader. This program grabbed all waiting BBS messages and e-mail and then logged off. This was considered good manners, as it allowed more people to connect. However, the most popular use for BBSs was file transfer. The BBS era was also the Golden Age of "shareware" (programs written and freely distributed with the idea that, if you liked it, you paid for it). The 1980s also saw the appearance of inexpensive scanners, and the photo content of magazines like *Playboy, Penthouse,* and *Hustler* quickly appeared on BBSs for downloading as files. The most popular downloads (from the BBS to a user's computer) were pictures of naked women and shareware programs.

In the mid-1980s, the BBS systems evolved into its own version of the Internet in the form of FidoNet, which at its peak (1995) had over 50,000 nodes (BBSs supplying messages from their local users). FidoNet was remarkable because it arose spontaneously in a universe of independently owned BBSs. Many BBS sysops (system operators, the guys who ran the BBSs) agreed to install the FidoNet software, which then collected the BBS's bulletin-board messages and e-mail and forwarded them to other FidoNet systems. Within a day, every FidoNet BBS had everyone else's bulletin-board messages, and had delivered e-mail as well. FidoNet was typical of the ideas and software that programmers created from the late 1970s to the early 1990s. Before the huge explosion in Internet newsgroups, there was an equally large expansion of topics in FidoNet (and several similar systems') interest groups. BBSs, and commercial systems, also hosted chat rooms before this became a hit on the Internet.

The kind of explosive growth of Internet software and concepts we all remember from the 1990s was played out in more primitive form during the 1980s with the BBS community. Since the arrival of the Web, FidoNet has shrunk (to about 10,000 BBSs, mostly outside the U.S.) because of the greater popularity of the Internet.

Meanwhile, through the 1980s, ARPANET continued to grow and evolve, but it was still essentially a government-funded research project.

The term "Internet" wasn't even coined until 1982—but once it had been, there was growing pressure to open it up to everyone. It wasn't until 1986, however, that ARPANET started opening up the Web to people outside of Department of Defense employees and their contractors. This is the point where the all-inclusive Internet became a reality. Now a standard set of electronic protocols made it easy for any network to connect to the Internet (which was all the Internet was, a collection of separate networks that could talk to one another).

ARPANET ceased to exist in 1990 and the Internet as a public network began. The introduction of the domain name System in 1988 made access easier; previous to that, reaching any Internet site meant typing in its numeric address (like 123.456.789.0). With the domain name server system, you could find a host computer with the old numeric address, or the name (mydomain.com).

Many businesses immediately saw the advantages of the Internet because what the ARPANET research project had done was to solve the problem of communicating between different networks. There was no standard for computer communication via telephones, and businesses were increasingly keen to communicate with suppliers and customers electronically. The many incompatible computer systems made this difficult, but the Internet solved the problem. After the Internet opened up to outsiders in the late 1980s, it was corporations that began to look into ways to make use of all this useful and free (the government had not patented the Internet it had paid for) technology. Making it free was done on purpose, for the idea was to get as many people as possible to use the Web. Meanwhile, into the mid-1990s, the major buyers for BBS software were corporations, who used BBS systems the way the Internet is now used at work. While the Internet was useful and its software was free, it was not all that easy to use.

But the Internet was basically a command line (think DOS, typing out arcane commands to get the computer to do anything) interface and was intimidating to many potential users. That changed between 1989 and 1993 as the Web browser was developed. The browser was a graphic front end for the Internet, having the same effect as replacing DOS with Windows software. All of a sudden the Internet was a lot easier to use. Increasingly, hosts were designed to be accessed only via a browser. After the first free browser (Mosaic) appeared in late 1993, the growth of Net users exploded.

At the end of 1988, there were 100,000 host computers, and it began to grow after that as the government let more people access the Internet. In 1993, when the browser showed up, there were 400,000 Internet host computers. By 1994 it was 600,000. In 1995 it was a million and 1.7 million in 1996. The next five years saw explosive growth. By the end of 2001 there were 12 million active Web servers. At that point, over a billion Web pages were available on the Net and there were 400 million users worldwide (135 million in the U.S. alone). The number of U.S. online users has surged from 6 percent of the population in 1993 to 42 percent in 2001. In that year, about one-third of economic growth in the U.S. was made possible, either directly or indirectly, through the Internet.

Several things happened at the same time to enable this explosive growth. Most important was the availability of cheaper and faster modems. In 1989, there were some 7 million modems in use, and that was after twelve years of companies shipping cheaper and faster modems. But in the 1990s, standard modem speed went from 9600 baud to 56,000 baud. The price of a modem went down to under $50 and shipments exceeded 50 million modems a year. In 1993, the U.S. had 12.6 million modem users, the next year it was 16.4 million. By 2000, over half the households in the country were online.

The Windows operating system (3.0) in 1993 was also a significant arrival on the Internet scene. This Windows software shipped with the majority of the millions of new computers bought each year. With Mosaic or Netscape Web browsers also available, all the user had to do was click the browser icon and they were online. With user-friendly Windows, far more people were willing to "play" with their computers, and once they headed to the Web with their browser, they were hooked.

In late 1994, the Netscape Corporation released its first commercial browser. It was available as a free download, but only 5 percent of the people who used Netscape initially downloaded it (although the download angle made for great publicity). Most people got it with their new computer, and Netscape made this happen by quickly cutting deals with all the major computer manufacturers. The manufacturers were only too happy to do this as it was obvious the Mosaic browser was an enormous success and that Netscape had managed to build an even better one.

Another major change brought about by the Web is that students no longer comprised the largest chunk of users. In late 1995, 3.3 million people connected to the Internet via a university. As a result, 6 percent of Americans eighteen to twenty-nine years old used the World Wide Web, but only 1 percent of those over fifty. While 8 percent of Americans with a college education used the World Wide Web, only 1 percent of those with a high school degree did. By 2001, the characteristics of the average Web user much more closely matched the demographics of the general population.

As the '90s went on, computers got cheaper, the Web grew larger, and there was more and more to do with a browser. BBS use shrank as users found they could do the same things more easily on the Web. The BBSs themselves either turned into ISPs (Internet Service Providers; to provide Internet service to their BBS users) or disappeared. Many of the BBS sysops (system operators) were happy to set up Web sites, which did what their BBS did, but with a lot less hassle. Moreover, a Web site gave the sysop a much wider audience. This was not all positive, for the BBS communities were often local and clannish (even if they rarely met face-to-face). But on the Web, all manner of odd, and often abusive, characters could, and often would, come by. Expenses were a lot lower, and BBS experience often provided users with a head start to golden opportunities in the dot-com boom. Overall, the sysops made out just fine.

Commercial services either turned into ISPs or went out of business. AOL connected to the Internet in 1994, although they had been using the Internet to transfer e-mail for several years. The e-mail connection, in fact, was forced on the commercial services by their corporate customers, who told them one way or another to get this kind of interconnectivity or else (or else the corporations would do it themselves and maybe not need all those thousands of commercial user accounts). Many businesses already had used commercial networks and BBS technology, but they found the Internet much easier to surf via a browser.

Unrealized by most people was the fact that the security on the Internet was not nearly as strong as it was on the commercial networks, or even BBSs. There was a dark side to all this, and it turned out to be a lot darker than anyone realized.

The Dark Side

Computer viruses were not unique to the Internet. They first appeared during the BBS heyday. The first PC virus appeared in the early 1980s, meant as practical jokes and as a way for programmers to show off. The viruses even displayed messages telling users that they had been infected. But by the mid-1980s more damaging viruses began to appear. These spread quickly because of the millions of files traded each day via BBSs. While many sysops were experienced computer professionals, most were not software experts. The whole idea of viruses caught most sysops by surprise. Worse yet, only the larger and better-staffed BBSs checked uploads for viruses, and it took time. Because most BBSs were hobby endeavors, all most sysops did was to post a virus warning to users, and to tell people they were on their own and to be careful. The Internet was in the same boat except for a few FTP (file storage sites) where someone checked uploaded programs for "infection." Fewer viruses got loose on the commercial systems because they had the staff to check all uploaded programs before the public was allowed to get at them.

Until the late 1980s, the Internet was literally a work in progress (many insist it still is). The experimental nature of the Internet made for rapid progress in solving a mass of technical problems and developing lots of new software. The system was set up so that anyone on the Net could gain access to other computers that were also on the Net. Security was a low priority because nearly all the people working on it knew one another (or knew of each other). Moreover, the ratio of computer experts to users was very high in those days. Anyone engaging in destructive acts would be quickly caught and suffer the humiliation of being chastised by their peers.

By the 1990s, the Internet was international and adding millions of new users each year. The playful and energetic spirit that had made technological progress so swift now came back to haunt cyberspace. Many of those playful "hackers" had decided it was more entertaining to bring down the system than to expand or maintain it. While the people running the individual computers attached to the Net were aware of their vulnerability, not everyone upgraded their systems as quickly as they should have to keep the vandals out. Moreover, there was the larger question as to whether the Net could be made secure at all.

The Internet had developed as a loosely organized project, and the U.S. government officials financing the work encouraged the Net to be designed as a very "loose" Net. That is, if large portions of the Net were knocked out by, say, a nuclear war, the surviving elements would still be able to function. While the government was not silent about the "surviving the nuclear war" aspect of the Internet, they didn't play it up either. The people building the Net, many of them on a volunteer basis, also saw the advantage of a network that was free from the control of one central authority. It was like a swarm of bees. You could kill parts of it, but not all of it. The more traditional concept of a network was an elephant on parade, where one large bullet in the right place would bring the entire show down for keeps.

The Internet is millions of individual computers, joined by telephone lines and common software and formats for transferring information. A computer connected to the Internet can be a desktop system used by one person, or a mainframe shared by thousands of users. Each computer (or group of computers) on the Internet has its own address, like brown.edu for a university, army.mil for the U.S. Army, exxonmobil.com for a corporation, or aol.com for a large, commercial network. While all these computers use common software to talk to one another, they still use hundreds of different operating systems on the individual machines.

By the 1990s, however, the Internet had become so large and complex that no one really understood the entire system. It was not known for sure what vile things you could do to the many different types of computers attached to the Internet. Some of these computers were more vulnerable than others. All you had to do was sneak into one Internet computer and that would often reveal passwords and other information that would give you easier access to many other systems. In response, many companies began to develop for themselves, or for sale to others, "firewall" software that isolated the portion of your computer connected to the Internet from the other parts of your computer system. But because just about any type of computer (from PC to mainframe) could be attached to the Internet, not all firewall systems were the same, nor were all equally effective.

To further complicate matters, local area networks (LANs) came into wider use during the 1970s. As the name implies, LANs are computers in the same building hooked together via wires. When one of the computers on a LAN became part of the Internet, all the other machines on the LAN were also, usually, reachable by anyone on the Internet. Earlier networks attached to the Internet had professional staffs and better security. But LANs were simple to set up and run, making it easier for their intended buyers, low-tech users, to handle them. These users, ultimately, were not able to deal with security problems, making LANs a preferred playground for Net vandals.

In 1988, the first major Internet worm hit. This was the Morris worm, which ended up affecting 10 percent of the 60,000 host computers then connected to the Internet. Like the early PC viruses, the worm was not meant to do a lot of damage. Mr. Morris was creating a little hack to see if he could create a program that could spread itself throughout the Web and secretly run on as many computers as possible. This was a typical hack. No one gave permission or supervised the work. On the Internet, you can do whatever you want if you have the skills, and the nerve. The author also had a legitimate (although dangerous and much criticized) reason for creating the worm: distributing software or upgrades. But the worm had some bugs in it, a common occurrence. It's difficult to test an Internet virus or worm without turning it loose on the larger Net. The Morris worm's flaws caused it to replicate on the computers it hit, tying up all the machines' computing powers. Fortunately, the worm only worked on machines with specific hardware and software configurations, but it still spread over the Net to other computers.

While the Morris worm was a media event, it was also notable for several other reasons. Knowledge of worms had existed since the early 1980s, that's where Robert T. Morris got the idea. What Morris paid insufficient attention to were the previous incidents of poorly prepared worms running amok in LANs. In general, worms were meant to do good things, like update software, put idle computers to work at night, or spread urgent information. No one, until Morris came along, thought of attacking the Web with a worm. The earlier Trojan horse programs that were spread via infected programs posted to BBSs and consumer network libraries were slow; they took time to get around. Worms used built-in Internet software to spread themselves to servers using the same type of software. Yes, the Internet was more efficient than the earlier BBS and commercial networks, but now the electronic revolution was running into the dark side of efficiency. Morris had, in fact, not intended to attack the Internet, he did the damage by accident. But as a result of this accident, the Internet set up CERT (Computer Emergency Response Team) and several other organizations to study Internet security and provide fast and effective support should something like the Morris worm happen again in the future. Which, of course, it did. Therefore, the next step was to believe that by fixing software flaws, problems would go away on their own. Instead, the nature of the Web software was such that all new software provided a constant supply of flaws for hackers to exploit. The problem has become seemingly unending. Whatever happened to Mr. Morris, the man who began the vicious circle? He was convicted, fined, put on three years' probation, and later became a dot-com millionaire.

The phone networks have also changed. For one thing, they carry a lot more information now, and in many different ways. Satellites and microwave transmitters now carry a lot of telephone traffic, as well as data. Increasingly, the messages are made by robots talking to robots. Yes, robots. For over half a century, the popular conception of a robot was a vaguely human-shaped machine that could move, talk and, to a certain extent, think. In reality, more and more things have been automated over the last few decades using computer-controlled devices that come in many different sizes and shapes. The "robots" are generally found in metal boxes, large and small, often stuck in small rooms or closets. These "thinking machines" control power, communications, and a multitude of jobs in factories and anyplace where simple, repetitive jobs are found. While the jobs these robots perform are simple and repetitive, they are often vital. If one of these robots makes a mistake, or is sabotaged, power can go out in a city, phone service over a wide area can be disrupted, or a bank can be robbed.

What the military calls Information War has been going on to a greater degree since the robots began taking over a lot of dull, routine work. You see, as hardworking, uncomplaining, and efficient as these robots are, they are not very bright. If a human can get into contact with these robots, the human can often override the robot's decision making. Even though "police" and "guard" robots are put in place to protect the "worker" robots, a human still has the edge. So far, anyway.

Because it is easier to use, a lot of the remote-control robot work is done over the Internet. This scares people, although it shouldn't. While many utilities (power, sanitation, and communication) allow for remote access to the robots, there is no "robot-control central." A saboteur would have to go out and find out where a lot of robot-control sites are, figure out how to hack into them, and then do the damage on a large scale. The odds against this are very high. The remote-control sites constantly change, so what you know about a site now might be useless information in six months. Yes, the Internet is vulnerable, but it is also vast and constantly changing.

Now it's one thing to goose the phone robots to make free long-distance calls, or grab a few million dollars from a bank's automated money-transfer system. This sort of thing isn't going to get anyone killed. But the military also uses many of these automated systems. For example, over 90 percent of military communications goes over commercial data links. You, your bank, and the Department of Defense use the same phone lines. Although much of this data is being sent from one machine to another without human intervention, humans can intervene if they can get access to the system. Sure, you can send the data in a secret code ("encrypted") but these codes can be broken. Everyone who uses networked computers is vulnerable. Exploiting that vulnerability is largely what Information War is all about.

The military, at least the American military, cannot afford not to use computer networks these days. Too many weapons, radars, supply dumps, and headquarters depend on the speed of computer networks to keep them going. Anyone who tries to run their armed forces without these nets will be at a major disadvantage against someone who is fully networked. Remember, the first thing attacked during the 1991 Gulf

War was the Iraqi communications networks. Once those nets were cut up, the Iraqis never really recovered. That was Information War with bombs. But you can also wage Information War with a personal computer and a telephone line.

Rather than cringe in terror before the prospect of hostile personal computers and the evil hackers behind them, many in the military have begun looking for ways to outhack the hackers. This is going to be a rather unique fight. There has never been a time when war was open to anonymous individuals sitting at distant locations armed with computers and other electronic devices. Oh, there were nerds heavily engaged in other wars in this century. World War II had nerds designing, and often operating, radars and electronic countermeasures. Other geeks cracked codes and invented arcane, but quite lethal, tools like operations research. But all of these fellows (they were mostly men, then as now), were organized, if not highly disciplined, and worked under tight security. Their current counterparts, at least the feral ones, are largely unknown, and no one is sure of their loyalties. One thing is certain, the black-hat hackers are out there and have been raising hell, and blood pressures, for over two decades. Most of those that have been caught are, arguably, the usual suspects. That is, they are disaffected sons of the middle class. The former Communist nations also turned out to have quite a few of these cyberthugs, some of whom were on a government payroll. But as far as anyone can tell, it was not the organized hackers who were writing all the computer viruses and breaking into "secure" networks. No, all this mayhem was being done by freewheeling freelancers. Some of these independents would do business with spy agencies, for ideological, monetary, or "just for the hell of it" reasons. Some were caught; uncertainty over how many were not caught is driving the current mania to acquire a commanding Information War capability.

What gets lost in all the fear and desperation over cyberwar is that most of the damage to information systems is, and always has been, caused by human error. The flubs are either by the users, or by the programmers, hardware designers, or "integrators" (who put the hardware and software together). Often, it is impossible to tell if a system failure is a result of some bad programming, sloppy chip design, or the consequence of someone's cyberwar attack. This has led to work on developing techniques for sorting out the usual system failures from real (really real) cyberwar attacks. What makes this angle interesting is that a clever cyberwar attack would try to introduce failures into enemy networks that looked like failures from hardware or software problems. But the more popular cyberwar thinking is to hit the other guy hard and fast with everything you've got. Bring down the enemy's information systems as completely as possible.

Many nations, however, see cyberwar as a way to level the playing field. Sort of another version of "getting a nuke." Alas, it doesn't work that way. The industrialized nations have most of the computers, and most of the hackers. There are exceptions. The former Communist nations educated more people than they could put to work and this created a lot of computer specialists with time on their hands and a grudge against society. Bulgaria, for some odd reason, has been the source of a lot of computer viruses since the 1980s. Non-Communist nations that produce educated people and no work, like Pakistan, have also produced a lot of malevolent hackers.

India, on the other hand, has put much of its programmer talent to honest work. While this has lowered the percentage of programmers who turn to malicious hacking, it does provide India with a pool of cyberwar talent. It is also possible, and has already been done, to hire hacker mercenaries. But as with any weapon, victory goes to the best organized, led, and has, as the saying goes, "the bigger battalions." While a handful of "superhackers" working for a smaller nation might possibly inflict massive damage on, say, U.S. information systems, the likelihood of that happening is pretty remote (as is getting hit on the head by a falling meteorite). The industrialized nations have taken the cyberwar dangers seriously, far more seriously than the opposition has been in developing cyberwar weapons. Cyberwar makes good copy; nothing like a frightening lead story to spice up a slow news day. But cyberwar is nothing more than the same old use of deception against an enemy that has been with us since the first recorded battle, 3200 years ago. There, in Syria, the Hittites successfully "compromised" the Egyptian "information systems" with lots of bad and deceptive data. That was cyberwar, or, as it is sometimes called, Information War.

CHAPTER 3

The Internet: Built to Be Nuked

45

tain as commercial products (like Microsoft Windows), the software itself is free.

TCP/IP is the set of standards for any computer to communicate over the Internet. Any computer with software that adhered to the TCP/IP standards could be connected to the Internet. This was a radical idea at the time (the 1970s), but was needed to put the "inter" in the Internet.

Wireless Internet Devices—They look like slightly oversize cell phones, but they are attached to the Internet instead of the phone system and use e-mail instead of voice messages.

The Internet was an accident. It began as a government project to develop some interesting ideas about data communications. Things got a lot more interesting than anyone expected and after twenty years, people outside the small, Internet community began to notice that this could be something very big, and very different.

Packet Switching Takes You Anywhere

What telephone systems have in common with the Internet is the transmission of electronic data. Although they are tightly controlled and fast, destroy one telephone control center and thousands, or hundreds of thousands, of people lose service access. This happened in New York on September 11, 2001. Several hundred thousand telephone customers lost service. Millions more saw their phone service become irregular, and often nonexistent. The only exceptions were users of wireless Internet devices (Blackberrys, for the most part). Their messages got through because the Internet was designed to survive disruption. If you can get a message onto the Net, it will reach its destination (if the destination still exists) no matter how damaged the Net is.

What enables the Internet to survive anything is its use of packet switching, a technique that breaks data (e-mail, telephone conversations, or music and video) into small pieces, or packets, and sends each packet on its (sometimes separate) way to its destination. There may be delays, but eventually all the packets will find their way to their destination. With the older circuit-switching system used by the telephone companies, you either had a connection (a "circuit") with the person you were talking to, or you didn't. Like most new ideas, the concept of packet switching was worked out before there was sufficient money, and hardware, to actually do it on a large scale. Packet switching required more capacity (phone lines) than circuit switching. But as communications companies built more and more capacity, it was understood that eventually packet switching would be practical. And that's what packet switching needed, a lot of resources.

Packet switching breaks the information (which can be a sound, like the voice of someone speaking) into packets of data (averaging about 200 bytes, or characters, each). Each packet also has information in it about its destination. The millions of computers on the Internet send their transmitted data through a specialized computer called a router. These routers constantly communicate with one another and each maintains a current list of the most efficient routes for messages to travel from themselves to the destination address. The routers work with the local Web servers (PCs that store or "host" the Web pages and other stuff you find on the Net) and DNS (domain name system) database. DNS databases translate the domain name (aol.com or bigschool.edu) into the numeric address. Humans have an easier time with text, but machines prefer numbers.

For example, if you are working at a university, your computer is probably attached to the university computer network. Say your e-mail address is joedoe@bigschool.edu, and you send an e-mail to your friend mybuddy@aol.com. When you send that e-mail, your university computer system sends it to its router, which sends the packets comprising your message to a series of other routers until it reaches the AOL system, where the message would be held until your friend linked to AOL and checked his e-mail.

The beauty of the packet-switching technique is that the different packets containing, say, an e-mail message, could all travel through a different sequence of servers before arriving at their destination and being reassembled. As many users have noted, most packets arrive at their destination within seconds. But there are sometimes problems along the way (something else most users have experienced, usually when browsing the Web and things suddenly slow down) and it can take awhile before the packets arrive. Things go wrong on the Net, this is expected. Sometimes a server is out of service for some reason or another, or a natural disaster takes out one of the fiber-optic lines that carries a lot of the Internet traffic. This has happened; once because a construction worker accidentally cut a fiber-optic line. This sort of thing slows down, but does not stop, the Internet. Thus, the Internet's durability is constantly tested. These disasters serve a useful purpose, as they often lead to additional tweaks in the Internet to lessen the impact the next time a similar problem shows up.

The DNS (domain name system) was a latecomer during the development of the Internet. It was set up in 1987 to help enable the Internet to move from a government operation to a public entity. Some organization had to keep track of new Web addresses (domains) and the idea of having easier-to-remember names to match the numbers had been kicking around for some time. The Domain Solutions company got the contract to do this work, although there are now several services authorized to register new Internet addresses.

DNS and the Root Servers

While there are DNS databases all over the Internet, the ultimate authority are the thirteen DNS root servers around the world. They are a key element of the net. There is one master root server that updates the information on the other twelve root servers once or twice a week. These root servers contain the master list of registered domain names and the numerical addresses that all other DNS databases consult. Hacking a root server could, for example, redirect Internet traffic to a false site posing as a bank and, say, collect credit card information. With regard to a cyberwar, if all the root servers were physically destroyed, the Internet could actually continue to function as the vast majority of domain names don't change. You wouldn't be able to add new Internet addresses, however, until the root servers were reconstructed.

E-mail Takes Over ARPANET

The Internet could have been built on telephone (circuit switching) technology. This was the case in 1969, when the first network went online, connecting four computers in different parts of the country. However, in the 1970s programmers realized that software used with packet-switching technology, not telephone wiring, was going to change the world.

With this understanding in mind, e-mail was developed. Before the first message was sent in 1971 and ARPANET users began using e-mail in 1972, messages could only be sent from one computer to another, not one person to another. Roy Tomlinson added the idea of using individual e-mail addresses with the now familiar "@" to separate the person's name and the computer system that person was operating on. Individuals could now have a personal e-mail address. Before, all you could do was send messages from the Columbia University computer to the Penn

State computer. Someone at Penn State would have to look at each message to see what person it was for. The new system allowed you to send e-mail directly from joe@columbia.edu to bill@pennstate.edu. This became the first "killer app (application)."

It was working. By 1975, 75 percent of ARPANET traffic was e-mail. By the end of the 1970s, ARPANET users generally agreed that e-mail changed everything and would become a major use for the network. This was unanticipated and unplanned. The original purpose of ARPANET was to allow people to use one anothers' computers and send data files back and forth. This unexpected development also made everyone on the project aware that they could probably expect some more surprises along the same lines. They were right, and security issues and the use of the Internet as a weapon turned out to be some of them.

The concept of mailing lists, which allowed a group of people to share all their messages with one another (now generally known as listserv, which was developed in the 1980s) quickly followed. Interestingly, the most popular mailing list discussed science fiction. This was indicative of another unexpected direction where ARPANET found itself heading. In 1979 the first multi-user dungeon (MUD) game, MUD1, was started in Britain (at the University of Essex). Many more networked games were to follow. There had been games played on ARPANET before, but the MUDs were unique in that they involved role playing. Players not only solved puzzles and wandered around the MUDs' mazes, but also interacted in entertaining ways with other players. Students in computer science departments were prone to immerse themselves in the MUDs, leading to a constant stream of new ones; in fact, there were infinite variations possible. Programmers started honing their programming chops on the time they "wasted" creating and tweaking their MUDs. Then again, more than a few computer science or engineering students flunked out of school because of their obsession with MUDs. Eventually, many engineering schools developed counseling programs for this particular form of addiction. Not that schools had no experience with this kind of issue; students who got an e-mail account in the 1970s were also found to spend an inordinate amount of time with their new toy, or tool, depending on how you look at it.

Saved by an Open-Source Apache

E-mail communities led ARPANET's enormous growth; all that communication created ideas, with which people wanted to work. This eventually led to Usenet, which was the Internet version of what Compuserve was doing with its forums and the BBS systems with their bulletin boards. Actually, the bulletin board idea had been around for some time, but as the number of people on the Net increased, mailing lists were being overwhelmed (too many people on the lists sending too many messages). So a bunch of the netheads got together and created a solution. The sense of community, and the fact that the government was paying for all this (making it "free") led to the Open Source Movement. This was nothing less than thousands of programmers writing and maintaining (fixing problems and adding new features) software for free.

The Open Source idea wasn't just another idealistic, but unsustainable, movement from the '60s; it actually served a useful purpose (and still does). The popular Linux operating system and the Apache server software are both open-source products. Apache is the most widely used (and safest from Web attacks). Linux is one of the flavors of the Unix operating system that Apache runs on. Linux is also more secure than Microsoft Windows. Linux (actually GNU/Linux) didn't appear until 1993, after ten years of work. The GNU project began in 1983 to create a free operating system. There were plenty of Open Source tools already available, but without an Open Source operating system, you could be subject to a company (like Microsoft) crippling your Open Source tools with an unexpected change in the operating system (like Windows). Things take longer when you're using volunteers, and the first releases of Linux and Apache didn't come out until the mid-1990s. While Linux is running only about a quarter of the Web servers (in early 2002), its growth has been impressive. Apache, however, beats even Microsoft, running over half the Web servers. And for good reason, as Apache has only a fraction of the security problems that Microsoft's more expensive, and more bug-ridden (but much more aggressively promoted) Web server does.

This points up one of the major dangers for Internet users today: security. The Open Source software, like Linux and Apache, use more robust code; users are building and maintaining it as opposed to a corporation (like Microsoft). Problems with Apache can be fixed within hours by many eager, skilled, and responsive volunteers. Microsoft's Web server, IIS, requires at least a few days (usually a few weeks) to fix a security-related flaw.

But the reason why there was an Open Source Unix in the first place was because Unix was such a good operating system. Long (and somewhat justifiably) castigated as the operating system "by geeks, for geeks," Unix was developed in Bell Labs in the early 1970s. The engineers there wanted to build an operating-system that could handle many users at once (a rather advanced concept at the time) and be easily adaptable for different computers. Up to that time, operating-system code was written tightly, to get maximum performance on one model of computer. This meant that it was very difficult to adapt an operating system to run on more than one model of computer. But Unix was meant to be the operating system of the future, so it was written in a looser fashion, making it much easier to adapt Unix to run on just about any computer. This was a radical idea at the time, but proved to be an accurate prediction of where computing was going. Naturally, Unix was favored by the ARPANET crowd. In the 1980s, the basic Internet software (called TCP/IP) was built right into Unix. This made Unix even more attractive for anyone setting up an Internet server. The TCP/IP software to do that was a part of Unix, all you had to do was plug your Unix computer into the Internet and you were on the Net.

Before the Internet could become the monster that it is today, the pioneers had to build tools and basic functions. Many of these tools did (and still do) things users never see, or simply take for granted. E-mail was originally developed as a tool, one that quickly turned into much more. In 1973 came another: FTP (file transfer protocol), and it was a major improvement. Before the Web, using FTP meant typing a lot of commands to transfer a file from a distant computer to your own. FTP was refined and enhanced to a point where, today, anyone can click an icon and the file will be sent. It's interesting to note that such a profound change in the way we share information, based on speed, was developed because the Internet was not being policed. Today, however, this ease of use also provides opportunities for crooks and crackers (black-hat hackers) to get into your PC. We are still trying to plug the security holes opened twenty years ago when Internet tools were first developed.

Insecurity Included

As we're seeing, if security had been a major factor in the beginning, the Internet would not exist, or at least it would not exist as we know it. Another example of a security issue that never got a chance to impact the early Internet was the Telenet company's commercial exploitation of packet-switching technology in 1974. The commercial (business to business) networks created by Telenet, Tymnet, Compuserve, and other 1970s companies operated very differently—and more prohibitively—

than the budding Internet, even though they used much of the same technology. Their security was tighter, but their users had a lot less flexibility. You could not create tools for these networks on your own, as with the Internet, but had to ask the network company to do it for you. The commercial nets also cost more to run and were more expensive for their customers to use. One could see the differences starkly in 1979 when Compuserve began its consumer-level service. While this service was expensive, it was also less confusing for users (there were fewer choices) and a lot more secure than the Internet.

The 1960s and 1970s also brought forth the minicomputers. Computer components were getting cheaper and it was now possible to build a less-capable computer, one that was also smaller (the size of a refrigerator, or even a fifth of that size). Although each one was priced at over $100,000 in today's dollars, the minicomputer, like e-mail, was another unanticipated development that changed the computing landscape in unexpected ways. Because of minicomputers, there were now a lot more computers out there. The original developers of the Internet did not see the Internet as being a consumer purchase, at least not until (they estimated) sometime in the twenty-first century, when hooking up to a mainframe computer might be cheap enough. But in the late 1970s, minicomputers begat personal computers and modems and brought technology prices down and into middle-class homes.

The arrival of PCs also divided the kingdom of the geeks into two factions, the "big iron" (mainframe) crowd and the PC people. This epic battle ended only recently, with both sides winning (or both losing, depending on how you look at it, but that's the subject for another book).

The developers of ARPANET grew up with, and worked on, large computer systems that had "dumb terminals." Little more than a black-and-white CRT, a keyboard, and just enough electronics to keep it talking to the mainframe (which stored all the data and did all the computing), these attachments were low priced. Recall that in the 1970s, electronics were expensive; the dumb terminals only cost $5,000–15,000 in today's money as compared to a mainframe cost of half a million dollars each (and up, into the tens of millions of dollars). At the time, however, this was the most practical way to enable people to have computer access. The Unix operating system, which powered the Internet almost from the beginning, was built to handle multiple users on one computer. The Internet then added the capability to do that for users communicating via a modem over the telephone network, as well as those using a dumb terminal attached by cable to a nearby mainframe. The first PCs that appeared in the late 1970s were even cheaper than dumb terminals (costing $2500–5000 in current dollars), but were still seen as expensive toys by most computer professionals. By 1980, it was common for PC users to be using equally inexpensive modems to connect to bulletin-board systems (BBSs) run by the PCs. A foothold was being established. It wasn't much longer before ARPANET users realized they could use this combination to connect cheaply from home. In 1982, a pair of teenage PC users from Los Angeles figured out the same thing. There was only one problem: they weren't authorized ARPANET users. The kids ran amok and this reinforced the attitude of many ARPANET developers that PCs were tools of the devil.

The "data processing" (DP) professionals that ran mainframe systems tried to keep PCs out of their organizations up through the 1980s. They did not consider PCs "real computers" and saw the spread of PCs as a threat to their control over how computing was done. They lost that battle. Then, local area networks (LANs) arrived, powered solely by PCs. Again, the data processing community looked down on this pitiful development and wished it would go away. It didn't. The DP professionals thought it was dangerous if a bunch of amateurs got their hands on their own computers. The users, in this case departments in large corporations, saw the price differential between PCs and mainframes, and ultimately that lost the mainframe community the battle. Along the way, it also changed the idea of what a mainframe was.

For all practical purposes, the mainframe was becoming a dinosaur, even though its proponents insisted that PCs were less reliable, which they were. But that was beside the point. PCs were sold on price, cost was low, and users were more willing, and able, to accept less reliability. Mainframes also still had expensive communications gear that allowed connections with dumb terminals and for remote users via ARPANET or other networks. Of course, they were larger, too, (and very expensive). For example, a state-of-the-art seventy-five-megabyte hard drive in the late '70s cost some $40,000 in today's inflated dollars. The early PC users didn't need all those expensive extras.

This wasn't a "you're for us or against us" kind of war, however. Many longtime mainframe pros had a PC at home, or even suggested bringing them into the DP department. At the same time, many pro-PC geeks had no trouble using mainframes (Compuserve and the Internet, after all, were run on mainframes). What finally settled the dispute were advantages gained from hooking those PC LANs up to mainframes. The concept of a mainframe, however, then changed. Designers noticed that PC manufacturers would add on analogous mainframe components (like bigger hard disks) for little cost. Into the 1990s the trend reversed:

you saw mainframes being built from PC-type components. You might say that the PCs kept growing in capability to meet the needs of engineers and scientists and, currently, the most powerful PCs are called mainframes to describe themselves.

There was a downside to this. One of the many points the PC and mainframe partisans butted heads over was "control." The older mainframe advocates came from a time (in the 1950s) when computers were new, expensive, and cranky. They had to be protected and used carefully. Time was money, access for the uninitiated or inexperienced was not allowed. The PC partisans, on the other hand, espoused personal freedom, fought to bring down the wall of technophobia, and sought to use their personal computers any way they wanted. The battle began being waged over good security practices versus hardly any. Sure, there were security elements built into many PCs, but all of them were easily circumvented by any geek worthy of the name. To mainframers, security was a religion. To PC users, security was a joke. Then came the Internet. People went shopping online, banked in cyberspace, and traded stocks via a Web site. Network security was no longer something that just old mainframe farts would bust your chops about, especially if you were bidding up collectibles on eBay and doing all your banking via a Web site. It was too late to go back, and repairing the damage was going to take some time.

The weak security of the Net is not only due to the war between PCs and mainframes. The ARPANET culture played a part in it as well. Although the Open Source community has done a lot to shore up Net security, the freewheeling, cooperative, and trusting nature of the Internet's early days also contributed to the current Net security problems. For the Internet to work at all, a lot of this openness and cooperation was necessary. But back then, you could trust just about everyone to leave the Web the same if not better than the way they found it. Not so today.

ARPANET Breaks Free

While ARPANET was a crude, and very experimental, network, in the 1970s, it did work. And it was addictive. People wanted it. The increasingly louder demand for access to the Internet led to the establishment of NSFNet (National Science Foundation Net) in 1985 for those in academia who were not part of the ongoing ARPANET project. Agitation on campus had already led to the establishment of the Computer Science Network (CSNET) and BITNET (Because It's Time Network) in 1981–2. In 1985, the Department of Defense, which had split from the ARPANET in 1983 to produce MILNET (just for the military), gave up control of the ARPANET altogether.

Another crucial development in the early 1980s was the establishment of TCP/IP as the standard ARPANET communications software. TCP/IP had evolved since the early 1970s as a robust and flexible set of software rules ("protocols" in geek speak) that made it relatively easy for any kind of computer network (and there were dozens of different types and variations) to connect via the government's ARPANET. BITNET didn't use TCP/IP, but CSNET did, and it was subsequently connected to ARPANET in 1983 with great success (and a few headaches). In 1984, the NSF (National Science Foundation) took over management from ARPANET, or what was now being called the Internet. In the same year, the domain name system (DNS) came into use, making it easier for users to identify and get to an Internet site. In 1985, ARPANET officially became NSFNet (National Science Foundation Net). The Net was now a civilian operation. More was changed than the name; suddenly there were a lot more people on the Net. In 1981, there were 213 host computers (think of them as servers) connected to ARPANET. In 1983 that went to 562 and doubled in 1984 to 1024. In 1985, the year the Internet was opened to the public, there were 1961 hosts. But by 1987 there were 28,174 and in 1988 over 56,000. By 1990 there were over 300,000 hosts. At this point, ARPANET was disbanded and all that was left was the Internet. You no longer had to scrounge an account from a university or research center to get on the Internet, for now it was possible to buy monthly access through an ISP (Internet service provider). This led to tremendous growth. By 1995, when the World Wide Web took off, there were 6.6 million hosts.

The sudden, rapid growth of the Internet led to the development of new tools to deal with all the neat new stuff that was showing up on the Net. The first search engines were tools called Gopher, Archie, Veronica, and WAIS, which allowed people to search the Net and retrieve documents or files. Roaming around the Net was first called "surfing the Net" in 1992. Most users didn't have a graphical interface like Windows or Macintosh. This was before the World Wide Web had arrived. It was simpler and harder to use than the Web (which is what people called the World Wide Web when it did arrive, as well as the Internet in general). But the NSF didn't see it coming. At the time, the

NSF believed that what the Web needed was to expand its infrastructure and get the Net into as many hands as possible. The NSF brokered a lot of arrangements that had far-reaching implications, such as:

TCP/IP was made mandatory for anyone wanting to link to the Internet (and by now everyone was calling it that). This avoided a protracted fight between several other commercial protocols. On the downside, TCP/IP is not as secure from hackers as many of the commercial competitors. But with TCP/IP, more people were going to get on the Net faster.

Government and corporations would cooperate to form the "Internet backbone" (the high-capacity telephone lines that would carry most of the Internet traffic long distances). In effect, this was a private telephone system. The regular telephone system was only used for the "last mile" from a backbone connection to individual users or local networks.

There would be no metered cost between the various nets. This was a risky proposition as the Internet was still not a commercial operation. But it simplified things and helped make the rapid growth of the Internet possible. The backbone would pay for itself by charging middlemen (Internet service providers, or ISPs, or large-end users—corporations, universities, government agencies) for direct access.

The establishment of the Internet Activities Board (IAB) to oversee and encourage cooperative research (in the U.S. and overseas) and to develop the new technologies the Net would need to grow. This was sort of an official Open Source movement and the IAB was a direct descendent of a similar organization (Internetworking Working Group) established in 1972 to do the same thing.

It was a start. Then came the first crime wave on the Net. A survey of 300 major corporations and government agencies in 1987 showed that 5 percent of them had been victims of computer crime in the past year. Overall, loss estimates ranged from $145 million to $730 million. Most of it was embezzlement, electronically sending money to a crook's bank account (the account was promptly cleaned out so the thief could make his getaway). A survey of 3000 computer sites in 1991 indicated that 72 percent had suffered a "security incident" in the past year. By this time, site operators were becoming more alert to the danger, and only forty-three said that the security incidents had gotten far enough to be a criminal offense. Other surveys showed that only about 5 percent of computer-crime incidents were even reported to the police.

The early '90s were a chaotic time for the Internet. New users were coming online by the millions. New software was being introduced to deal with the increased activity, and the increasing security problems. The most common problem had to do with passwords. While the outsider hacking into networks received most of the media attention, studies indicate that some 90 percent of computer crime is committed by insiders. Most companies just considered the security losses as another cost of doing business, and worked to improve their security. Government agencies, however, were concerned in a different way, fearing politically harmful media exposure. All of this was something of a "good news, bad news" situation. The good news was that there were no major disasters. This despite the fact that sites controlling dams and other utilities were hacked into. The bad news was that these sites were compromised, and it was obvious that not a lot of talent was needed to do it.

The World Wide Web Tidal Wave

In the early 1960s, when the term "Internet" was first heard, another fascinating new technology was dreamed up. It was hypertext, and it languished as an academic curiosity until scientists at CERN (a scientific research institute) in Switzerland began looking for an easier way to exchange technical information on the Internet. This often included illustrations and photos or heavily footnoted technical articles. In response, Tim Berners-Lee basically invented the World Wide Web by developing the idea of HTML (hypertext markup language) and URLs (universal resource locators). These are Internet addresses that begin with HTTP, which stands for hypertext transfer protocol. Naturally, a special communications program, soon called a browser, was needed to enable HTML instructions to communicate with the Internet. It took three years of work before the first HTML and the software to make it work were released. The first Web server (an Internet host computer programmed to answer requests from browsers) went online in 1991. At first, the Web was all text; graphics, which took longer to retrieve, came later as faster modems were more widely available. The Web was an instant hit; by 1992 there were fifty Web servers. By 2001, there were over 24 million Web servers and over a billion Web pages available.

In 1993, the first graphic browser (Mosaic) was developed by faculty and students (including Marc Andreesen, founder of Netscape) at the University of Illinois. Mosaic browsers were released for Windows, Macintosh, and Unix systems. In 1994, Netscape was founded, but the gold rush was already on. Cheaper PCs and a version of Microsoft Windows (that worked reliably) all combined to create another bit of popular technology that changed everything. Like the telegraph, radio, and television before it, the PC/Web combination brought computing to the masses in a totally unexpected way. The U.S. government hopped on the bandwagon by putting $1.5 billion into the NSF to help keep the Internet infrastructure growing fast enough to keep up with the demand. The Internet had grown from about a thousand networks in 1985 to over 60,000 in 1994. No one, however, had a clear idea of how many people were on the Net in 1995, but it was obviously in the tens of millions (perhaps as many as 40 million) and growing fast. The major commercial networks, like CompuServe and AOL, connected to the Internet in the same year the NSF got out of the Internet business and the Net became an entirely commercial operation.

As early as 1995, a survey of existing Web sites showed that this new "information utility" was doing what everyone had hoped. A breakdown of 1100 randomly selected sites went like this:

Web Site Function	Sites Using that Function
Public Relations	21.93%
Advertising	20.70%
Data Bank/General Information	9.74%
News	9.74%
Service/Product Information	9.30%
Bulletin Board	8.86%
Archives/Exhibits	6.93%
Entertainment	6.84%
Commentary	4.65%
Miscellaneous/Other	1.32%.

This was before Personal Web pages, e-commerce, and porn hit the Web. Something else came along as well: the increased use of scripting. This was an ancient tool for experienced computer users and administrators. The DOS batch files (.bat files) were the most widely used scripting language, but others are so powerful that they require real programming skills to handle. In 1995, JavaScript showed up. HTML was very flexible, but it cried out for scripting, and JavaScript allowed experienced Web designers using scripting to make their sites even more useful. JavaScript, however, (and similar scripting tools) also gave the increasing number of malicious hackers and other Web vandals a powerful tool with which to cause damage.

The Web delivered an even more lethal capability with the huge amount of new software being developed to work with the Web itself. All of this software tended to have flaws (all new software has flaws) that allowed hackers to gain illegal access to the sites. The programmers of this stuff didn't find many of these flaws because these problems did not affect what the program was supposed to do. But the bad guys knew an opportunity when they saw one and began building tools to sniff out the security flaws. Put simply, the World Wide Web was a much less secure version of the Internet.

But there was no going back. The Internet did not belong to any one organization. In effect, no one was in charge. So there was no authority that could impose security standards. The Internet was meant to be inspired anarchy, and the breakneck rate of growth in the late 1990s would have made it difficult to implement any security policy anyway.

The Web was also bringing commerce to the Internet. While e-commerce had not arrived yet, in 1996 ISPs raked in over $3 billion. And a third of that was outside the United States.

By 1997, there were over 50,000 E-commerce Web pages, and a growing number in private, corporate, and government networks. By the end of the century, the number of hosts had grown to 93 million (from four in 1969). There were some 4 million registered domains, and it was estimated that some 23 million people were on the Net on any given day.

But the Net was not secure. Maybe it was not meant to be secure, and maybe it was robust enough to withstand any assault, but the dangers were real and users were increasingly getting uneasy over exactly what the worst would be that could happen.

CHAPTER 4

Cyberwars Past

The Internet provided a new way to communicate, and not much later it became a battlefield. A real battlefield. Since the American Civil War, it had been obvious that electronically transmitted information plays a role in winning wars. In the past, information was important, but now, with the telegraph, messages moved at the speed of light.

The military realized that they had more than just another communications and propaganda tool.

There are two types of combat on the Web. There is the traditional Information War, which does all sorts of thing with the news that was not possible before the Web arrived. Then there is cyberwar, which uses the Web to, as the infantry likes to put it, "break things and kill people." Technically, cyberwar means using electronic devices in combat. That, it turns out, is not a recent idea. Cyberwar, as defined in this way, already has a sixty-year history.

The Largest Cyberwar Ever

The worst that can happen in the future is that some major cyber-warriors go at it big time. A major cyberwar would be unprecedented. Well, no, actually it wouldn't. A major war using the Internet would be unique, but a major military operation featuring electronic weapons happened a long time ago, during World War II. From 1940 to 1945, the air over Europe was filled with hundreds of thousands of aircraft. Most used radio, many had their own radars, and many others had a growing collecting of jammers, electronic-navigation equipment, and what we would today call electronic-warfare gear. This was the first cyberwar. It was huge. It went on for six years. And we can learn a lot about a future cyberwar by looking back at this World War II experience.

At the beginning of World War II (1939), aircraft had little electronic equipment onboard except a radio, and many nations didn't even equip all their warplanes with radios. But there was a lot of new electronic gadgetry being developed in the laboratories and universities during the 1930s. The needs of wartime quickly brought a lot of that speculative and experimental gear into use. This brought about an electronic arms race that has never been matched for speed (of innovation) or violence (in how the stuff was used).

We have a very similar situation sixty years later. We have a new technology (the Internet) that has yet to be tried in wartime, and we have a lot of potential to rapidly modify and rework the Internet to meet wartime needs. The Internet was built to be quickly modified. So what will happen? Let's find out how by taking a look at the first big electronic war.

What started the electronic war over Europe in the 1940s was the efforts of Germans and Allies to bomb one anothers' cities and factories.

Again, this was something unique in history. There had been some small, more annoying than destroying, raids at the end of World War I (1914–18), but now the bombers were bigger, more numerous, and had a longer range. Some of the things they did lack would be supplied by a long list of electronic devices.

One of the first of the modern electronic devices to be introduced for combat over Europe was the German Knickebein in February of 1940. This was an airborne navigation system using signals from ground transmitters. This allowed bombers flying at night to find targets, and accurately bomb them. This was a classic, and oft repeated, case of an unexpected military situation (bombing at night) bringing forth a technical solution to a seemingly intractable problem (finding targets at night).

While the Germans pioneered the bombing of cities in the 1930s, particularly during the Spanish Civil War (1936–39), they always assumed that they would first clear the air of enemy fighters and then bomb accurately by day. When the Luftwaffe (German Air Force) ran into the RAF (British Royal Air Force) in 1940, it was quickly obvious that British fighters could make bombing in daylight a very expensive proposition. Bombing at night avoided the fighters, but created seemingly insurmountable navigation problems. Thus the rapid development and introduction of Knickebein. But while it didn't take much time to create Knickebein, it took even less time to break it. The British, in September 1940, introduced their countermeasure: Asperin. This was nothing more than electronic jammers that sent out a lot of noise on the same frequencies as Knickebein, rendering it useless.

The Knickebein was something that aircraft engineers were interested in for purely commercial reasons before the war. Such a system could just as easily move commercial aircraft from city to city. Even before the war, such a system was in use to allow aircraft to land when the weather was so bad that they could not see the airfield below. Based on that World War II experience with electronic navigation devices, the LORAN (LOng RAnge Navigation system) was constructed after World War II and is still in use. The shortcomings of LORAN also led to the GPS, which uses the convergence of signals from three space satellites to pinpoint where you are. This shows how military and civilian technologies can switch quickly between wartime and peacetime use. No one has yet figured out all the military uses one can put the Internet to, and this is what scares the military most about the Internet.

During 1942 and 1943, the Germans and British rapidly improved their radars and communications systems. Radars were developed with longer range and the ability to more accurately locate aircraft. But with thousands of aircraft in the air on any given day, it soon became clear that the radar operators needed a way to tell the good guys from the bad guys. This led to the invention of IFF (identification, friend or foe). This was a small, radio transmitter (called a "transponder") that constantly sent out a coded message identifying the aircraft as friendly (the message was changed frequently so the enemy could not copy the message and use it to sneak past your defenses).

By the late 1990s, the Internet rediscovered a need for IFF. The Internet uses a form of IFF in the way it authenticates who is who on the Net. Not just passwords, but also the control data sent between servers and the software that runs the Net all use a form of IFF to prevent someone from shutting down or taking over portions of the Internet. In the beginning, Internet communication was based on a certain amount of trust. But the Internet is no longer a tight group of researchers, but hundreds of millions of people, and not a few governments, that see the Net as a potential battlefield. "Spoofing" (editing an item, even an e-mail, to make it look like it's coming from somewhere else) has become a major problem. The British World War II IFF was a simple solution compared to what must be done on the Internet to obtain the same kind of assurance that what you see is what you get. But the effort to develop better Internet IFF continues, and the Net won't be a whole lot safer until more reliable IFF is developed.

The World War II Germans eventually picked up on IFF and used it themselves, but in other cases, the Germans never realized that the Allies were using superior technology. A good example was microwave radar. This was a basic improvement in radar technology that made radar equipment more powerful and smaller. What's interesting here is how vital electronics technology was not discovered by nations that really, really needed it. The Germans grabbed the secret of microwave radar from the British as soon as they had the chance, but the Japanese had not bothered to share their earlier discovery of microwave radar with their allies. The Internet, and cyberwar, will also be full of such nasty little technical surprises. The problem is, we're going to have to wait for some kind of war (a regular, bang-bang kind, or a purely cyber-type conflict) to find out who's got what. It won't be long before Hollywood picks up on this and you'll have spy movies where the big secret is some kind of devastating Internet cyberweapon. In this case, it won't be a Hollywood fantasy, but a very real fear in the cyberwar community.

The World War II cyberwar also showed that low tech could still be used against high tech. For example, the Germans developed a way to use searchlights (set up in a long line) to serve as a primitive, but effective, form of unjammable radar. The Allies also discovered that if you dropped hundreds of pounds of aluminum foil strips (called, then and now, "chaff"), you created a huge cloud on enemy radar screens. In effect, you blinded the enemy radar. This was low tech, but it made the high-tech radars useless, at least until all the foil strips drifted to the ground. Some low-tech ideas were less successful. For example, the British knew that the Germans also relied on a network of ground observers who, at night, simply stood outside and listened for the sound of bomber engines overhead. The observers then phoned in this information to a central headquarters where all the reports were assembled and showed where the bombers were coming from, and their probable heading, too. The British tried to disrupt this system by modifying some of their bomber engines so that they made a louder noise than usual. It was thought this would cause the ground observers to provide erroneous reports. Didn't work. But you have to keep trying.

Chaff was an approach to technology that worked in 1942, and will do just as well in the twenty-first century. There are still low-tech ways to deal with the enemy's high-tech advantages. For example, when you want to maintain a network that can communicate with the Internet, but will be immune to attacks via the Net, many organizations have resorted to a "sneakernet" connection. That is, the internal net uses Internet technology, but all e-mail, coming and going, is copied to a CD and carried (by some clerk wearing sneakers, thus the "sneakernet") to a PC that is connected to the Internet. There, a special program takes the e-mail messages and sends them out over the Net. Incoming messages for people on the sneakernet are then carried back to a PC that is part of the sneakernet, checked for e-mail viruses and such, and then sent to the recipients. No attachments are allowed (although some sneakernets do allow attachments, which must be scanned before being let loose on the sneakernet). Crude, but effective. Perfect for sysadmins whose paranoia is not misplaced.

From 1943 until the end of the war, the Allies and Germans developed new radars, new devices to detect radars, radar jammers, more electronic navigation equipment (including radar that could create a map of what was on the ground), and devices that detected the use of the electronic navigation gear, or simply jammed it. By the end of World War II, the electronic warfare people expected a new item to last but a few months before the enemy came out with some countermeasure. This set the tone and tempo for electronic warfare that persists to the present.

Jamming and spoofing (making something seem what it isn't, like increasing the engine noise) have become standard weapons for cyberwarriors. The DDOS (distributed denial of service attack) is a popular form of jamming that shuts down the targeted Web site. Spoofing is a key element in hacking as it is a collection of techniques that hide what the hacker is doing, and make it difficult to track the hacker down.

This back and forth, new measures followed by countermeasures, is typical of the way cyberwar is being fought right now. Sometimes it is even done in the open, as when Microsoft tried to get its own instant messaging system connected to AOL's much larger instant message system. While the lawyers had it out in court, the MSN programmers kept finding new flaws in AOL's software that allowed MSN users to send instant messages to AOL users. This was followed by the AOL programmers patching the hole and cutting off the MSN instant message users. The MSN programmers then went and found another way in. Eventually the lawyers won, but it was fun to watch while it lasted.

The World War II experience also provides encouraging examples of how you can create an electronic system that can't be jammed. At the very end of 1942, the Allies introduced Oboe. This was a 430-kilometer-range radar that calculated a friendly bomber's precise location and sent signals to the bomber telling it when the bombs should be dropped at night or during bad weather during the day. This technique was limited by the range of the Oboe radar (sitting on the English coast), and was of no use for the many targets deep inside Germany. But most important, it was, for all practical purposes, impossible to jam. We see the same thing happening today. As DDOS attacks became more popular (via easy-to-use DDOS tools on the Net) after 2000, there soon appeared software tools for sysadmins that provided them with a lot of resistance to this form of jamming.

The promptness with which both sides responded to each other's new electronic weapons during World War II is typical of how cyberwar works. The big difference was that during World War II, new weapons went into action right away, and an enemy countermeasure was expected soon after. Since we have not had a cyberwar yet, the best new weapons will be kept secret. No point in giving the enemy a chance to cancel out your new tool, before you get to use it, with a clever response. This is particularly important because one thing that air forces learned from their World War II experience was the primacy of "threat alert" equipment. These devices simply told the pilot that his aircraft was being hit with radar signals. More sophisticated threat-alert equipment interprets the radar signals and tells the pilot if it's friendly or enemy radar, or the kind of radar a missile uses as it closes in for the kill. In today's cyberwar, "threat alert" equipment is represented by a growing number of intrusion-detection devices on Web sites. These will tell you that someone is trying to sneak into your site. That's what threat alert is all about.

Another World War II lesson being relearned is how lethal a bunch of independent operators can be. At night, in the air over Germany during World War II, most of the 12,000 bombers destroyed were brought down by a few hundred night fighters. While there were thousands of antiaircraft guns on the ground, it was the few night fighters, piloted by some pretty skillful and resourceful pilots, that did most of the damage. This spotlights the basic difference between the attacker and defender in cyberwar. The Web sites are large and often well-armed (with hacker defenses) targets. The attackers, the hackers, capitalize on being small, fast-moving targets. A hacker who is too slow to realize he has wandered into a well-protected site is going to get nailed before he can disconnect. But the odds are in the hackers' favor, and the best of them don't get caught.

Hackers also look to nail sites when the sites are most vulnerable. This is usually when a new flaw in a Web server has been discovered. The prime target sites will usually get patched quickly to eliminate the flaw. But a sharp hacker will move fast to catch a site before that happens. There are always sites that are a little too slow to upgrade their defenses, and they often get hit.

The rapid development of new electronic tools and countermeasures between 1943 and 1945 was a sign of what was to come in cyberwar. Since World War II, there hasn't been a sustained period of electronic warfare. But now we're seeing it on the Internet. Even without a full-blown cyberwar, the battle between sysadmins and hackers is generating the same kind of measure/countermeasure activity. Moreover, the World War II tools were electronic; you had to design, manufacture, test, and deploy an electronic device. While there is some hardware used in cyberwar (especially routers and hardware firewalls), most of the equipment is software. And these tools can be designed, manufactured (written and compiled), tested, and deployed in hours. The process usually takes days or weeks, but that's still ten times faster than during World War II, and can be a hundred or more times faster if the heat is on.

Although the World War II Germans had much success in the aerial cyberwar (downing 11,965 of the British night bombers), the Allies simply had more stuff. And this points out another aspect of cyberwar. Today's defending Web sites number in the millions, and their unique configuration (of hardware and software) number in the thousands. An organized and massive cyberwar attack would be hard put to bring down a lot of them. Remember, the Internet was designed to survive massive damage and keep on functioning. Most Web users would notice a massive attack. A lot of sites would be off the Web for a while and everything would slow down. But the cyberwar attacker, like the Germans attacking the massive, Allied, bomber fleet, has to do an enormous amount of damage to score any kind of meaningful victory. And the Web sites of the world are not totally unprepared for the attack. Numbers do count, and quantity does have a quality of its own.

By early 1945, Germany lay in ruins, in good measure because of the 955,000 tons of bombs dropped by the British night bombers and the 623,000 tons dropped by the U.S. daylight bombers. The American air force officers that planned and flew all those missions over Germany came away with ideas and expectations that have resonated for sixty years and form the core attitudes of air force technology and tactics to this day. The flying networks used over Europe in the 1940s were the first major cyberwar. But it wasn't called cyberwar back then, even though the use of electronics and information was what it was all about. The bombers needed a constant supply of information on where they were and where their targets, and defending German aircraft, were. The Germans were trying to find the bombers. And both sides were trying to deny the other side information. Today, the targets are no longer German cities or bombers flying overhead. Now we have cyberwarriors moving around the Net at the speed of light seeking sites to knock off the Net, or information to corrupt or steal. Airspace has been replaced by cyberspace and the bombs and weapons are all electronic. If all this induces a sense of déjà vu, it should. And that is good, because this exercise shows that, while cyberwar can be scary, it is not new. It's been fought before. Then, as now, victory goes to the side with the most brains and tools. America has the most of both. Sure, the little guy can win, and he sometimes does. But victory usually goes, as Napoleon put it, "to the bigger battalions." We can snatch defeat from the jaws of victory if we get lazy and underestimate the enemy (whomever it is). And we don't have to wait for a cyberwar to happen to do that. The Web is in a constant state of low-level conflict. This is good because it constantly reminds us of what is in store if we stop defending ourselves.

Cyberwar Case Studies

Cyberwarfare caught the FBI's attention during the 1990s. Below is how the feds described the three attacks that motivated them to organize and go after Internet crime. What follows is the exact text of the FBI report.

AIR FORCE ROME LAB (1994)

In March 1994, system administrators at Rome Lab in New York found their network under attack. The Air Force dispatched two teams to investigate further. The attacks were traced to an ISP (Internet Service Provider) first in New York, then in Seattle, Washington, where the Internet path dead-ended (the attackers used dial-up lines). There was subsequent monitoring at Rome Lab and two hacker handles or aliases were identified—Kuji and Datastream Cowboy. Informants were solicited and someone recognized a hacker from the United Kingdom; this hacker had bragged that he had broken into various U.S. military systems. The United States then contacted Scotland Yard. Scotland Yard discovered the hacker was "phreaking" through Columbia and Chile to New York, defrauding telephone companies and using the New York ISP as a jumping-off point to attack Rome Lab. The U.K. hacker was later observed targeting other sites such as NATO headquarters, Goddard Space Flight Center, and Wright-Patterson Air Force Base. At least eight countries were used as conduits for these attacks. Scotland Yard had enough information to issue an arrest warrant and proceeded to make the arrest after data from the South Korean Atomic Research Institution was accessed. In all, over 150 intrusions were monitored at Rome Lab from 100 different points of origin. More than 100 other victims reportedly were hit.

Datastream Cowboy, a sixteen-year-old British student, pled guilty and was fined. His mentor, Kuji, a twenty-two-year-old Israeli technician, was found not guilty because no laws in Israel applied to this incident.

ELIGIBLE RECEIVER (1997)

Eligible Receiver was the first Information Warfare (IW) exercise in this country. Thirty-five people participated on the Red Team over 90 days using off-the-shelf technology and software. The scenario was a rogue state rejecting direct military confrontation with the United States, while seeking to attack vulnerable U.S. information systems. Some of the goals of the rogue state were to conceal the identity of the attackers and to delay or deny any U.S. ability to respond militarily.

A number of cyberattacks (all simulated) were made against power and communications networks in Oahu, Los Angeles, Colorado Springs, St. Louis, Chicago, Detroit, Washington, D.C., Fayetteville, and Tampa. Although reliable, unclassified results are hard to come by it is generally believed government and commercial sites were easily attacked and taken down. This exercise served as a wake-up call for many. General Campbell, head of the Pentagon's Joint Task Force—Computer Network Defense, wrote Eligible Receiver "clearly demonstrated our lack of preparation for a coordinated cyber and physical attack on our critical military and civilian infrastructure." Then-Pentagon-spokesman Kenneth Bacon said, "Eligible Receiver was an important and revealing exercise that taught us that we must be better organized to deal with potential attacks against our computer systems and information infrastructure." Senator John Kyl said in 1998:

Well, cyberterrorism is surprisingly easy. It's hard to quantify that in words, but there have been some exercises run recently. One that's been in the media, called Eligible Receiver, demonstrated in real terms how vulnerable the transportation grid, the electricity grid, and others are to an attack by, literally, hackers—people using conventional equipment, no "spook" stuff in other words.

SOLAR SUNRISE (1998)

In February 1998, a number of Department of Defense networks were attacked using a well-known vulnerability in the Solaris (UNIX-based) computer system. The attackers probed Defense Department servers to see if the vulnerability existed; exploited the vulnerability and entered the system; planted a program to gather data; and then returned later to collect that data.

Some of the initial probe activities appeared to originate from Harvard University and the United Arab Emirates (UAE), moving on to Pearl Harbor and a number of Air Force bases: Kirtland, Lackland, Andrews, Columbus, Gunter, and Tyndall. Later intrusion activities were monitored from the UAE, Utah State University, and a commercial Internet Web site to some of the same Air Force bases. Further activity was monitored at dozens of other U.S. military sites and universities. International activity was monitored in Germany, France, Israel, UAE, and Taiwan. Over 500 computer systems were compromised, including military, commercial, and educational sites, by attackers using only moderately sophisticated tools.

In the end, two California high school students were arrested and pled guilty. Their mentor, an eighteen-year-old Israeli, was also arrested and indicted. Although the Department of Defense called it "the most organized and systematic attack to date," many dismissed its seriousness because "the Justice Department claimed that no classified information was compromised." And details of precisely what the hackers did are not publicly available.

Lessons some have drawn, however, are that Solar Sunrise confirmed the findings of Eligible Receiver: U.S. information systems are vulnerable. Additionally, others indicate that various legal issues remain unresolved (e.g., statutory restrictions and competing investigative needs and privacy concerns that hinder searches), there are no effective indication-and-warning systems in place, intrusion-detection systems are insufficient, and there is too much government bureaucracy that hinders an effective and timely response.

—U.S. National Infrastructure Protection Center

Kosovo Capers

During the 1999 Kosovo War, the U.S. Air Force tapped into Serbian communications networks using satellites and EC-130 Compass Call aircraft. They wanted to insert false messages into the Serbian systems about nonexistent air raids and other attacks. Encouraged by their success, and wanting to improve their skills, the air force allocated more resources into these cyberwar activities.

Since 1999, new satellites, with more capabilities, have been put into orbit. The Kosovo experience, however, has Department of Defense lawyers nervous. The problem with using signals from satellites and high-flying aircraft to interfere with military communications systems has a drawback: it's often impossible to avoid interfering with civilian communications as well. What the military calls "collateral damage" (civilians accidentally hit with attacks meant for military targets) has become a political hot potato: some NGOs (nongovernmental organizations) are trying to establish international war crimes courts that might declare some cases of this as war crimes. This is more of a problem in wars that aren't really wars yet. Such was the case in Kosovo in 1999, when NATO warplanes began bombing in an effort to stop Serbs from attacking Albanians. It was a murky situation and no one was sure who was explicitly in the right. After the Serbs shot down an American F-117 bomber, however, the electronic weapons were unleashed. The collateral damage on Serb civilians didn't catch the attention of the media, and there was no embarrassing headline mongering about "inhumane and indiscriminate electronic weapons." Still, the danger is always there. Since 1999, U.S. cyberwarriors are under standing orders to get planned, offensive, cyberwar operations cleared with representative lawyers and public affairs experts (media damage control).

Although mostly a media ploy, the Serbs did get positive press by announcing their own cyberwar efforts. A great story for the world media, it caused momentary consternation in the Pentagon and White House, so it wasn't a completely wasted effort. Foreign reporters were invited into a roomful of Serbian college students banging away on Internet-connected PCs. The students were strictly amateurs, however, using script-kiddie tools to launch harmless attacks.

A more formidable group of cyberwarriors mobilized against the U.S. when the Chinese embassy in Serbia was accidentally bombed. Thousands of young Chinese hackers went to work on American Internet targets, while officially the Chinese government simply looked the other way. No serious damage was done, however. The Chinese government saw the defaced American Web pages and shut-down Web sites as a warning to the United States about the cyberthreat from the East.

The U.S. Air Force saw the Kosovo War as vindication of their earlier cyberwar efforts. The air force subsequently set up cyberwarfare organizations to continue speeding up weapon development in the cyberwar arena. New schools and courses were set up—along with the extensive school system already set up in electronic warfare—to train cyberwarriors.

Perhaps more important, an air force cyberwarfare officer was added to the staffs that planned and controlled combat operations. This was an important move for cyberwarriors, for it meant that commanders would always have pertinent information available to them in the war rooms.

Based on the experience in Kosovo, the air force looked more carefully for cyberwar opportunities. They found there were a lot more of them out there than they expected. For example, many nations, including China, use the civilian communications network for controlling air-defense systems (and military communications in general). Wealthier nations build separate, and less vulnerable, military communications systems. The civilian communications systems are built with off-the-shelf components and common principles (to keep the costs down, it's a competitive business). This made it easier to plan and execute cyberwar attacks on these systems. And there's an important difference between a cyberwar attack on enemy communications and an electronic-warfare attack. Cyberwarriors don't want to just bring down the system, as the electronic-warfare lads would do. No, they want to gain some control over the enemy communications. This way you can mess with the enemy's messages, as was done in Kosovo. Planting false or misleading information is more valuable than just shutting down the enemy electronic communications (which is useful, but the enemy will just find another, less efficient way to communicate). Moreover, there is one advantage to a civilian communications system, especially a large one like in China (which serves over a quarter of a billion customers): These systems are almost impossible to destroy. You can damage large parts of it, but, like the Internet, modern communications systems are built to take hits and keep on functioning.

Electronic Warfare over the Balkans

The U.S. has a flying radio/TV transmitter called Commando Solo (the EC-130E aircraft, a specially equipped C-130 transport). It got its first real workout during the 1999 Kosovo War, but didn't do so well due to the hilly terrain in the Balkans. The basic theory for Commando Solo was sound enough, though. Destroy the enemy radio and TV transmitters and then send in the plane to put out your message on the frequencies the locals were used to. Another specialized C-130, the EC-130H Compass Call aircraft did better: its purpose was to soak up and sort out enemy electronic transmissions. This bird could sing, too, and was the means of planting false messages into the Serb air-defense communications system.

One shortcoming of the EC-130H, however, is that it is a large, slow aircraft that has to get relatively close (a hundred kilometers or so) to enemy transmissions to do its work. But the mere presence of this new capability makes enemy air-defense operators and commanders less sure of themselves, and that is also a small victory.

The Keys Report

After the 1999 Kosovo War, air force Major General Ronald Keys (one of the senior officers who directed the air operations) prepared a report on what happened during the Information War/cyberwar portion of the Kosovo War. Interestingly, Keys's superiors said the report did not represent the U.S. Air Force's official views, but just those of General Keys. This was an interesting Information War gambit itself (meaning the air force wanted the information in the report to get out, but did not want it presented as official air force material). The Keys report was unclassified and delivered some harsh lessons on how successful and (more important) unsuccessful everyone's Information Warfare efforts were. A principal target for this report was the U.S. Congress, which has to come up with the money the air force wanted to increase their Information Warfare capability. The Keys report also demonstrated the large number of items included in the concept of Information Warfare. According to Keys, Information Warfare covers managing how (and what) information is passed to the news media as well as compromising enemy communications systems. While the report spoke of "NATO Information Warfare" efforts, it was mainly dealing with American Information War and cyberwar operations. Keys concluded that NATO was better at the technical (wide array of tools and capabilities available) aspects than in how the weapons were applied (the "tactical aspects").

The Serbs (representing what was left of Yugoslavia) had much less Information Warfare equipment to play with, so they had to do more with what they did have: a long history of using deception to foil more powerful enemies. Despite all the American electronic sensors (in aircraft and satellites) taking pictures night and day and picking up any electronic transmission in Serb territory, the Serbs managed to use a more powerful array of low-tech tools. On the ground, their troops knew how to hide themselves and their vehicles. Even with all that American stuff watching them, they were still able to move around. They used decoys and fake vehicles that we did spot, and bomb. The Serbs played up the few times smart bombs hit civilian targets. They played on American sensitivity to civilian casualties to the extent that they began to look like victims. The Serbs succeeded with the "civilian casualties" to the point where many of the NATO nations insisted on reviewing any proposed targets for U.S. bombers, and often exercised a veto. This approval process reduced the effectiveness of NATO bombing, as mobile targets had often moved by the time approval was received. The Serbs also played a mean information game, getting true and false rumors into circulation, causing confusion and dissention among NATO members. The Serbs were quite good at playing the public relations war, and NATO never really was able to score many points in that area.

The extensive array of Information War tools available to NATO actually backfired in many respects. The vast amount of visual and electronic information collected by the aircraft, satellites, and ground stations flooded into NATO headquarters, overwhelming staffs and commanders. Key information was often lost in the flood of data. Sometimes useful items were found, and it was suspected that a lot of valuable information was never found. The superb communications system turned into a curse for commanders. For American generals, it meant they could get a phone call from the president at any time. Since the president could get to the satellite reconnaissance stuff first, the flustered general could only steam while his boss in the White House told him what to do and how to do it.

General Keys concluded that there had to be a better way to deal with the flood of information and the curse of micromanagement from above. This complaint, unfortunately, has been heard periodically since the 1970s. The problem, however, seems to have been addressed during the Afghanistan War in 2001.

The Balkans Syndrome

The Internet often provides the jumping-off point for cyberwar skirmishes that no one expects. In early 2001, the Italian media took an unsubstantiated Internet item and published a bizarre, but powerful, story involving Italian peacekeepers dying from leukemia as part of the "Balkans syndrome." Half a dozen Italian troops had died from the disease after and another two dozen Italian soldiers (out of 60,000 who have served in the Balkans since 1995) came down with various similar illnesses. The reason given was depleted uranium. For weeks, the Italian, and then the European, press ran with the story. No one, apparently, bothered to check with doctors or scientists who knew anything about depleted uranium.

Depleted uranium—denser and heavier than other metals—is used to pierce tanks when shot by 30-mm cannons usually carried by A-10 attack aircraft, as well as 120-mm tank guns. US A-10s fired some 30,000 30-mm shells in Kosovo. Not only does the depleted uranium go through armor, it also burns when it hits armor at high speed (a mile a second). This increases the damage within the tank, but when the depleted uranium burns, it also creates many tiny fragments. Italian scientists reportedly felt that these fragments, emitting alpha rays, were causing the Balkans syndrome problems.

Depleted uranium replaced tungsten, another (nonradioactive) heavy metal for armor piercing work. Tungsten can also cause health problems if it gets inside of you, as does another, more familiar heavy metal: lead.

Depleted uranium is what is left after the highly radioactive U-235 is removed from uranium for use as nuclear fuel or for atomic bombs; U-235 emits dangerous gamma (and other) radiation. U-238 is what is left, which, while still radioactive, emits much-less dangerous alpha rays. Thus less radioactive than the original uranium, depleted uranium is not much more radioactive than many other rocks. Thousands of American soldiers and civilians have handled depleted uranium in the last half century with no noticeable increase in health problems. Moreover, there has been no increase in cancer cases among the civilian population of Kosovo since 1999. Specialists also point out that it takes five to ten years for leukemia to develop from a radiation exposure. The Italian troops had only been in Kosovo since 1995, or three years. Nuclear medicine specialists also point out that depleted uranium's alpha rays would be stopped by skin. Leukemia is a cancer of the bone marrow, something depleted uranium's alpha rays could not reach.

There has been an increase in cancers in Kuwait and southern Iraq since the 1991 Gulf War. The area was subjected to several weeks of burning oil fields. These fumes are a known carcinogen and were far more abundant than the remains of depleted uranium shells. Moreover, the thousands of armored vehicles that tore up the pristine desert created an unprecedented (even for Arabia) dust cloud containing a very fine, talclike sand. Local doctors were not surprised at the increase in illness because they knew, from long experience, what oil fumes and sand can do.

So what made depleted uranium a credible news story in Italy, and throughout Europe? Part of it was the eagerness of the media to follow a frightening story. In Italy there was also much public displeasure with the NATO actions in the Balkans. Italy, in particular, has been the destination of many Albanian refugees, from Kosovo as well as Albania itself. Most of the air attacks against Serbia and Kosovo came from the Italian air bases. When it was reported during the air campaign that returning warplanes would be dropping their bombs in the Adriatic (rather than risk landing with them), the Italians were incensed. Although not armed, the bombs were still highly explosive and a clear danger to Italian fishermen.

The Internet also played a part in the Italian displeasure with their involvement in the Balkans. The depleted uranium story first became news after the 1991 Gulf War as another bit of Iraqi propaganda. It would have quietly faded away were it not stored on the Web and quickly referenced through search engines. It also became a pro-Iraqi/anti-U.S. discussion point there before the Italian media decided to pick it up—with plenty of easily accessed backup material.

This is Information Warfare. Italian politicians knew it would be an unpopular stance to go along with the rest of NATO in attacking Serbia and taking over Kosovo. The flood of refugees would head straight for Italy, increasing an already unpopular (with Italian voters) refugee population. What better way to deflect some of the negative feelings than to get solidly behind the Balkans syndrome. Moreover, the real story of the end of the war, about veterans with additional physical and psychological illnesses, would probably not get much play, although the true nature of depleted uranium would eventually erode the visibility of Balkans syndrome as a news story. Ultimately, the politicians will suffer no ill will from their involvement in supporting the public outrage over a war fought with misinformation.

The Y2K Scare

The Department of Defense shut down many military Web sites over the year 2000 New Year's holiday weekend. This was to avoid exposing them to attacks by hackers who might have somehow found a Y2K flaw that could only be exploited when the clocks turned over from 1999 to 2000. Nothing happened.

The Y2K (geekish for "Year 2000") situation was turned into a major scare by the clueless media and some rapacious software companies. The problem arose in the 1950s, when the first commercial software was being developed for computers. By today's standards, they were tiny computers, with only a few thousand bytes of memory to play with. Since space was so tight, it became common to keep track of year dates using only the last two digits ("1957" became "57"). Now everyone knew at the time that eventually, in the year 2000, these two-digit dates would become a problem (the computer would not know if it was dealing with 1900 or 2000). Actually, the problem was going to arrive even earlier than that. Many commercial firms have to plan ahead and use future dates. Think of a bank keeping track of thirty-year mortgages on their computers. This kind of software had to be Y2K ready in the late 1960s.

These early programmers assumed that the software they were writing would be replaced with stuff using four-digit year dates before 2000. Well, it didn't happen. A lot of that early software wasn't replaced. It was just upgraded so that it could run on newer and more powerful computers. The watchword was "if it ain't broke, don't fix it." But as

2000 loomed, it became obvious that a huge flock of chickens were coming home to roost. The major problem was no one knew exactly where the problems were and how many there were. This enabled the media to assume the worst (this sells more newspapers) and there promptly appeared many software consultants to assist nervous managers on how to fix the problem.

FUD (fear, uncertainty, and doubt) caused a lot more anxiety than was warranted. What actually happened was that software managers finally got the money to upgrade a lot of ancient code. By the 1980s, most new stuff was being done with four-digit year dates. Most banks and financial institutions had been dealing with the Y2K problem since the 1970s. But the programs that needed the most attention were really ancient code written in computer languages (like COBOL) that hardly anyone used anymore. Lots of retired programmers had to be paid big bucks to get them off the golf courses and back into cubicle land.

What worried people the most was seriously dangerous things going bad because of Y2K problems. By December 1999, the Department of Defense announced that the 2,101 computers that were essential to running the U.S. military were "Y2K ready" and another 5,488 (well, all but ten) "pretty important" computers were also ready.

But fear of serious Y2K problems in Eastern Europe caused the U.S. State Department to evacuate 352 diplomats (and their dependents) from U.S. embassies and consulates in Russia, Belarus, Moldova, and Ukraine. American also paid to bring Russian experts to the United States (and send Americans to Russia) to stand by in command centers for 2000 to show up. There was fear (unfounded, as it was in nearly all cases) that something would go wrong with nuclear missiles or space satellites.

Okay, some things did go wrong. In what the Department of Defense called "one serious incident," a U.S. spy satellite (a Keyhole bird) lost about three hours of data when a ground station had a Y2K problem. The U.S. satellite recon system was crippled for two days until the Y2K problems were resolved. That was it, at least as far as "major" problems went.

There were smaller problems that were noted. A cash register at a PX on Okinawa was out of action for a while because of Y2K issues. Some computers that had been "fixed" proceeded to present the year 1900 when 2000 was intended. There were some similar problems at many nuclear power plants (where every little thing tends to get reported), but nothing serious enough to interrupt operations.

The military was so relieved that it awarded Meritorious Service Medals to the project managers who led the effort to get the army's thousands of computer systems Y2K ready. Those who had spent at least a year working on Y2K issues received the Army Commendation Medal. To recognize the hundred of troops drafted for the last few months of furious effort, anyone who labored for at least two months on the Y2K effort, and distinguished themselves, received an Army Achievement Medal. Others who took part in Y2K projects received certificates or souvenir coins to show that they had served in a rather massive and, most important, successful, operation.

While much of the hype was just that, hype, you didn't hear any of the software professionals complaining out loud. These folks went along with the scam because they were finally getting money to repair some very old software. This had been a major, if unseen (by the public) controversy between software professionals (programmers and their supervisors) and senior management for several decades. Once it became clear that the 1950s and 1960s software was not going to be replaced, or thoroughly upgraded, the software community knew that there were going to be serious problems down the line. In the 1990s these problems began to surface. The software pioneers who had written this stuff were retiring, and their managers often made sure they kept in touch with these guys (most programmers were, and generally still are, men). Even before the Y2K crises, retired programmers were enticed back (with consulting contracts or high day rates) to fix old software that none of the current programmers could really understand. Actually, the day of reckoning was delayed somewhat by the end of the Cold War. Russia was one of the few major nations that still used the ancient computer languages, and this provided some new hires to maintain ancient code. But the noticeable number of Russian programmers in American companies also raised another fear in the wake of the Y2K work. It was pointed out that all these temporary hires brought in to plow through old software looking for, and fixing, two-digit year dates could also add code that would allow someone to later get into the systems these programs ran on. This was especially the case with government and banking systems. There were a lot of suspected cases of this, but few actual occurrences showed up. This scare was more the last gasp of the fear mongering that proliferated throughout the Y2K scare. For one thing, most of the programs in need of Y2K attention were not connected with the Internet or any other kind of network. And those that were tended to be watched over by regular staff or trusted subcontractors. Still, you never know.

Code Red from China

Information Warfare struck hard in July 2001 when thousands of Web sites got hit with the Code Red virus. Initially, no one knew where Code Red came from, although when it hit a vulnerable Web server (a PC running a Web site), it changed the Web site page to a page that read "Hacked by Chinese." Code Red provided an example of how Information War would be fought.

First, Code Red only worked because of a flaw in Microsoft's Web server software. On June 18, Microsoft issued a security bulletin about a vulnerability in that software and provided a patch. But by announcing this problem, Microsoft also let the bad guys know there was a way to sneak into servers and do damage. On July 13, the first reports of Code Red were received. The virus was quickly taken apart and it was discovered that it had a number of interesting features. First, it operated completely in memory, not putting anything on the hard drive. This made it harder to find, even though it defaced the server's Web page. Second, it immediately began randomly calling other servers, looking for vulnerable ones to infect. At the time there were about 3.5 million servers out there that were potentially vulnerable (the 21 percent of the world's 17 million active servers running Microsoft software). It was estimated that Code Red could infect half a million servers in twenty-four hours. As it was, only about 300,000 were infected. This was because the random search was not completely random, a feature that could have provided the authors of Code Red with a larger list of vulnerable servers, but a week after the first Code Red appeared, a modified version appeared that went after every server it could reach. It's not known if every vulnerable server was hit, or what percentage of the Microsoft servers were patched to keep Code Red out. If a server administrator just fixed the defaced Web pages and did not reboot their server PC, Code Red went dormant and then became active again on certain days of the month to either try and spread or execute a denial of service attack on the U.S. White House server. This was avoided by changing the IP address of the White House server and simply dumping the junk data that went to the old address.

Apparently the U.S. military felt vulnerable as they closed many of their Web sites for several days to make sure the servers were patched to keep Code Red out.

What's special about Code Red is that it wasn't anything special. Worm-type programs like Code Red are known to be fast. Code Red was dangerous because of the easy access the defective Microsoft server software provided. The "index server ISAPI vulnerability" that Code Red exploited was one of many in this particular software. Microsoft server software is notoriously buggy, with about one new vulnerability being found each month (and forty bugs of all sorts in the seven months preceding the Code Red Attack). Attempts to get Microsoft to be more serious about system security had limited success. Meanwhile, the original Code Red was hibernating on servers where it was not detected. These Code Red sites reactivated at 8 P.M. EDT, July 31, 2001. But this second wave proved much less troublesome than the first attack. Meanwhile, mutant versions of Code Red were released. There were perhaps a million servers out there at the end of July that were still vulnerable and capable of being turned into Net-choking, spamming machines when the second wave hit. But sites that might be widely noticed (government and e-commerce) managed to get their defenses up.

The U.S. government has been a major customer of Microsoft products, mainly because the stuff is easy to use. This is important, because the government cannot compete with the commercial sector when it comes to hiring the best computer talent. Any future wartime use of cyberwar will use programs like Code Red because all servers using the Microsoft software will not be patched. Well, at least not until a new version of the software is released and all servers upgrade. Put another way, hostile nations will have access to some U.S. servers for years to come. Wartime versions of Code Red will not deface Web pages or let its presence be known. No, the combat version of Code Red will hide out until instructed to launch a denial of service attack, or some other mischief, on American servers.

One wonders if Microsoft will ever be tried for treason.

The Code Red worm was described as the perfect media software. It doesn't do much damage, although a mutant strain could be pretty deadly, and will stay around for years (until all servers running NT or Windows 2000 are upgraded or patched). If you're having a slow news day, Code Red will always be there for another scary headline. But Code Red has also done a public service by making more people (especially clueless sysadmins) aware of the importance of keeping server software up to date. Another side effect was a repeat of the call for some fundamental changes in how the Internet operates. From the beginning, it was easy for users to hide their identity on the Net. No one foresaw the enormous growth, and commercialization, of the Internet. So in the beginning, security was not a critical issue. That has obviously changed. Reconfiguring Internet software to eliminate the anonymity would be a major task, made more difficult by getting so many people to sign off on it. It has been proposed many times before. This would be a bitch to do considering the "legacy code" that would have to be changed. Making everything traceable would not be a panacea, though, for there would always be ways around that. Still, making things harder for the black hats is a good thing.

In late August, 2001 a U.S. government study concluded that the Code Red worm probably originated in a university in Guangdong, China. A nongovernment research organization, Computer Economics, estimated that the cost of cleaning up Code Red damage was $2.6 billion ($1.1 billion for inspecting and cleaning servers and $1.5 in lost productivity while servers were down). This was based on an estimate of some 1 million servers being infected.

CHAPTER 5

Cyberwars Present and Future

Several cyberwars are going on right now, and several more are brewing.

Cyberwar Is Already Here

The idea of cyberwarfare hasn't been picked up by most people's radar yet. At worst, most people see hackers and a few archcybercriminals. But year by year, more Internet users encounter cyberwar personally. This often just means getting a computer virus, or having the office network shut down for hours, or days, while damage from some cyberterrorism is repaired. But is the problem really big enough to start a race for Web security? There are signs that it is. In 2000, when China and Taiwan were going at it over the Taiwanese independence issue, pro-Taiwanese Web pages were getting trashed regularly. The culprits were traced back to servers in Beijing.

A similar activity happened with recent snooping in Department of Defense servers. The culprits were operating from Moscow. When the DOD called them on it, the Russians responded that they would not be so clumsy as to be caught, if they indeed had done such a thing. Rather, they blamed thrill-seeking amateurs. There may have been some of that, as many of the attacks were made with tools and techniques that weren't advanced. But the Russian-based attacks were all done 9–5 (local time) and never on Russian holidays. Government employees always leave a trail. Freelancers generally work different hours, often at local nighttime. During the 1999 Kosovo War, the Serbs made no secret of the local crackers they had mobilized to fight back. There was some mischief done, but no serious damage. And these Serbian hacker volunteers worked all hours.

Whoever began the hacking, both the Russians, hackers, and the rest of the world know one fact: America is the most vulnerable nation with regard to cyberwarfare. America has taken the lead in hooking essential services and business operations up to the Internet. This is often a convenience for staff; so that when there's an emergency, the people in charge can just log on to the company Web site and take care of business. An example would be a water-reservoir system. If there's a problem on the weekend, an engineer can be alerted at home. The engineer can log on to the reservoir-system Web site, check to see how the dams and waterways are doing (via sensors and controls also hooked up to the Internet), and make adjustments without having to drive the many miles to a dam. Another benefit of something like this is that several technical experts can log on at once, examine the data, discuss the situation via a chat room or conference call, and then quickly take action. The same system also applies to factories, research labs, or large office buildings. The downside is that if any of these facilities do not have adequate security on their Internet connections, their system can be hacked and someone could do a lot of damage, something like opening up a dam to release all its water or manipulating factory controls to cause an explosion or other damage.

Information is now recognized as a great source of power, and increasing amounts of data, especially military, is online. Fortunately, most Net experts in the world are Americans. And then there is the American tendency to pile on in a crises situation and beat it to death. Don't underestimate this, for it is the major reason the U.S. won the Cold War, not to mention World War II, the Space Race, and so on. Anyone launching an attack on American commercial or military facilities will find themselves dealing with some of the best Internet talent on the planet. So far, attacks on American dams, factories, or military databases has been largely theoretical. Department of Defense sites containing military information have been under attack for over a decade, and some of these attacks make the news. This war goes on all the time, although most of the action takes place out of the public view, but occasionally bits and pieces will surface. We know that the Department of Defense keeps improving its defenses, and businesses that make heavy use of the Internet also work constantly to make themselves less vulnerable.

Cyberattacks on the U.S. Defense Department

The U.S. Department of Defense computer systems have increasingly been the target of cyberwar attacks from all over. It started in the 1980s, as more people got online. The popular 1984 movie *Wargames* encouraged the trend. The movie featured a teenage hacker getting into a system that didn't exist; and almost (in the movie) launching nuclear missiles. A lot of teenagers never realized that the movie was total fiction, and attempting to "hack into the Pentagon" has become a popular indoor sport the world over. In the last few years, the attacks on Department of Defense Web sites have become more numerous, damaging, and often, it would appear, training exercises for foreign hackers getting ready for a major war. The number of attacks has increased steadily through the 1990s.

Annual Attacks on Department of Defense Internet Sites

Year	Net Attacks
1994	225
1995	559
1996	730
1997	780
1998	5,844
1999	22,144
2000	24,501
2001	30,000

These are only the attacks that are noted. The most dangerous ones don't get detected, and no one has any idea how many of those have taken place. Very few of these attacks result in any noticeable damage. The army, for example, reported that in 2001, for every thousand attempted Internet break-ins, 6.69 were successful. In 2000, there had been 11.6 break-ins per thousand attempts. Very few of the break-ins of military Web sites have been serious because the most critical military computers tend to be better protected. But there is, obviously, risk. However, the army Internet experts noted that 98 percent of the successful break-ins were a result of hackers taking advantage of known weaknesses that could have, and should have, been fixed.

Attacks dipped considerably after September 11, 2001, aided by most military networks being pulled off the Internet for a while. The military also maintains networks independent of the Internet. By the end of the year, attacks on U.S. military networks was up, way up, however, running at an annual rate of 40,000. There may be more than 40,000 attacks in 2002 if the number of daily attacks keeps going up. The earlier years probably undercounted the number of attacks, as many failed (or even successful) ones passed unnoticed. Better defensive technology (intrusion detectors and monitoring systems) are catching more attempts, and stopping many that are near to success.

Worse, the attacks are increasingly more sophisticated (it's hard to detect them) and damaging (the bad guys are getting to the good stuff). Think of intrusion detectors as Internet versions of silent burglar-alarm systems. Same principles, and just as vulnerable to being defeated by very good burglars or, in this case, hackers. More experienced hackers know about intrusion detectors and try to get in without being discovered. If you can do this, you have a good chance of getting to classified military information. This can include anything from where troops are, where they are going, details on how weapons operate (so you can more easily defeat them) and to the holy of holies, control over military communications systems (which use a lot of space satellites).

Although many attacks are simply thrill seekers looking to score points with their peers by "hacking the Pentagon," some are rather more serious, coming in a pattern and with specific, and dangerous, goals in mind. At the end of 2001, the Department of Defense reported attacks that were apparently from Al Qaeda and other Islamic fundamentalist groups. Although the groups don't yet possess the highest level of hacking tools, there's a lot of "how to hack" info and tools available on the Web, and the terrorists do attract many educated people to their organizations. The first widespread computer virus, in fact, was written by Pakistani programmers in the 1980s.

No one is releasing data on the number of cyberwar attacks made by the American military. Obviously, you don't want potential enemies to know what you are doing and how, or how often, you are doing it. Because no nation has a larger military and government presence on the Internet, the U.S. has invested heavily in developing cyberwar weapons and technology. Unlike other weapons, you can't identify ones used on the Net, much less describe them, without compromising their effectiveness. This continues to cause disputes within the Defense Department when some senior leaders ask for the use of the formidable cyber-weapons, and the cyberwarriors resist, claiming the target is not worth the use of their formidable, valuable, and scarce assets. This argument makes sense. Once some of these cyberwar technologies are used, and their techniques revealed, they are no longer useful, or as useful. Sort of like a hand grenade, you can only use it once. Undoubtedly, there are not many of these magic hand grenades in the American cyberarsenal. And when they are used, they have to be replaced at great expense. Moreover, even existing weapons quickly become obsolete as Internet technology changes.

Many of the attacks on U.S. military computers are caught while they are underway, making it possible to trace the source of the attack. In many cases, the PCs the attacks were launched from are training centers operated by governments, including Russia, China, and Iraq.

One example was a computer virus that invaded U.S. Marine

Headquarters PCs on October 21, 1999. The attack destroyed files and brought down several machines. The virus exploited scripting language vulnerabilities in Microsoft Word and Microsoft Excel. Although details on how the attack was carried out were not released, the way it was executed indicate that it was deliberate. The marines never reported if they were able to trace the source of the attack.

More worrisome are the large-scale attacks made on U.S. military networks. Since March 1998, they have been undergoing sustained attacks from Russia. The Russian government denies responsibility, even though the United State formally protested to the Russians in 2000. It's quite possible that the three-year assault is being undertaken by criminal gangs. This is a professional effort, sneaking into military servers and leaving behind zombie programs that can be easily activated to provide the hackers with access. Similar attacks have been made on university and research organization computers.

Going After the Big Guy

Hacking some nets gets you more points than others. The biggest score is the U.S. military. The Department of Defense runs some 10,000 different networks—most linked to the Internet—using nearly 2 million PCs. Some 2,000 of the Pentagon's nets are critical, controlling essential functions like command and control, logistics, nuclear weapons, research, and intelligence.

In 1999, the Pentagon detected some 22,000 attempts to hack into their systems. Most of these were amateurs, often teenage script kiddies employing easy-to-use tools widely available on the Web. In 2000, there was about a 10 percent increase in attempted hacks. About 3 percent of these caused some Web pages or local nets to be shut down for a short time. About 1 percent of the hacks actually got into a site, but none were able to get into classified databases or take control of critical functions. Or at least no such hacks were detected. What worries Pentagon computer-security experts is the number of professionals who are trying to get in. Even during the 1980s, before the Internet and the World Wide Web became widely available, Soviet intelligence agencies were hiring hackers to get into Pentagon networks. Some of these attempts succeeded, or at least they got in and were later found out. A professional hacker wants to get in, take information, and not be caught. Classified information stolen that way is a lot more valuable than when you get it and your hack is detected. Some of the recent successful ones were traced back to military organizations in China and Russia. Both countries deny that they were trying to hack the Pentagon.

It was the military that created the Internet, but they did not use it until civilians got access in the early 1990s and the World Wide Web appeared in the mid-1990s. No one expected the Web to have such an enormous impact on how people communicated. Soldiers, as well as civilians, eagerly took advantage of the many opportunities presented by the Web. Faced with all the clamor for military Web use from their own troops, the generals gave in and began using the Web everywhere, even on the battlefield. Very quickly, however, everyone was reminded of how easy it was to hack into other people's Web sites and the computer servers they ran on. Hacking wasn't the only problem.

In early 2000, a Pentagon task force took a close look at 800 major military Web sites. They found 1300 instances where sensitive, or even classified, information was available. Shortly thereafter, most U.S. military Web sites were shut down for "reorganization." When these sites came back online, there were a lot more restrictions on who could see what. Either you needed a military account (.mil) or a password to get to the good stuff. Less visible were the frantic changes made to try and keep the hackers at bay.

The best defense against hackers is well-trained systems administrators (sysadmins) keeping your network software up to date and secure. Most hacks, especially the professional ones, are the result of software that was poorly installed or not updated with the latest patches and protections. The demand for good sysadmins made young soldiers who had these skills immediately employable in the civilian job market. In fact, the military had a hard time getting them to reenlist. Having such a hard time keeping enough sysadmins, the services often used civilians who admitted to knowing "something about PCs."

The sysadmin shortage was addressed by providing better centralized support for military Web sites. Then the military began, in the late 1990s, using their own teams of hackers to periodically attack their own sites and networks to see how secure they were. The weak sites got more attention. It wasn't a perfect solution, but it was better than the earlier anarchy.

At the same time, the Pentagon went on the offensive. The most sensitive sites were given the most attention, something that was not always done in the past. To cut down on the amateur attacks that succeeded, false files, labeled as top secret, were placed on servers' hard disks. Obvious decoys, these files enticed intruders to stick around long enough for them to be traced and caught, or at least identified (usually

as Chinese or Russian). A few well-publicized prosecutions would discourage many casual hackers. The professionals are another matter.
These hackers are careful and skillful. They will hack into a site and just
look around to find traps and see how security is set up. The professional hackers will then come back and do some real damage, knowing
how not to set off alerts. As discussed, it's not just stolen files that are a
worry, but the planting of programs that can be set off later to trash the
network and its files or send operational data to the enemy. This last
item is particularly scary, as it means that the hacked computer will pass
on to the enemy details of what that particular computer is doing for
your war effort.

No one has pulled off a major network attack yet, but the potential
is there. Because the United States has more PCs and networks than any
other nation, it appears to be the most vulnerable to such an offensive.
But most of the work on network security is being done in the U.S. No
one knows how likely Web warfare is, but no one believes it is impossible. Someone will eventually become the victim of a "Pearl Harbor" attack delivered by hackers. Until that time, everyone is eligible for this
dubious honor.

The Internet Goes to War

There was no magic involved in the rapid adoption of the Internet
for military use. The pressure and expertise was coming from below.
Soldiers bought PCs with their own money before the brass got around
to making such purchases officially. The troops immediately saw the
laborsaving potential of PCs and e-mail. Then, when the Department of
Defense finally allowed the Internet to be "commercialized" in the early
1990s, the troops ran with it. As long as the Internet was tied to phone
lines, however, most of the military use was restricted to military bases
and soldiers using their home PCs to stay in touch with one another.
Even before the Internet became available to the general public, soldiers
were using ARPANET (the DoD predecessor of the Internet) and commercial networks to discuss military issues, plan operations, and generally operate faster and more efficiently. The generals were usually the
last to know what a powerful new tool they had available. Indeed, many
of the generals in the 1990s had gotten their first taste of the Internet
when they were college students and junior officers. This played a large
role in the rapid escalation of Internet and e-mail connections between
themselves and military organizations back in the States. Generals no-

ticed that this approach was quicker and more effective than traditional methods of communicating (telephone and paper documents).

After the Gulf War, the buzzword du jour was "netcentric operations." Officers began searching out Internet-savvy young troops and turning them loose. The senior brass had seen their own kids, as well as the junior officers that worked for them, take to the Internet in a big way. Moreover, many military officers have a bit of the "gadget freak" in them anyway and are science-fiction fans. The Internet hit a responsive chord, which speeded its use on the job. Officially accepted technology began to catch up. For example, satellite-dish equipment was tweaked to better handle Internet data. The military came up with a secure (encrypted) version of Internet data so they could send sensitive material from browser to browser. The navy upgraded their communications so that every sailor could use e-mail as much as they wanted. This not only made everyone's work much easier and quicker, but vastly improved the morale of those forced to spend months at sea. Army battlefield commanders used Web browsers to replace field telephones and maps with plastic overlays (and grease pencils), which had been their chief tools for nearly a century.

Online games and instant interactive voice and graphic communications provided troops with the concepts and working technology to create battlefield techniques that speeded up operations to the point where a nonnetcentric opponent simply could not keep up. There is always a need for speed on the battlefield and the Internet tools provide more speed than anyone had imagined.

Potential opponents, however, also have access to Internet tools, so it was not a luxury for the military to adopt this technology. Whoever implements the Internet in combat will have an edge, an edge that can mean the difference between life and death. In the aftermath of Silicon Valley dot-com start-ups, few people think of browsers as lethal weapons, but they are. Whoever gets to the battlefield first with the most Internet technology will survive and win.

The Threat from the East

The Cold War was supposed to have ended in 1991, but on the Internet it continues. Consider the battle fought between Russian criminal gangs and Cold War–era software experts in 2000. The gangs broke into some three dozen heavily guarded e-commerce sites and financial institutions and stole data from over a million credit card accounts.

These gangs are considered some of the most dangerous ones in cyber-space. Although the Russian government has started to crack down on these groups in 2001, the gangs are so rich, well connected, and violent, that any such crackdown will be very difficult. That other Cold War foe, China, is not interested in reining in its hackers at all. In April 2001, Chinese hackers began a popular movement to deface U.S. Web sites in protest of the American patrol plane's downing of a Chinese fighter that month. The Chinese didn't do so well, defacing, at most, 300 sites while American hackers, in retaliation, defaced over 900 Chinese sites. Unbowed, Chinese hackers apparently unleashed the Code Red worm, which brought down over 300,000 (mostly American) Web sites. The Code Red was traced back to a university in China. China openly pro-claims its belief that cyberwar is one area in which it can achieve world-class capability and meet America on even terms. Because of an increasing number of Net attacks on U.S. targets that have been traced back to Chinese locations, including Chinese-government servers, it can only be concluded that the Chinese are serious.

Doomsday Via the Internet

In 2000, two Russian college students in Kaluga were arrested, tried, and convicted for an Internet hoax. The students tried to pass them-selves off as missile control officers with the power to authorize the launch of Russian nuclear missiles. The two wanted to nuke Western Europe. Both of the young men were sentenced to a year of hard labor. The implications are what are at issue here—for everyone. In theory anyway, it is possible to hack sites to do something as far-fetched as launching nuclear missiles.

Electronic Guerillas from China

Because new technology tends to produce change governments can-not control, China entered the twenty-first century nervous. For cen-turies, the country had solved such problems by outlawing change. This may seem odd to us, but it has worked in China many times, and Chinese leaders see nothing implausible about this approach. China is still a police state, and the government is fearful of a popular movement to overthrow the Communist party control of the country. To this end, the government insists on controlling the media and communications.

The government's biggest problem, however, is corruption, not revolutionaries. The growing corruption, especially among members of the ruling Communist party, makes unregulated communications among citizens a source of unwanted political change for the government. Twentieth-century media developments changed the way politics operates in China. Electronic media, especially radio, made a largely illiterate population more aware of the world beyond their villages. The spread of television in the last twenty years only intensified this. Then came the pagers, cell phones, and Internet in the 1980s and 1990s. This was, for a totalitarian government, a truly scary development. Centrally controlled media like radio and TV made running a police state easier. You could tightly control the message, and keep most people from knowing, for example, how badly the Communist party was doing. Even telephones can be controlled by limiting who has them and letting everyone know what a phone tap is. Pagers and cell phones were mobile, and thus more dangerous. The Internet was worse, for it allowed access to the outside world. Worst of all, there was no historical experience of how to deal with these new technologies. The Communists rule much the same way the emperors did for thousands of years before them.

In the late twentieth century, the Chinese restricted the Internet, faxes, and cell phones. Although these efforts are not completely effective, Chinese dissidents or criminals know that there's always a chance they can be overheard; there is a little fear. The Chinese cyberpolice have, in effect, driven much of the Net expression underground and created a generation of electronic guerillas. E-mail, faxes, and cell phones get around this somewhat by using code words. Web sites containing forbidden information are set up outside China. When the cyberpolice find out about it and block it, the site is moved and coded messages explain where the new location is. Internet users within China have to be careful, however. It's illegal to use encryption. Get caught and you have a close encounter with the secret police, plus the possibility of a long stay in jail. In China, cell-phone systems are set up so that the location of users can be quickly found. If you are one of the usual suspects, you have to use your cell phone carefully. Constantly getting new ones can get expensive, and can also alert the police. Fax usage can be traced to a specific phone line.

There are wireless gadgets that the Chinese cyberpolice do have hard times with: pagers. This was the first form of wireless communication introduced into China, and it remains very popular. It's much cheaper than a cell phone and early on the Chinese worked out codes that perform complex communications with simple two-way, or one-way, pagers. By 2000, there were some 1,500 pager systems in China, with 52,000 base stations (antennas) and over a hundred million users (compared to 60 million cell-phone users, 12 million Internet users and 130 million regular phone users in that country). Policing the pagers is difficult because there are so many separate companies providing the service, and so many codes. It was, for all practical purposes, impossible to capture all, or even most, of the messages. Even if that were done, sorting out which messages said "pick up some snow peas on your way home from work" from those that say "the demonstration will be at 1 P.M. tomorrow" would be beyond current technology. So Chinese freely use their pagers to communicate without Big Brother eavesdropping. It's with pagers (and most new cell phones, which also allow text messages) that the persecuted religious group Falun Gong has been able to maintain its organization and the ability to continue mounting demonstrations. The downside is that criminal organizations also use the pagers, complicating police work.

As inexpensive and useful as pagers are, their use is declining as cell-phone service spreads in China. By the end of 2001, there were 135 million cell phone users and only 50 million pager users. Internet use, although more expensive than cell phones and pagers, is also growing at a rapid clip, reaching 22 million users by the end of 2001 (up from less than 2 million in 1997). Much to the cybercops' dismay, former pager users bring to all the cybertechnologies in China the custom of using codes and specialized slang. While many more Chinese have cell phones, they liked to keep the messages short. With so many people using codes for practical (economic) uses, it's difficult for the cops to figure out when such use is innocent or not.

Yet the police do come off with one unique advantage. China's cybercops are the most expert and experienced in the world when it comes to messing with and monitoring the Internet and wireless communications. This has implications beyond the needs of running a police state in the Internet age, it gives you an edge beyond your borders. Working as a hacker for the police is seen as a prestigious job in China. The government has been playing up nationalism for the last ten years and this has been well received by the younger folks. The propaganda stresses China's remarkable recovery from a century of calamities and the need for other nations to show China proper respect. This is the same sort of nationalism that got World War I and II started. The Communist politicians running China are playing with fire, but it works. So the hackers eagerly sign up to serve the fatherland. Remarkably, few have been "polluted" by Western ideas. Democracy is an alien concept in China, and few people see much need for it. All they want the government to do is leave them alone so they can get rich.

China does have one problem with its hackers, though. Unlike India, that other growing software powerhouse, China teaches its students programming in Chinese. Indian students learn programming in English, giving India an enormous advantage. Moreover, Indian students tend to be more familiar with Microsoft products, which are the most widely used. In China, the standard is Unix, more specifically, Linux. In fact, Chinese universities allow only Linux to be used. So Chinese cyberwarriors must later learn how to use Microsoft software (the most vulnerable in the world, and the most widely used in U.S. government organizations).

Although the Chinese now have the most formidable ability on the planet to deal with pagers, cell phones, and the Internet, they know this may not be enough. This capability will probably prove more useful as a weapon against foreign enemies. Taiwan and the United States have already gotten an unpleasant taste of what the Chinese-government hackers can do. Meanwhile, the grassroots hackers in China move in ways no one can predict. If China spins out of control, you can be sure pagers and cell phones are at the root of it.

Iraq's Starving Cyberwarriors

Not all examples of cyberwar involve a lot of technical skills, but they do require a certain amoral boldness. Here's an example that went off right in front of you. Iraq continues to protest that the UN embargo is killing Iraqi civilians. The embargo has been in place since the end of the 1991 Gulf War, and will not end until Iraq allows weapons inspectors to certify that Iraq is not producing nuclear, chemical, or biological weapons. Iraq refuses to allow the inspectors in, so the embargo continues. In particular, the embargo prevents Iraq from buying certain kinds of heavy trucks, computers, chemicals, and industrial equipment. The UN says that this type of equipment is dual use; that it can also be used by the military or for the production of chemical weapons. The Iraqis are also keen to build up the capability to do some serious cyberwarfare. Iraq has a lot of underemployed engineers, many of whom are skilled and quite patriotic, all they need is the equipment. Actually, it's the United States that's vetoing the shipment of this stuff to Iraq. The main reason for that is because when America allowed the shipment of these items to Iraq in the 1980s, it was later accused of "arming Iraq." This became a popular myth on the left. A typical book of this ilk was *Arming Iraq* (by Mark Phythian and Nikos Passas): "How the U.S. and Britain Secretly Built Saddam's War Machine." The Northeastern University Press published this book, which was basically about gun-running during the Iran-Iraq War and how Iraq ripped off aid programs to buy weapons, plus how Iraq exploited dual-use equipment. PBS also did a show in September 1990 using the same evidence blaming the West for arming Iraq. Somehow, no one ever came up with tangible evidence (except for the French, but that was hardly a secret) that Iraq had any American weapons. All this paranoia was turned into "Iraqgate," a vast American conspiracy to build up Iraq's armed forces. The only actual "weapons" that could be identified were the nonmilitary equipment (medical equipment, trucks, industrial chemicals, etc.) that were turned to military use, particularly the production of chemical weapons. When the U.S. tries to withhold such dual-use equipment, the same people who invented "Iraqgate" accuse the United States of abusing Iraqi civilians. Who says you can't have it both ways? But the Internet makes it easier to spin a story any way you want and mobilize worldwide support. While Iraq has not been able to build a large cyberwar capability, they have cleverly peppered the Internet with lies, misinformation, disinformation, and lurid fabrications. This material has attracted a sizable amount of worldwide support for what is essentially a murderous police state. Yet the Iraqi government is clearly responsible for any increase in death rates since 1991, and this can be seen by the much better living standards (and lower death rates) in northern Iraq, where the UN has kept the Iraqi government out since the early 1990s (to prevent the government from conducting another massive massacre of the local Kurdish population). You don't need a lot of computers to wage a successful cyberwar campaign.

Meanwhile, trying to keep PCs out of Iraq is impossible; there are too many smugglers operating across Iraq's borders. But blocking large shipments of the stuff, especially the more expensive servers and routers that Saddam's hackers-in-training would like to play with, limits the lethality of Iraq's cyberwarriors. Every little bit helps.

Loose Links Sink Ships

Consider that most troops now have e-mail accounts. Although it is unlikely that those out in the field get to use it much, those who are stationed in one specific place do. For sailors, who never lose their e-mail access while they are aboard their ships, the navy has set strict guidelines over what can be sent. The navy also monitors and scans outgoing e-mail for keywords. Still, an innocent remark (that doesn't contain words the scanner will catch) about a ship's whereabouts can get back home. Before you know it, the bad guys know something they shouldn't. Enemy cyberagents don't even have to rely on e-mail. There are hundreds of support bulletin boards for the families of troops. Here, people in the military and members of their families discuss matters of mutual concern. An enemy agent can scam their way onto these, keep an eye on them, and pick up all sorts of useful information. It might not be the sort of thing that would attract a reporter, but there can be potentially deadly information there nonetheless. If the people using the bulletin boards are not careful, enemy agents can pick up information about troop morale, the location of units, and what they are doing. It's an old problem. During World War II, there were posters on the walls of stores and saloons with the slogan "Loose Lips Sink Ships." Little has changed in sixty years, except that people now hang out on the Internet, where someone from anywhere in the world can listen in.

National Infrastructure Assurance Council (NIAC)

One of Bill Clinton's last acts as president was to appoint yet another advisory organization on security: the National Infrastructure Assurance Council (NIAC). This brings to mind the old joke about how a politician deals with a problem he doesn't want to deal with: appoint a "blue-ribbon panel" (composed of blue-blood worthies) to study the problem to death, or at least put it into a black hole where the media will lose interest. The blue-ribbon panel is now competing with outfits like the NIAC, which say much, mean little, and are generally ignored. The growing media attention to Internet and communications security has brought forth dozens of panels, committees, and studies. For example, these are just a few of the similar organizations (that oversee national Internet policy) that the NIAC joined: Computer System Security and Privacy Advisory Board (Department of Commerce), National Infrastructure Protection Center, Critical Infrastructure Assurance Office, National Science and Technology Council, Cyber Incident Coordination Group (CIA, NSC, CIAO, FBI, and others), National Security Agency, Department of Defense, National Security Council, Federal Networking

Council, Office of Management & Budget, Federal Public Key Infrastructure Steering Committee, President's Export Council on Encryption, Information Technology Industry Council, President's Information Technology Advisory Committee.

People in the industries being studied and advised generally consider all these efforts useless or, sometimes, counterproductive. None of the advisory groups speak with the same voice, or enough authority to counter the others. Thus you get a muddled murmur that no one can understand and no one pays attention to. Now you know.

Patriotic Hackers

The September 11 terrorist attacks may not have brought instant retaliation in terms of traditional military action. But there were a lot of cyberwar operations that took place immediately. Web sites associated with Islamic radicalism were attacked by persons unknown (but thought to be antiterrorist Americans), usually just resulting in Web pages being defaced. The Web site's usual main page was usually replaced with an antiterrorist message and image, or some American patriotic symbols. Perhaps the most damaging attack was an unusual one. In Germany, a hacker calling himself Anonyme Feigling ("Anonymous Coward") cracked into a server hosting a listserv (an e-mail discussion group) supporting Islamic Holy War and terrorism. He took 500 names on the mailing list and published them on the Internet. The hacker also alerted the police and revealed his real identity to them. No police action was taken against the hacker. One of the people on the mailing list was already being sought by the U.S. FBI. This sort of attack is unusual in several respects, as many listservs feel it is essential to keep the identities of participants secret in order to foster free discussion. But pro-terrorist (or other illegal action) listservs exist. Most Islamic radical listservs tend to be pro-terrorist, as are many that discuss leftwing politics. Many of these listservs disappeared or changed their discussion topics after September 11, 2001.

Pro-Taliban and related Web sites were under constant attack throughout September 2001. The normal content has been replaced, again and again, with wanted posters for Osama bin Laden, and similar visuals. Also used were denial of service attacks. Some of these sites have shut down, and others have been booted off the Net by their service providers. Other hackers went further, in one case hacking into a Sudan bank, finding information about bin Laden bank accounts, and sending the information to the FBI. This hack was publicly announced, but other, similar ones are suspected. There have been no reports of any of these hackers being prosecuted, even though the hackers admit that what they have done is illegal.

This particular part of the war went on, although without much publicity. There were apparently several official hacks into pro-terrorist sites, looking for names, bulletin-board messages and all sorts of useful information. The law, especially international law, is still pretty vague on governments hacking into Web sites and other forms of Internet attacks. But since just about every nation on the planet signed on for the war on terrorism, the lawyers and courts have remained rather quiet about these issues.

Hackers have increasingly joined in, on a freelance basis, whenever their nation is involved in some armed, or just diplomatic conflict. Russian, Chinese, Indian, Pakistani, Arab, Israeli, American, and other nationalities of Internet enthusiasts have joined the fight on their own. A recent example (early 2002) occurred in Tomsk, Russia (in Siberia). The FSB (Russian FBI) discovered seven hackers in the town that have been waging their own war against Chechen rebels for the last three years. One of the seven was from Grozny (the capital of the Russian republic of Chechnya). Like many Russians living in Chechnya, he had fled to avoid the ethnic Chechen's murderous campaign to drive non-Chechens out. Thus inspired, he got six other Russian computer users to join him in their own private war against the Chechens. The seven, all students, attacked any pro-Chechen Web site they could find. One of the larger pro-Chechen sites, "Kavkaz," was forced to switch ISPs three times and is still under attack. The students are recruiting more Russian hackers for their effort. The FSB has left the kids alone.

Afghanistan

The war in Afghanistan began in early October 2001, with air strikes on Taliban military targets. At about the same time, U.S. and British commandos went in on the ground. But this was also the first war that saw the Internet (and other networks) playing a major role. Ten years earlier, in 1991, the Internet was still a minor operation; one of many computer-based networks available. The World Wide Web had not been invented yet. But in 2001, everyone was on the Internet, or knew about it. In ten years, the concept of being part of an electronic communications network was taken as normal. That attitude soon showed up on the ground in Afghanistan as American special-forces troops landed and went to work. These troops instantly set up a unique network on the ground using American bombers, satellites, recon aircraft overhead, and various American military and political leaders outside Afghanistan. The purpose of this particular network was to quickly put one-ton bombs on enemy targets.

The major weapon used was the JDAM (joint direct attack munition), a one-ton bomb guided by satellite signals (the GPS system) to a target selected by a guy on the ground using a laser range finder and a radio to pass the target location to an aircraft overhead. The people on the ground also received information from recon aircraft and satellites overhead, giving them, literally, a look behind the hill in front of them. Satellite communications also sent these photos (and motion pictures), as well as the conversations of the soldiers on the ground, back to the Pentagon and the White House. All of this was taking place as it was happening—in real time.

Right there you have a pretty complex network (team on the ground using radio, GPS, and laser, talking to the bomber overhead, which is also using GPS and radio, and the bomb itself, which uses the GPS to find the target designated by the ground team). The radio and GPS signals can be jammed. But in Afghanistan they weren't because the enemy was not up to speed on that kind of technology. Not only can the relatively weak GPS signal be jammed, it can also be modified. That could be done to direct the JDAM onto friendly troops. Just because the low-tech Taliban didn't "hack the JDAM network" doesn't mean someone else won't, or that others won't at least try.

American troops know they had an easier time of it in Afghanistan because no one was trying to interfere with their battlefield network. The next time, however, it will likely get more interesting as the enemy tries to interfere with the network, and the secret defenses that network has are put to the test.

Al Qaeda Web Assets Attacked
Before the War

Even before September 11, 2001, there was a cyberwar campaign against the Al Qaeda terrorist network. Bank accounts were reportedly being hacked by American intelligence agencies and funds deleted or transferred. Although in most cases the hacking was just to collect information on the location and extent of Al Qaeda's resources, when an opportunity to attack presented itself, it was often taken.

Cell and satellite phone communications were also jammed.

There were up to 200 Web sites supporting Al Qaeda and other Islamic terrorist groups and these were also hit, or hacked to provide access to computers containing more information. In this way, information on terrorists, their supporters, and contributors was obtained. Despite all this work, nothing was detected about the planned September 11 attacks.

The terrorists caught on to the attacks on their Internet communications in the mid-1990s and responded by increasing their cyberdefenses and using more encryption. Al Qaeda had always used code words, and since the mid-1990s, had been using encryption. It was later discovered that for key operations (like the September 11 attacks), messages were only sent by courier, and never via cell phone or Internet. But the FBI and CIA was unaware of this additional layer of security in Al Qaeda and thought they were on top of the terrorists' communications.

Most of this snooping was done in the shadows, as the legality of some of the Internet monitoring is still murky. For example, you need a court order to monitor cell-phone conversations in America, but not overseas. Technically, the government can monitor Internet traffic without a court order, but can expect lawsuits from civil liberties groups whenever this sort of surveillance is made known.

The Geneva Conventions that for over a century have provided some legal guidelines for warfare have yet to be amended to cover cyberwarfare. The civil law for Internet tapping is in the process of being changed and this process will no doubt go on for several years.

Run Over by the Internet

While over 20,000 Islamic terrorists flocked to Afghanistan during the war on terrorism (and other countries where training camps existed), most of them were trained as infantry, used as ground troops to fight the Northern Alliance for the Taliban and, if they survived that, sent home to "do what they could" to strike a blow for Islam. Most of them restricted their militant activities to a lot of lively talk at the local coffee shop or mosque.

How do we know this? It seems that among the subjects taught at the Al Qaeda terrorist schools, operational security was not the big favorite.

OPSEC (operational security) is doing what is needed to keep the enemy from finding out what you're up to. The Al Qaeda trainees understood the need for OPSEC, but many did not understand how much OPSEC had to be applied to remain undetected. The biggest weakness among Al Qaeda operatives was careless use of telephones (especially cell phones) and e-mail. These two items are very popular among students and younger people everywhere, and the younger Al Qaeda zealots are no exception. It turns out that the ease of use that makes cell phones and e-mail so popular also creates many situations where Al Qaeda business is conducted without proper OPSEC safeguards. Even though most e-mail systems make available strong encryption, Al Qaeda members have been caught using the weak, old, forty-bit encryption. Organizations like the U.S. NSA can easily crack forty-bit encryption. Worse yet for terrorists, much Al Qaeda e-mail gets sent with no encryption at all.

And then it gets even worse for them. Al Qaeda members are picked up carrying address books and computer files that use no encryption at all. If these lads expected Allah to see to their encryption needs, perhaps they should be told they are undergoing a religious crisis. No point in having faith in encryption unless you use it. One could understand this sloppiness in Afghanistan, where a lot of unencrypted material (hard disk drives, paper documents) was found in Al Qaeda strongholds. The collapse of the Taliban was so swift that one would expect a lot of stuff to be left behind as everyone rushed for the exit. Religion may also have something to do with it. When you believe you have God on your side, you tend to believe the Lord will provide (security for your data, or whatever). But the Al Qaeda outside of Afghanistan should have been better trained. They weren't. The "terrorist training" provided in Afghanistan was often haphazard and concentrated more on military, religious, and anti-West indoctrination than about the details of running secret operations.

Al Qaeda was probably unaware that there are a relatively small number of Internet (IP) addresses in Pakistan, a favorite place for Al Qaeda to take care of their e-mail. If the U.S. was not checking every item coming out of Pakistani Internet connections before September 2001, they probably have been since. Actually, there apparently was a lot of surveillance of Al Qaeda e-mail and Internet operations before September 11, 2001, but this was unable to catch the elite Al Qaeda agents. Although some 20,000 recruits went through the Al Qaeda training camps between 1996 and 2001, only a few hundred were selected as elite agents. These guys did pay attention to OPSEC, or at least did so a lot more than lesser agents. It is these elite agents that are being sought all over the world. Some were killed in the Afghanistan fighting, and some are still loose in Afghanistan. Others are captives in Afghanistan and Guantanamo Bay.

The remaining agents, perhaps 100–200, are on the loose outside of Afghanistan. Without the Al Qaeda organization back in Afghanistan, these agents are largely on their own. Apparently they are contacting the less-capable graduates of the Al Qaeda camps, and this is where some of them are getting caught because of careless use of e-mail. Adding to their problems are the thousands of documents being collected in abandoned houses, apartments, camps, and caves. These identify many who have been through the camps and are now elsewhere. While the Al Qaeda agents on the loose are extremely dangerous, they are also vulnerable. And we owe a lot of that to the Internet.

CHAPTER 6

Information War

mailer and it gives you an anonymous return address. In some cases, the remailer retains information that can, if forced by court order, reveal the true identity of those using a remailer. Other remailers destroy all evidence of the true identity of their users. Police and antiterrorism agencies are not happy with remailers, but they can be set up anywhere and would be very difficult to stamp out completely.

While cyberwar is the kind of Internet combat that most worries people, we tend to forget that it's really a subset of Information War. The Internet is all about information and Information War is all about who controls that information.

While cyberwar concentrates on software and hardware, most Information War is about playing games with the information itself. Often you can accomplish your goal of controlling information by simply manipulating the information. We've all heard of "spin." Think of Information War as spin on steroids. Why resort to cyberwar when you can do it the easy way? Often the easy way has to be combined with the more rough and tumble world of cyberwar in order to send a stronger message. As the old saying goes, "When the talking stops, the fighting starts." But the Internet allows for a lot more talking, and many more opportunities to use nothing but information to wage war. The Internet is the fastest communications system ever invented. Anyone can use it, and use it anonymously. Information War will never be the same, and the Internet is the reason why.

A recent example occurred during the Afghanistan War, when public opinion in Muslim countries was largely controlled by the terrorists and their followers. Rumors and outright (but catchy) lies were used to convince a lot of Muslims that the September 11 attacks were an Israeli plot and the "War on Terrorism" was an excuse for a war on Islam. The Internet was a major player in this war of lies and spin.

Information Is Fundamental

Information, and its use in combat, is fundamental to Information War. Often the Information "War" is nothing more than getting the information faster and analyzing it more quickly using computers.

For example, back in the 1970s, the U.S. Forest Service set out to create a game for fighting forest fires. The basic idea was that forest fires are fairly predictable if you receive a constant supply of information on an area with regard to weather conditions (wind speed and direction), the types of trees and vegetation, moisture situation, etc. The game allowed you to play "what if" with your fire-fighting resources and weather variations. What it ultimately demonstrated was that firefighters needed to move their fire-fighting efforts to where the fire was most probably going to be, not where it is at the moment. Fighting forest fires is all about staying ahead of the fire so you can use your limited resources (firefighters and equipment) to stop it. Information War tools enable you to see the future faster and more accurately than your opponent. Anyone who trades stocks is fighting an information war. And unless you work on Wall Street, where you are a lot closer to the most important information about individual stocks, you are operating at a disadvantage. The trader with better information will make more money, often at the expense of those who are not getting the crucial information as quickly.

The Forest Service went on to computerize their fire-fighting games and use a lot of technology to fight fires. Gadgets included better airborne cameras to track the progress of fires and keep track of weather conditions (wind intensity, direction, and humidity, items which make a big difference when fighting large fires). There are a lot of similarities between fighting fires and fighting human adversaries. But there is also an important difference. Fires are a force of nature and follow the laws of nature. Human adversaries are more unpredictable because humans can think for themselves and fires cannot. Therein lies one of the potential problems with Information Warfare.

With a lot of information on a fire, you can predict, with a high degree of probability, what the fire will do next. More important, the computer model can provide an accurate prediction on what the fire will do if different strategies are used to fight the fire in the next few hours or days. The control of information thus allows you an accurate peek at the future.

But when your opponent is human, things become less predictable. A fire moves in whatever direction the winds and availability of fuel (unburned trees or brush) takes it. But a human opponent will try and outthink you. And this is where the Internet comes in. There are often technical problems with the Internet and the many smaller networks connected to it. Hardware components fail or software turns out to have flaws. If that was all it was, technicians could quickly track down the problem and fix it. But what if, as is increasingly the case, a problem on the Internet is the result of some hacker trying to break something? Figuring out whether an Internet problem is broken hardware or software, or a hacker attack, can only be determined if you can get enough information on what is going on. The skilled hackers will protect themselves by making their damage look like "natural" events (broken hardware or software).

Military opponents go out of their way to prevent others from collecting information. A battlefield foe will try and feed you bad data. With that in mind, it makes sense that using more computers, high-speed communications (like cellular phones) and sensors (like satellites) for combat operations is called Information War. In the old days, this sort of game was simply called deception. But with the Internet, the quantity and speed of information flying around is much greater. It's a whole new world.

The Internet is the ultimate Information War battlefield. As every month goes by, more things are plugged into the Net. Since the object of warfare has always been, first, to destroy your opponent's ability to make war, the Internet is shaping up as a key battlefield. But like the more traditional battlefields, the Internet is full of civilians. That's us, folks. And you know what happens to civilians caught in the middle of a battle. The cyberwarriors, like all soldiers in all wars, will be concerned primarily with accomplishing their mission. If large numbers of civilian Net users get cut off the Net, or even have their PCs trashed in the process, well, that's why they say "war is hell." For the cyberwarriors, speed in getting their jobs done is more important than anything else. If they are too slow, the opposing cyberwarriors will get defenses up, and trash your own Internet resources first. Information War isn't just about information, it's also about speed, and trashing the other guy before he zaps you.

Deceptions

Never forget that the best-equipped electronic weapons can still be defeated by rather crude countermeasures. The U.S. Air Force is still annoyed at how they were snookered by simple deceptions in Kosovo and Iraq. We were dropping bombs in Iraq throughout the 1990s and there is concern over whether we were hitting what we thought we were. But even before Iraq came along, the air force had had long experience with such deceptions in Korea in the early 1950s, where they again may be faced with the same problems encountered fifty years ago.

After the Cold War ended, the CIA published detailed reports on Chinese and North Korean deceptions against American airpower during the Korean War (1950–53). For three years, the U.S. tried in vain to cut off supplies to Communist troops along the frontline in central Korea. Much of this failure was due to a simple and successful Communist deception. Bridges that appeared, from the air, to have been knocked down, were repaired in ways that allowed them to still be used (if only at night), but still appeared to be unusable from the air. Another favorite deception technique was to equip trucks with barrels full of oily rags or straw. When American aircraft attacked the convoy, the barrels were set on fire whether or not a truck had actually been hit, producing a lot of smoke. The drivers were then instructed to quickly move off the road and bail out of the truck. From the air, the pilots marveled at their accuracy and flew off looking for more targets. Once the enemy warplanes were out of sight, the tops were put back on the barrels to put the fires out and the convoy proceeded on its way. A few trucks actually would have been hit, but not as many as if the aircraft came back for pass after pass of bombing and strafing.

The air force insists they can beat these half-century old deceptions with better sensors (more accurate cameras). Maybe, but this also assumes that the enemies have not upgraded their deceptions during the last half century. It's unlikely that the warplanes have gained an edge here. Airpower was unable to keep the Serbs from supplying their forces in Kosovo in 1999. Americans thought they had successfully used airpower to cut off the Iraqi forces in Kuwait during 1991. Later it was discovered, however, that most of those troops were Kurdish and Shia reservists, just the kind of people Saddam wanted to be rid of. Even in the best of times he did not supply these "disposable" troops on a decent level and was not interested in making efforts (like deceptions) to keep the food and water coming to them out in the Kuwaiti Desert. In fact, these troops not only got their supplies, but came and went on leave. The troops on the ground have always come up with simple ways to avoid getting hit by marauding warplanes. This should not be surprising, for the ground troops either come up with good deceptions, or they die. That has proven to be a very effective incentive program.

The situation is worse than it appears because the air force has never taken the ground-based deceptions seriously enough to make a real effort to deal with them. There is no rational reason for this, but it's been going on for over sixty years. Not just in the U.S. Air Force, but in the air forces of other nations as well. So the cycle of, "we got the problem beat," and, "oops" seems likely to continue into the age of cyberwarfare.

We are already seeing indications that the same pattern is emerging with cyberwar. The concept of "Honey Pots" (servers set up to look like attractive targets, attract, and distract, skilled hackers from the real targets) is already in use Many firewall and other Net-security programs also use forms of deception to ward off serious damage from hackers. As good as the offensive tools of cyberwar are, never forget that an energetic defender is not without techniques to thwart the attacks. System administrators, like enemy infantry trying to avoid getting bombed, have a major incentive to figure out ways to keep their systems up and running. The hackers think they have an edge, as they can choose when and where to attack. And the media tends to pick up on successful hacker attacks rather than the more frequent hacker attacks that fail. An old military truism is that, for every offensive weapon, there is a defense, and the defense is, overall, more likely to prevail than the offense.

Psychotic Victims of Cyberwar

Information War and cyberwar have opened up new opportunities for older, and somewhat exotic, forms of warfare. A long known, but infrequently used, aspect of warfare is psychological warfare operations (psyops). Put another way, this is playing mind games with the enemy. Considered sexy, and much talked about, psychological warfare isn't practiced nearly as much as you would expect. There are several reasons why psyops has not been used more, or used successfully when it does get into play. First, psyops is scary (it can backfire in embarrassing ways for the user), as it is little understood by most senior military leaders. Even if psyops is understood, it is often elbowed aside by more vital matters (like logistics, combat operations, and communications with allies and political leaders). Moreover, the field has gotten more complex during the twentieth century. You now have Information Warfare (mass media and electronic media games), and public affairs (dealing with media on a professional level) as well as psyops. What this means is that you now have three different military bureaucracies fighting over who does what, often with the same resources. For example, the psyops crowd has found out that the U.S. Air Force Commando Solo psyops aircraft (it can broadcast radio and TV signals) doesn't have a strong enough signal to really make a difference. This was discovered in the Balkans during the 1999 Kosovo operations. At least, now, they won't have to fight with the Information Warfare people over who gets to use Commando Solo. Both the psyops and IW now want access to satellites for broadcasting more powerful signals. First they have to convince the bean counters that their message is worth the high freight costs.

Deciding what the new Information War crowd deals with and what the psyops crew gets to do is still a work in progress. Information War professionals started out in Internet deceptions and political spin. The Information War crowd is a combination of Internet geeks and people who have worked for the CIA and state department. Then there are the public affairs (PA) officers, who release official information to the media. Often the psyops and IW folks want to doctor up the official word (insert useful half-truths or outright lies) as part of a deception. If they do that, they do it at the expense of the credibility of the PA people. The public affairs personnel like to stay on good terms with journalists while the IW and psyops are less inclined to do that. All of this internal strife and confusion is getting in the way of anything getting done. It's uncertain if things will somehow be made all better anytime soon.

The Internet has created many new psyops opportunities. Unfortunately, most of them aren't being used by the psyops professionals (who prefer older techniques like dropping leaflets from the air and setting up radio stations). The Internet provides the perfect vehicle for getting a buzz going for whatever idea or cause someone wants to run with. It took awhile before the Internet activity regularly connected with radio, TV, and print media. But since the mid-1990s, print and electronic journalists have increasingly seen the Internet as a source of exciting (if not always accurate) information. As always, those who have a talent for saying the right thing, in the right way, at the right time, to the right audience, can get people's attention. What it comes down to is that you can do all this a lot faster and cheaper by moving your message (whether its true or not) at light speed across the Web.

So far, the people with a real talent for this sort of Internet psywar are doing it for commercial purposes. Marketing movies, music, or whatever on the Internet has proved very lucrative. It's cheap, meaning you don't risk much. And if it works, you end up with a lot of very cost-effective advertising.

Psyops on the Internet will probably come to everyone's attention only when there actually is a cyberwar. In a situation like this, you can add panic and demoralization to the effects of crashing servers and broken nets. Get the right disinformation out and your victims will be slower to get their systems up and running again. To do this you've got to spread convincing fear, uncertainty, and doubt over the Net, and it needs to be done quickly. The more convincing someone using psyops methods are, the longer it takes the victims to discover they're being scammed.

This is a powerful weapon. Unfortunately, few people in the military have yet figured out how to use it correctly. This is largely because, unlike their civilian counterparts (fondly called "marketing weasels"), the military psyops don't get much real practice. You need the feedback of real action to learn what works and what doesn't. The civilian marketing weasels get this practice and thus are a lot more effective. Perhaps the best solution is to draft a lot of the civilian marketers in wartime and turn them loose.

Information War and PAO Competence

Traditionally, most of the military's Information War effort is directed against journalists. The chief weapon for the military is the PAO (public affairs officers). These folks are the ones that journalists have to deal with. Naturally, not all countries, or services in a nation's armed forces, are equally effective. A year 2000 survey of ninety-two journalists (who regularly cover defense issues), found USAF PAOs the most competent. Marine PAOs were a close second, and were considered the most cooperative and credible. The navy was third and the army was last. The army is the only service that does not have PAOs in a separate career field. The army instead takes officers from their primary job (infantry, artillery, etc.), gives them a little training (on dealing with the media) and has them spend a few years dealing with the press. The army finally realized that this was not really working all that well and is in the process of creating career PAOs.

Information War for More Money

One of the military applications of current Information Warfare is right in our own backyard. Since the end of the Cold War in 1991, the Pentagon has been the scene of a furious publicity battle between the air force, navy, and marines. All of these American services are striving to present themselves as the combat force of the future. Especially, they all want to be able to claim they would be able to fight America's future wars most efficiently and with the least number of casualties. They hope that technology will be able to give them the edge. So far, the air force is winning. Sexy-looking jet fighters and stealth bombers, using flashy electronics and smart bombs, generate crowd-pleasing images. The army has responded with new, more easily transportable (to distant hot spots) brigades using armored cars instead of heavier tanks. Although the navy has not come up with exciting visuals or compelling pitches, all branches are fighting over a larger piece of the defense budget, as well as a bigger say in how future wars are fought.

The air force, for example, is pushing the same line it has for the past sixty years; we can do it all from the air. Time and again since World War II this has not worked, but with all those spiffy warplanes and associated technology, the air force has been able to convince the public it works. It won't, and when the underfunded army and marine troops go in to "mop up" (as the air force likes to put it), the guys on the ground are going to take a beating. The air force makes this work by always putting their spin on any military operation. The 2001 war in Afghanistan is a case in point. While the use of air power against heavily armed tribesmen was impressive, the same thing was done against Iraqi tribes by the British in the 1920s. This points out another weapon in the air force Information War arsenal: forget about history. Or, more important, make sure no one else brings up embarrassments from the past. Hey, history is boring. As noted historian and aircraft manufacturer Henry Ford put it, "History is bunk." Remember what that other noted historian (and first general to use air reconnaissance via hot-air balloons), Napoleon Bonaparte, said, "History is the lie mutually agreed upon." But history also has a nasty habit of biting you in the ass when you least expect it.

The backside of this is that everyone takes it for granted. In the PR business, reliability and consistency are good deeds that do not go unpunished. The glory goes to the glitz, not the most effective. Information War is all about deception. And when you begin to believe your own press releases, you are in big trouble.

Reading Other People's Mail

Information War doesn't just take place between nations. It also goes on between smaller organizations, and even individuals. High-speed Information War began, in fact, with the telegraph networks in the nineteenth century, and the rapidly expanding telephone networks of the early twentieth century showed the way. In the early days of the Internet, Information War and cyberwar feuds between individuals were not unusual. The original hackers were individualistic, but tended to operate in the open. There wasn't a lot of sneaky stuff for the very good reason that everyone had good hacking tools and access to software on the Internet in those days was pretty open to everyone. Do something nasty and you would be quickly found out and dealt with. This period of openness and straight talk ended in 1988 with the appearance of the first anonymous remailer. This was an Internet program that hid the sender's true identity. Originally, anonymous remailers were developed and made available so that people could freely discuss sensitive or embarrassing subjects (like childhood sexual abuse or odd hobbies). While some predicted a flood of libelous and malicious messages from these now anonymous Net users, this never happened. There was some abuse of the anonymous remailers, but it was pretty minor.

Well, "minor" is relative. Use of anonymous remailers by individuals has never become a noticeable problem. But organized, Information War–type anonymous campaigns were another matter. Stock-market fraud, commited by pumping up the value of stocks via anonymous messages (and then selling the stock before the truth sets in and the bottom drops out) still happens. Although the SEC often catches up with the perpetrators and prosecutes them, which discourages some, people continue to "pump and dump." There are also legal scams like having a lot of people leave messages all over the Net praising a new music CD, book, or movie. Not exactly illegal, but not ethical either. It's called "viral (as in a virus that spreads all over the Net) marketing." The way the low-budget movie *The Blair Witch Project* was marketed via the Web is considered one of the best examples of viral marketing.

Internet users are less anonymous than they think, which has led to a lot of inept fraud attempts by people who are increasingly located and picked up quickly by Internet-savvy police and FBI. But there are many cases when Internet users do have a degree of anonymity. When you are in a chat room, the name you use typically means nothing, but someone with a little technical knowledge can find out what IP address you are using. Every time you log on to the Internet you need an IP address (think of it as your Internet "phone number"). If you dial in via a modem, your ISP will automatically provide you with an IP address from a pool of IP addresses they keep for just that purpose. If you use ISDN or a cable modem, you will probably have your very own unique IP address. It usually takes a court order, or query from the police, to find out the name and address attached to an IP address. So if all your Net activities are innocent, you do have a degree of anonymity. If you cross the line into illegal activities, your anonymity can quickly disappear.

But there has developed a unique Internet culture that encourages people to say things they normally would not say to someone in person. It affects everyone, regardless of age, gender, or social status. In many cases, like on newsgroups or in chat rooms, this sort of exuberant behavior is a minor pleasure, and not a problem. Where it is developing into an issue is when the exuberance extends to e-mail. Not private e-mail, but the increasing quantity (the majority, in fact) of e-mail that is sent via business or government e-mail accounts. Users have discovered, the hard way, that there are very different rules for business and personal e-mail. The reason is simple. When an individual says something via their personal e-mail account, they are speaking for themselves. When they say the same thing via their work account, they are implied to be speaking for the organization. After a few lawsuits were settled in the 1990s, it was established that your business or organizational e-mail account was yours to use, not to own. The organization owned it and had a lot of control over what was done with it.

This rush of organizations to develop rules for e-mail use was not just the corporate control freaks and lawyers running amok. If an individual says the wrong thing via their company e-mail account, the company can get sued. But it got worse. Lawyers suing the company over non–e-mail issues found that this newfangled e-mail often contained compromising statements that they rarely found in printed correspondence. Again, there's that attitude that what you say via e-mail is somehow less permanent or binding than something you mailed out via the post office or distributed locally, on paper, as an office memo. Additionally, business e-mails are routinely saved by most corporations. So even if an employee deleted electronic documents, hostile attorneys could later recover them from backup tapes in the IT department.

Something had to be done; e-mail had to be tamed. Technology was put in the service of taming . . . technology. Screening software is currently being put in the workplace to monitor the kind of e-mail users are sending, and receiving. Although the American military has long monitored all the e-mail coming and going to .mil e-mail addresses, similar systems are becoming increasingly popular in all kinds of businesses and foreign militaries to look for certain words or phrases indicating a message that shouldn't be there. What is being objected to is not just bad language, but also unauthorized discussions of secret material or indications of disloyalty. Terrorism anxiety in the U.S. is making this much more common and it will, no doubt, increase.

The e-mail (and even chat room) monitoring software sometimes goes over the top. Political correctness, or simply very conservative attitudes toward "acceptable speech" annoys many employees who find that an outgoing e-mail with the word "bitch" in it (referring to a discussion about breeding purebred hunting dogs) gets bounced back to them for "unacceptable speech." What many don't realize is that this same technology will soon be available to monitor phone calls as well.

U.S. law has long protected the right of organizations to keep their business records (correspondence has long been accepted as a "business record") away from prying eyes and under the control of the corporate officers. The appearance, and popularity, of e-mail has provided new opportunities, however. In the past, it was tedious for senior management to review all the documents the corporation was generating. Often the big shots were then nailed for something they not only didn't know about, but had no way of knowing about. In any case, once the other side's lawyers had finished plowing through tons of memos and correspondence, they usually had plenty of incriminating evidence.

This is no longer the situation with e-mail and electronic documents. Business leaders were quick to appreciate the fact that they now could not only monitor the documents and e-mail generated by their organization, but within minutes could also go back and check illegal or irregular behavior. For honest companies, and most are honest, this age of electronic documents not only enables the brass to sleep more easily, but also to make it more difficult to do something illegal (and get away with it). While it's true that there are now firms that will sell software that guarantees the "shredding" of electronic documents, there are still those pesky backups and the fact that some messages get cached or saved in out-of-the-way locations. Crooked businessmen and government officials would like e-mail to go away, but that is not likely to happen. Anyone who shows a preference for communicating only via face-to-face meetings or over the phone is increasingly seen to be acting suspiciously (and perhaps showing ignorance of wiretapping technology).

There are still a lot of paper documents out there, but the trend is to scan the ones that need to be saved for electronic storage. This takes up less space, is less of a fire hazard, and provides a format that is more "search friendly." Oddly enough, this use of electronic documents has not led to the long promised "paperless office." Instead, people print many of their electronic documents, either because they are more comfortable reading on paper rather than on a computer display, or because they feel safer if they have a paper backup of the document. In fact, the electronic copy is safer, easier to find, and likely to survive longer than the paper copy.

Internal Information War

Not all the information warriors are concentrating on the enemy. The military version of "office politics" went on even during the Afghanistan War, or, perhaps more accurately, because of it. The air force was most upset that it was getting only a minuscule share of the action (and good press) in Afghanistan during the early stages of the war. During the first month, for example, some days saw only a dozen air force heavy bombers over Afghanistan, but up to eighty navy aircraft operating from carriers. The navy made sure that journalists got onto their carriers and had plenty of opportunity to film the warplanes flying off to war. Numerous interviews were set up with sailors and aviators. It looked like the navy was doing the air war over Afghanistan all by itself.

The air force was at a big disadvantage with no airbases close enough to Afghanistan for most air force warplanes. Some AC-130 gunships and F-15Es began operating from bases in the Persian Gulf, but the nations involved did not want that publicized. This was because all of the anti-American propaganda rolling around the Internet and other media had made the average Arab decidedly anti-American. The air force also had heavy bombers flying from the British-controlled island of Diego Garcia in the Indian Ocean. These bombers were actually dropping twice as many bombs as the navy, but even there the air force could not get any publicity as the British would not permit reporters on the island; the original inhabitants of the island had been bought out and moved years ago when the island was turned into a military base, so there wasn't even anyone to bribe for information.

The air force was never able to get a buzz going to spotlight the decisive impact of their heavy bombers over Afghanistan. This could have serious consequences in a future war because those few bombers (just sixteen B-1 and B-52 aircraft dropped two-thirds of the bombs) were far more effective than the several hundred warplanes operating from carriers. However, the navy is already cranking up its PR machine to make sure that in the next ten years it gets more money for carriers, at the air force's expense. The air force would like, in fact, to build more long-range bombers, but would prefer to build shorter-range fighters. In ten years, the results of which arm of the service wins such a skirmish may well be a matter of life and death for Americans.

The Television Information War

One of the little understood, but quite important, aspects of Information War at the beginning of the twenty-first century is the role played by the American media. In particular, how American movies and television shows impact the world because of their portrayal of

Americans and the United States. What does this have to do with cyber-warriors and Internet combat? Quite a lot, actually. Foreigners (as well as most Americans) obtain a lot of their impressions about cyberwar and cyberwarriors from the electronic media (mostly from the huge out-pouring of American movies and TV shows, which feature them). By the end of the twentieth century, as Information War became a full-fledged military tool, the Department of Defense began to pay attention to what was being shown, and how cyberspace was being presented.

The military has had a long relationship with moviemakers, mainly because movies on military themes are a lot cheaper to make when the Department of Defense cooperates and provides military equipment free or for reasonable fees. Naturally, the Department of Defense was not willing to lend assistance on a movie that was going to make the military look bad. They didn't even think of this as part of the Information War until the 1990s; it was just good public relations. But there's a difference between maintaining a good image in the movies and the actual practice of Information War. For example, a number of movies and TV shows on the American participation in Vietnam left the impression that nearly all U.S. soldiers were ineffectual and against the war. A look at any of the firsthand accounts of American combat in Vietnam tells just the opposite story. This gave people like Saddam Hussein and Osama bin Laden the idea that whatever they did, America would not, or could not, come after them because they were afraid of taking casualties. The world would have been a better place if both of these fellows had a better idea of what was going happen to them if they took on the American armed forces.

Since the late 1990s, the Department of Defense has been a lot more active in correcting producers of television shows portraying the government. While it's long been known that American movies play all over the world, U.S. television shows play over there even more. So more attention is now paid to what the troops look like on the tube. For example, in late 2000, the Secret Service let it be known that they were unhappy with the way the NBC show *JAG* portrayed the Secret Service as inept in guarding a fictional first lady. What the Secret Service feared most was that the wrong people would get the idea that the Secret Service were pushovers and attack someone they're guarding.

The producers of the popular NBC show *West Wing* were planning on doing, in effect, a slightly different version of that theme for a show set in the Pentagon. The new program never went into production, but the Department of Defense saw it as a potential opportunity for either making themselves look very good, or very bad.

Sometimes, even looking good can be a problem. In 2001, a TV production company announced that they were doing a reality show called *Combat Missions.* In this series, teams of current or former commandos (special forces, SEALS, airborne, police, SWAT, DEA, FBI, army rangers, and so on) would compete performing military tasks. The Department of Defense promptly forbade active-duty people from participating. The reason was a practical one: The TV show was going to concentrate on exciting and unrealistic stunts that pass for military operations in movies. Ever since movies began showing soldiers performing heroic deeds in an unrealistic way, generations of drill instructors have had to convince young recruits that if you do it that way you'll die real fast. For several decades, the drill sergeants would scream, "I don't want any of the John Wayne crap!" For the last two decades the cry has generally been, "I don't wanna see no Rambos!"

Ironically, when a movie faithfully recreates combat, as in the film *Black Hawk Down,* most of the critics lambaste it for being unrealistic. However, that film is one that infantry instructors recommend to their troops.

MTV Generation

Information War isn't practiced just against the enemy, sometimes you have to use it on yourself. In 2001 the U.S. armed forces are into heavy-duty marketing mode. Noting that the MTV generation is not much impressed by stories of past military glory, the brass tried to meet the kids on familiar ground. A new TV show called *Wargames,* complete with a music video–class soundtrack, was seen as an excellent advertising outlet for military recruiters. A new reality TV show, *Boot Camp,* was helped along by the marines, who allowed active duty marine corps drill instructors to add the right edge of authenticity. New recruiting commercials were redone to come on like music videos. Action and excitement was stressed. In the long history of military recruiting, stressing the fun (there's always some) and neglecting the tedium, terror, and boredom has always worked better than being up front about what military life is really all about. Stressing service, accomplishment, and pride in one's work has always been a hard sell. But the current campaign was actually not so much about recruiting as it was about just keeping people aware that the armed forces existed at all. Recruiters tend to be more forthcoming about what military life is really all about. The recruiters know that word-of-mouth from young people in the service, or who have been, is used by potential recruits to provide more realistic information on what it's like "inside." But many potential recruits are only dimly aware that the military exists. Thus the current flood of flashy military programming. It didn't appear to work. Even the patriotic fervor raised by the September 11, 2001 attacks didn't give a boost to recruiting. Then again, the numbers didn't fall, either.

News from Far Away

The proliferation of TV cable channels was initially seen as a good thing. More choices allowed people to see what they wanted, not just what was available. When cable news channels began to multiply, this was also seen as a good thing. Part of this proliferation was the worldwide availability of news networks from many different nations. This enabled immigrants to the United States to see news in a language they understood. But the war on terror in 2001 brought on an unanticipated downside. The September 11 attacks were covered by Arabic news stations very differently from the American media. The Arab take included things like Israel being behind the attacks on the World Trade Center and the war on terrorism actually being an excuse for a war on Islam. For many Arab Americans, these foreign newscasts were all they saw, or the bulk of the newscasts they were exposed to. This put many Arab Americans at odds with their non-Arab neighbors. We tend to believe a lot of what we see in the news, and if two groups of people are seeing radically different interpretations of the same story, there will be some unease and suspicion on both sides. But most Arab Americans caught in this situation quickly expanded their list of news sources, especially via the Internet, and at least came to understand where their non-Arab neighbors were coming from. At the same time, many people take advantage of all those newly available foreign news channels to actively look for different takes on the news. You don't even have to understand other languages to do this. Some foreign news channels broadcast a block of their news in English, giving English speakers a synopsis of the day's news as seen in that country. Many Americans are picking up on this, or at least the news junkies are, and obtaining a wider assortment of interpretations of the news.

Even before the cable news networks expanded their availability in the last few years, the Internet was showing the way. Newspapers were quick to get Web sites set up. Once publishers realized that they weren't going to lose a noticeable number of readers because the Net version was available, it became obligatory to have an Internet presence. Many major foreign papers followed as well, but for more than just prestige purposes. Nations that had a lot of migrants living in the United States saw an Internet version of their paper as a way to keep in touch with their overseas countrymen. The English-language Pakistani newspaper *Dawn* went online in 1996. The publisher knew that many of the Pakistanis overseas were well educated and could afford to be on the Net. In addition, many Pakistanis going to college overseas had Web access via their universities. Less affluent Pakistanis were already using Internet cafes as an inexpensive way to e-mail family back home. The *Dawn* Internet edition went on to become enormously popular. People the world over who were interested in South Asian affairs found that *Dawn,* though giving the news from a Pakistani point of view, was pretty evenhanded by any standard.

The newspapers on the Internet did not, however, counteract the propaganda and general silliness that passed for real information on other parts of the Internet, and especially some of the cable news channels. The war on terrorism brought out all the kooks and rumormongers and these folks found an eager audience on the Internet. Politicians could also play the game with some of the more excitable cable channels. A special case was Al Jazeera, an Arab-language cable news operation run out of Qatar and bankrolled by the emir of Qatar (who just happens to be the feudal ruler of Qatar). While hailed as one of the few free voices of broadcast journalism in the Arab world, Al Jazeera is only superficially an independent news organization. While the emir is a pretty mellow guy, and runs Qatar with a light touch, Al Jazeera tends to treat kindly nations (and politicians) friendly with the emir. Makes sense. But it's always open season on the West in general and the United States in particular. What gives Al Jazeera more stature and credibility than it deserves is the professional manner in which it presents its news. Since it's in Arabic, non-Arabic speakers can't judge the content for themselves.

It's a lot cheaper to set up a professional-looking Web site that covers the news. But you won't attract nearly as many eyeballs as with a cable news channel. Especially one that has the financial backing to be broadcast from a satellite. The Internet is great for starting stories (true or false) and flogging pet ideas. But if you want to get massive, and sustained, coverage, you still need to spend money.

As successful as Al Jazeera was during the Afghanistan War, where it first declared that Afghanistan would never be conquered, and that the Arab world would rise up in defense of innocent Afghans, Al Jazeera soon saw its credibility and reputation in tatters. While this was not surprising in the non–Arabic-speaking world, many were shocked to see how quickly many of Al Jazeera's transgressions were pounced on in the Arabic-speaking world. Most of this was on the Internet, mostly in English-speaking forums, but also in the growing number of Arab-language sites.

Some of the counterattacks against Al Jazeera were probably delivered by professional cyberwarriors. This sort of thing works best if the operators stay in the shadows and don't reveal that they actually work for the U.S. government. How effective this guerilla approach to the news is can be seen by the fact that corporate marketing departments have been using this stealthy approach for years. It was mentioned earlier: viral marketing. A more comprehensible term would be "creating a buzz on the Net." A "buzz" can be positive or negative and can be directed at a specific target. In other words, we've seen the birth of a new cyberweapon.

It Pays to Advertise

Taking a technique widely used in American politics, the U.S. government ran ads on Arab television stations in late 2001 espousing the American position about the war on terrorism with all the splash and dash that makes U.S. movies and television so popular in Arab countries. Al Jazeera is a commercial operation that, while doing much better because of the war coverage, has yet to make a profit and is considered rabidly anti-American. The American government has also enlisted the help of the film industry, which includes many of the people who make commercials. Many movie directors got their start directing commercials and music videos. While no ads were run on the Web, a lot of content was placed in circulation that supported the American position.

The Spin Game

The Information War in Afghanistan was fought as diligently as the one with bombs, and apparently with more skill and intelligence. For the first time, the Internet has been made a major theater of operations, with troops (both volunteers and assigned) working to give U.S. forces an edge in the battle for worldwide public opinion. The Pentagon first recognized the importance of the media battle, and decided to do something about it, in the 1980s. Year by year, more government organizations have joined in working out plans for this aspect of future wars. This media manipulation is hitting full force this time around, although Americans don't see much of it. For example, the message being beamed to Muslim countries concentrates on things like: Saddam Hussein has killed more Muslims than anyone else in the last century; most wars against Muslims in the last fifty years have been waged by other Muslims. America has, in the last ten years, sent in its soldiers four times to protect Muslims (Kuwait, Bosnia, Kosovo, and Somalia). America was the major supporter of the Afghans in their war against the Russians during the 1980s, and has been paying for most of the humanitarian aid ever since.

For a while, America was seen by many of our nervous allies (especially the Europeans) as losing the propaganda war. The Taliban, before they collapsed, were putting out reports of massive civilian casualties. Many of these statements were obviously false. But pitched to a receptive, or even neutral audience, the fanciful reports had a negative effect. The U.S. responded by increasing efforts to press a more evenhanded version of civilian casualties into circulation. Part of this effort was shooting down, as frequently as possible, a lot of the blatant misinformation rolling around the Internet. The overall effort worked and the biased and false reports faded away. Simply pointing out the vague or obviously false sources of many of the casualty reports did the job. With the Taliban gone from Afghanistan, this was easy to do. But without the use of the Internet to constantly keep the subject (actual civilian casualties) alive, most people would still think 20,000 civilians were killed (the Taliban claim), rather than less than a thousand (what was actually found when civilians in bombed areas were interviewed).

America is the home for millions of (as many as 8 million) Muslims and at least 4,000 Muslims serve in the U.S. armed forces. Arabic-speaking Americans are being used to speak on Arabic-language TV and radio to put the American message across. Although the CIA has been flayed for moving away from "people on the ground" (agents in foreign countries) over the last twenty years, this was at the insistence of Congress. Through the 1990s, the CIA has been recruiting more people for this dangerous and vital job. In particular, the CIA has been interested in recruits with language skills for Middle Eastern and Asian nations. The army has long maintained one of the best foreign-language schools in the world and has been turning out linguists for intelligence and special-forces units. The Internet proved a useful tool to recruit additional linguists. This was because Web pages with linguist recruitment information were not only available twenty-four/seven, but could be quickly updated if there was some new, nasty rumor attacking the re-cruitment effort. The most likely recruits were recent immigrants who, while they had mastered English, had not met a lot of people besides their fellow immigrants. Such excellent prospects for translator jobs might never have been reached by government recruitment efforts.

Such a mundane matter as recruiting translators for the CIA and FBI shows what a versatile tool the Web is. It's not just the recruitment itself, but also the ability to simultaneously battle efforts by pro-terrorist groups to discourage such recruitment and slander the CIA and FBI in general. This aspect of the spin game takes place out of sight for most people, but it is there and it is important.

Chasing Headlines

The Afghanistan War upset many journalists because they were not allowed free access to American military operations. Some of the older reporters remember the freewheeling days of the Vietnam War, when they could film along with the troops. This was not because of a gov-ernmental change of policy, it's because Vietnam was not, technically, a war (it was a military assistance effort for South Vietnam). Anyone could buy an airline ticket to South Vietnam. Because of the experience with such open access during Vietnam, during the Gulf War journalists were upset at the restrictions put on them. What few journalists remem-ber is that in America's wars during the last centuries, restrictions were the norm. The armed forces, even in Vietnam, were leery about journal-ists inadvertently leaking important information to the enemy. This was first seen in the 1860s, during the American Civil War. The military, after getting burned during the Spanish-American War (1898, and its aftermath in the Philippines Rebellion) and World War I (1914–1918), instituted a mutually agreeable system for World War II. To solve the problem, war reporters were put into uniform, although they weren't considered part of the military, and their newspapers and radio stations still paid them. The war reporters, however, were fed and housed as if they were officers and were subject to military law. Press officers accom-panied them, however, and saw that their stories went to the military censors before being transmitted back home. This had to be done so that there were no damaging leaks. And leaks did occur, with major op-erations like D-Day and the cracking of the Japanese communications codes being revealed in American newspapers. Fortunately, the Nazis and Japanese did not have quick access to these newspaper reports and the damage was minimized. But those incidents scared the generals, and with good reason. During the Vietnam War, the Communists regularly got useful information on American operations by monitoring the American media. The tight restrictions during the Gulf War and the Afghanistan operations were prompted by the problems encountered in Vietnam.

In the Korean War, the reporters were asked to censor themselves. But this didn't always work, and many journalists asked for military censors to check their work to make sure they did not release anything that could hurt the troops. While many journalists are not aware of this bit of history, most senior military commanders are. Now, because of the proliferation of electronic media (especially the Internet) life-and-death information is much easier for the enemy to obtain and publish. Journalists are able to get their stories broadcast in realtime, so any slip in the information department gives the enemy an instant advantage. It's no wonder the military comes down so hard on journalists. But since many members of the media don't comprehend the implications of what damage they can do, the danger is constant, and real.

Rumor War

The war on terrorism also sparked the first serious studies of how rumors spread on the Internet. Traditional gossip spreads slowly, as items are spread by one person at a time. Internet rumors can be spread to thousands, or even millions, in days, and they can be wrong. It depends on how juicy, believable, or outrageous the information is. Military and police have, for years, had people monitoring newsgroups, chat rooms, and listservs. These "casual" agents are apparently being organized to spread favorable information (putting a good spin on antiterrorism operations) or disinformation (false information that will hurt, confuse, or disrupt pro-terror groups). Information on the Internet has several advantages over the usual verbal information operations. For one, the material is in writing. People still have a greater respect for written data than for something they've heard face-to-face. This is why so many outrageous items are believed if they show up on the Net, but appear rather more foolish when repeated verbally. A recent type of false rumor was that the staff in many Arab-American businesses (especially restaurants) cheered as the image of the burning World Trade Center appeared on the television. None of these proved true upon careful investigation. But people believed it, not because someone in the neighborhood told them, but because they "saw it on the Net." If someone had told them face-to-face, a few questions about the incident would have revealed it as an unsubstantiated rumor.

The other advantage is that on the Net you can establish some credibility by passing on some demonstrably valid information before you move into deceptive material. A skilled operator can do a lot of damage with this technique. The best example is the "pump and dump" activity you hear about in investment bulletin boards. "Pump and dump" is an ancient stock-market scam in which you buy cheap shares of a poorly performing company and then go on the Internet to play up what an undervalued stock it is. Then the talk turns to how it will skyrocket. Successful players of this game have a gift for gab and, in many cases, have provided some good information. Do it right, and the victims run out to buy the stock you've "pumped." The price goes way up, at which point you "dump" (sell) your shares at a nice profit.

One of the favorite terrorist tools in the war on terrorism was the use of false information. Directed at the right target, this could have significant military impact. For example, shortly after September 11, stories began to appear that 4,000 Israelis who worked in the World Trade Center did not show up for work on September 11 and that the attack was actually orchestrated by the Israeli Mossad (secret service). While this is absurd to Westerners, opinion surveys in Pakistan early in the war indicated that this could indeed be possible; half the Pakistani population believes that the attack was the work of the Israelis. Rumors like this had military value in the Afghanistan War, for the United States needed bases in Pakistan to support operations in landlocked Afghanistan. Islamic fundamentalists made much of the Mossad rumor and American support in Pakistan was uncertain for a while during the riots and demonstrations the fundamentalists generated. It's also important to remember that the Web is indeed a worldwide Web. In Arab and Muslim countries, there are millions of individuals with Net access, and in poor countries, Internet cafés are more common. So you don't have to own a computer to have Web access. All you need is enough money to buy an hour or two of Web access each week or month in order to pick up the latest rumors on the Web. Afghanistan itself is one of the few nations on the planet without easy Web access (you have to use a satellite phone, or get across the border to Iran or Pakistan).

Another story, openly spread by Israeli authorities, was that the September 11 attack had all the hallmarks of veteran Hizbollah terrorist Imad Mughniyeh. There was no real proof of this, but Israel wanted to make it clear that the Hizbollah and Palestinian terrorist groups are somehow connected with bin Laden (which they are, but only occasionally). This Israeli story had most of its impact within Israel, where it added to the already intense bad feelings against Hizbollah by Israelis. With so many all-news TV and radio networks, eager consumers heard the most outrageous stories and, in true Information War fashion, many operators put stories out that supported their causes. What many information warriors knew, however, was that the easiest way to get a story into the mass media was to plant it in a few places on the Web. That way you could get a good buzz going and eventually the mass media (print and electronic) would pick it up. There were many stories spread on the Net that supported the "Mossad took down the towers" theory and helped keep it alive even after videos of bin Laden appeared taking credit for the attack. Those videos generated a lot of Internet discussion, including some learned descriptions of how "Hollywood" could have faked them. One of my favorite Internet disinformation bits on this topic was the one that declared the video of Osama bin Laden over dinner discussing the September 11 attacks was actually taken from an earlier bin Laden video of him at his son's wedding in Afghanistan. This was easily dismissed by examining the two videos, but the damage was already done.

Virtual Peacekeeping

It's become dangerous, from a political point of view, to have American troops near most international hot spots. A longtime case in point is Israel. The unrest there is seen as an Information Warfare opportunity by many media, political, and diplomatic players. Israel has long been an American ally, and U.S. officers regularly travel to Israel for meetings, research, and joint training. When things heat up over there, many U.S. troops scheduled for visits in Israel are told to reschedule, or civilians are sent if the event date cannot be changed.

Anytime there is unexpected political violence (rebels or terrorists) in foreign nations, the media looks for U.S. troops. If found, and even if they are doing something completely unrelated to military operations (like reserve engineers building roads as part of their annual training, or a medical team providing aid to victims of a recent disaster), someone starts to create connections. "U.S. Troops Are in the Region," go the headlines and readers are left to let their imaginations run amok. A lot of this isn't exactly Information Warfare in the military sense, it's just generating headlines that will snag more eyeballs and boost advertising income. Not everyone knows that, of course, and the unfounded stories generate a life of their own. Which is why a prudent general keeps his troops away from hot spots lest there be unwanted, and unjustified, side effects.

The Internet has provided a solution to this problem, which in turn has added yet another weapon to the modern soldier's arsenal. In the last twenty years (from the late ARPANET days), the military has become keen on what is called "distance learning." A lot of this is little more than taking a correspondence course over the Internet. The military approach also includes using realistic multiplayer combat simulations ("wargames" to civilians) and generating a lot of e-mail before (to plan the exercise) and after (to discuss lessons learned) regarding the game itself. Not all troops travel overseas to engage in combat; a lot of it is to see what allies, or potential allies, are doing and how they are doing it. Turns out that e-mail, accompanied by digital pictures and videos, can cover a lot of the same ground without taking a long trip.

Another bonus from this approach is that, because most soldiers are married, replacing many of these trips with Internet contact keeps the peace at home. Initially, the only nations you could do this with were the industrialized ones (with good Net access and a lot of Net users). By the time the World Wide Web burst upon the scene, it became apparent to American troops that the military in even the poorest nations was the most likely place to find a lot of Internet users. In the poorest nations, the military is, aside from the universities, the most high-tech operation around.

The idea of "remote wargaming" actually got started in the U.S. Army during the late 1970s. The way projects plod along in the military, it wasn't until the 1980s that the first of these networked training devices got to the troops. Once the World Wide Web came along, people in the military (not just Americans, either) realized that the technology they needed was being developed more quickly (and cheaply) in the commercial sector. The military has been buying technology from the companies that created commercial network games and training their troops with it. This has enormous military significance because until the Web came along, the United States had the edge in high-tech training. The pre-Internet training systems were expensive and only the United States, and a few other wealthy nations, could afford them. But now even the poorest countries can buy realistic and very visual wargames off the shelf and use them with many troops via the Internet. And even poor nations find that providing the troops with Internet access is a great morale builder.

The Future of Information War

How well will Information War work in the future? Look at what happened during the 1991 Gulf War. The Coalition (of nations fighting Iraq) had most of the Information War weapons, but Iraq was not defenseless. Armed with access to the world media, Iraq tried, with some success, to mold public opinion to aid its cause. In fact, the Iraqi cause remained popular among the general population in many Arab and Third World countries. The basic Iraqi line was that Kuwait really did belong to Iraq and that Iraq was standing up for Arab honor by resisting Western efforts to force Iraq out of Kuwait. Because of the way the Iraqi leadership played the situation on CNN and other international media, the Iraqi "Media Offensive" also had some effect on public opinion in nations they were fighting. Iraqi agents outside Iraq also made attempts to sabotage military computer networks in Coalition nations.

Not only Iraq, but many other nations who might go to war, took the lessons of Iraq, and Information War, to heart. Future wars will have the weaker side making the most of the CNN angle of Information War. The TV news business is always eager for outrageous stories that will attract eyeballs, and many nations now realize there is a military advantage to be gained in playing this game. We've already seen quite a lot of it since the Persian Gulf War. The Afghanistan War saw the Taliban working from Iraq's playbook. The Afghanistan War also showed another key element in Information War: time. That war was over before the Taliban's Information War efforts could produce any results.

There was also another Information War going on during the 1991 Gulf War, or at least being prepared for. This was the one that could threaten the millions of messages that went back and forth between Coalition units inside Saudi Arabia, and between those units and their supporting organizations back home. The Iraqis were not able to cause much damage in this department, but it was not for want of trying. What is most troubling are those Information War techniques that would be difficult to spot until it was too late. For example, what if a foe was able to delete some of your messages between the sender and receiver? It would take you awhile to figure out that this was happening and even longer to sort out the resulting confusion. The damage would be serious. Spare parts would not be sent, leaving equipment idle. Units would not get their orders to move, or to change their direction.

This problem of the enemy getting into your communications network and deleting messages became a hot topic in the early 1990s, when it was realized how vulnerable the world's communications links were to this sort of attack. There are supposed to be fixes in place, or on the way. But who can be sure?

Yet another potential problem arose out of the Persian Gulf War experience. It was realized that air, land, and naval units had become much more dependent on their own, local, computer networks. The navy found that it was particularly vulnerable, for a naval task force could not quickly bring in nearby technology experts or resources to deal with an attack on its computer networks. Not only does each ship have several nets, but all the half dozen or more ships in the task force are linked into an even larger network so that all the task force's defenses, and offensive weapons, can be massed against the enemy. When the U.S. Navy took a close look at its network setup, it found that it was quite vulnerable. You didn't hear much of this vulnerability because no one knows who is on to them. The U.S. military networks were a lot more robust when they went into the Afghanistan War. Fortunately the enemy was not very well equipped to make an attack on these networks.

In 1999, NATO went to war with Serbia and the outgunned Serbs resorted to Information War because they had few other weapons that they could use. The Serbs actually got the best of NATO most of the time in that Information War. But the odds against Serbia were too great and eventually NATO won. Serbia made some feeble attempts at Internet combat, but nothing came of it. They were more successful in tweaking their air-defense system so that they were able to bring down a U.S. stealth warplane (a first).

During the 2001 Afghanistan War, the enemy was even less successful at Information War. The Taliban and Al Qaeda played their Information War options well, and the tide didn't turn until it became obvious that most Afghans were glad to be done with both the Taliban and Al Qaeda.

Iraq is still fighting the Information War angle in order to get out from under UN sanctions. They are unlikely to win, but because of the skillful way Iraq has gone about it, they are still very much in the game.

The U.S. armed forces in particular, and those of other industrialized nations as well, are increasingly dependent on electronic communication, and increasingly vulnerable to Information War attacks. The superior weapons used by American troops work so well because they rapidly pass data around the battlefield. Interrupt this flow of information and you cripple the high-tech edge. Zapping the flow of information is difficult, but not impossible for a nation with Western-educated engineers and scientists. Jammers and receivers to examine the signals used by U.S. equipment can, in the hands of determined and technically skilled people, make wonder weapons much less wonderful. A higher percentage of missiles will miss, communications will be interrupted or intercepted, and the bad guys will take a lot longer to beat. Friendly casualties will be higher and the good guys will be less trusting of their weapons and equipment. The latter is not such a bad thing, but these disasters are unlikely to be previewed in peacetime. It's difficult to recreate the pucker factor of a low-tech opponent about to get pounded by a high-tech army. Self-preservation is a tremendous motivator and many low-tech nations have been so motivated by the results of the Gulf War.

There may already be an example of this. In 2001, U.S. smart bombs, guided by satellite GPS signals, all missed their Iraqi targets by the same distance, and in the same direction. U.S. weapons experts feel that it was a programming error on the part of the bomb technicians. More ominously, there's also the possibility that the Iraqis were using GPS jammers. The GPS signal (from space satellites) is a weak one, and easily jammed. For several years, American smart-bomb manufacturers have been working on making their smart-bomb GPS guidance systems "jam proof," but weapons with this feature have not been put into service yet. Several nations advertise GPS jammers for sale, in fact, including Russia. The basic technology for the jammer is simple enough for Iraq to build its own. It's interesting to note that U.S. GPS smart bombs have a less accurate (but unjammable) backup guidance system if the GPS system fails, but the backup doesn't kick in if the GPS signal is simply being bent a bit by jamming. Did the Iraqis jam our GPS smart bombs? This "problem" with these bombs only happened once. Perhaps the Iraqis were just testing their jammers to see if they worked. A really clever GPS jammer would not trigger the backup guidance system. If the Iraqis have built (or bought) such a system, they are going to save it for a major attack by the U.S. If the Iraqis don't have such a system, someone does, or will. And American pilots will eventually have to deal with it.

The American troops closest to the fighting, namely the pilots and ground fighters, are most aware of how thin the high-tech advantage is. All the new gadgets are viewed skeptically by the combat troops, especially since the new technology is often just given to them with orders to "use it." The troops respond with the attitude, "If it doesn't do anything for me, it's a rock." In other words, the battlefield is littered with new equipment the troops don't trust. Pilots, being officers, are in a better position to argue back about new tools they don't trust. They usually don't get into action, however, until several other military men are lost in combat.

Information War brings a new kind of frontline soldier into action: the equipment operator or the technology expert. Of course, tank crews and many infantry are already operating a number of high-tech gadgets (laser designators, various kinds of radios, portable missiles, and sensors), but many new gadgets require specialists who operate their gear at, or very close to, the front. Electronic warfare apparatus is getting smaller and more portable. More of the equipment is at the front and more folks who thought they were just going to be "technicians" find themselves under fire much of the time. Aside from briefing the operators more accurately on their future working conditions, there is also a trend toward making the new electronic equipment simple enough so that most of the traditional combat specialists (infantry and tank crews) can operate it as well.

CHAPTER 7

Hackers, Sysadmins, and Codewarriors

Technical Terms You Might Not Recognize in This Chapter

A complete glossary, including the terms defined below, can be found at the back of the book.

Cyberpolice (or cybercops)—People in law enforcement (plus a number of Internet professionals who volunteer to help out) who have the skills to track down criminals operating on the Internet. In the 1990s, most of these were self-taught (cops who worked with computers as a hobby), but now there is a big rush to train a lot of law enforcement people to handle Internet crime.

Geek Magnet—Any organization, or activity, that attracts a lot of people with computer and Internet skills. Microsoft Corporation is a geek magnet, as are some types of software (like the Linux operating system).

OPSEC—The military term for operational security. OPSEC is the term given to all the things you do to keep the enemy from getting into your bases, buildings, or Internet servers.

Script Kiddies—Generally young men, often teenagers, out for illicit Internet thrills via easy-to-use hacking tools available on the Internet. More of a nuisance than a threat, but from this, some go on to serious, and often criminal, hacking.

These are the people who make the Internet happen, or not happen in some cases. Hackers love to write software, especially software that has anything to do with the Internet. Sysadmins are the people responsi-

131

ble for keeping the millions of servers (that provide the 2 billion Web pages we all use so much) running. Codewarriors are the people who attack, or defend, the Internet software. It's all about software, the thousands of programs that keep the Internet going. Hackers, sysadmins, and codewarriors are the people who create, patch up, baby-sit or try to destroy this software.

Who Are the Hackers, Sysadmins, and Codewarriors?

The people who are on the frontlines of any cyberwar are a special breed. Software, and the systems they run on, are created and managed by engineers and programmers who are not far from the seemingly comical characters featured in the Dilbert comic strip. That's because programming is part art and part science, which is why programmers tend to become consumed by their work. The part about being socially inept is generally overdone; it's just that programming tends to be the kind of work you take home with you.

Cyberwar is more than programming, there are also the systems administrators (sysadmins for short). Their job evolved with networked computers. In the early days (1960s), the computer networks were so complex, and newly created, that it took an engineer to keep them functioning. In the 1970s, relatively easy-to-use LANs (local area networks) began to appear and they were very popular (because they were cheaper and easier to use). By the 1980s, networking technology had been tamed to the extent that it wasn't unusual for some poor employee to be tossed a user's manual and told, "You're the sysadmin for the LAN, don't screw it up." Obviously, many of these casual LAN sysadmins didn't really know what they were doing. Or when they did, they didn't have the time to do it. Being sysadmin was often a part-time assignment. Most of the time, the networks worked okay, but when they broke, the part-time sysadmin often couldn't handle it. This produced a lot of work for LAN consultants, but didn't solve the problem that the system was not being properly administered. Mainly, this meant that the LAN software wasn't being updated regularly, or tweaked to improve performance and security. This has been the weak link in Internet security for two decades now, and it's not getting much better.

The bulk of the people working on the Web are technicians, help-desk folks, content providers, and others who do not create software, but who are involved in supporting the Internet on a daily basis. These are the eyes and ears of the Internet, the ones who first see when something is going wrong. If there's a cyberwar, these are the ones who will feel it first.

The codewarriors are the few thousand (mostly men) elite programmers and engineers who know a lot (but not all) about what's going on inside the thousands of computer programs that power the Internet. Most of them have worked on this software at one point in their careers. This software includes the Web-server software, the software that runs on many Web sites, and the software in routers and in the telecommunications sites that run the Internet backbone (the long-distance fiber-optic lines that carry most Internet data most of the way).

During the 1990s, Internet, and network, security became a big issue. While large organizations (major ISPs like AOL and the largest corporations) formed their own network-security operations, the majority of Internet computers were not regularly updating the security of the Internet software. Responding to this, there arose companies creating and marketing network-security software, as well as consulting firms that supplied skilled manpower for real or suspected network intrusions. The Internet is such a complicated beast that there are many places where it is vulnerable to penetration by some bad people. So far, the most popular solution is to add software that simply watches out for illegal entry and either stops it, or alerts sysadmins that something unwelcome is happening. But even installing the security software requires someone who knows a lot about Internet software (in other words an expensive consultant).

The problem was, and is, that there are far too many places in software that have flaws and are vulnerable to attack. Sysadmins are nervous and desperate for a solution to all this vulnerability. The network-security business pays so well, and provides more interesting work, that many of the good codewarriors leave firms that need them to join the network-security software and consulting companies.

Even the military has this problem. In the 1990s, many organizations within the Department of Defense set up cyberwar operations. But even bonuses and medals did not make an officers pay match up to what a network-security expert could make on the outside.

In the world of Internet security, there are four groups involved:

The largest one, numbering in the millions, are the script kiddies (usually teenagers out for illicit Internet thrills via easy-to-use hacking tools available on the Internet). Most of these guys grow out of it; very few get caught and prosecuted. A few improve their skills and join the ranks of the black-hat hackers (the skilled bad guys).

Sysadmins. Also numbering in the millions, most sysadmins are part-timers, and many have few, real computer skills. Systems administrators are the first line of defense on the Internet. For the big operations, the sysadmins are highly trained and skilled. That's why AOL, General Motors, or the major banks run relatively smoothly, although they are constantly under attack by thousands of amateurs and professionals. Smaller networks have less-skilled sysadmins, and the growing number of Internet users with cable modems or DSN connections don't realize that their individual machines are as vulnerable as a network, without the protection of even a part-time sysadmin.

White-hat hackers. There are fewer than a hundred thousand who belong in this group, yet they are the people with the skills to go after script kiddies and more dangerous hackers. No one has taken an exact census, and you'll get a lot of arguments over exact numbers, but these are experts who can handle (or figure out) serious Internet trouble. The top guns number only a few thousand, and the pyramid narrows to a few hundred world-class Internet code-warriors. Some of these folks are consultants, others work elsewhere in the software or Internet industry. They are known by reputation among their peers (software professionals in the Internet industry).

Black-hat hackers. Many work for criminal organizations, yet they have the same skill sets as the codewarriors. Others are official cyberwarriors for governments planning cyberwar against the United States (China, in particular). There are as many as five to ten thousand people in the group, depending on how skillful you feel someone has to be to do serious damage.

Programmers are the people who create the software that makes computers useful. Programmers usually have little trouble finding a job, and there never seem to be enough good programmers to go around. In 1983, when the PC was becoming popular, the U.S. Bureau of Labor Statistics counted only 278,000 programmers. Just as the World Wide Web became a cultural phenomenon ten years later, there were 639,000, and a major shortage. By 2000, there were 1.1 million programmers, and an even bigger shortage. Current projections call for 2 million programmers by 2010.

Unfortunately, there will continue to be a shortage, even with millions of programmers outside the United States willing to immigrate. The reason for this is that programming, as a career, is difficult. It's an art and a science, and it's plain hard work. Most people who train as programmers, and acquire enough skills to do the work, leave the field within ten years. Employers have discovered, the hard way, that it's better to have a few (even just one) really good programmers than to use mediocre talent.

Fortunately, many competent hackers don't work on the Internet full-time—the only full-time employment in the field is with government cyberwarfare operations, or criminal operations. When they see something interesting happening on the Web (a software flaw, or the need for a new tool), they get involved and make things happen. The government jobs are growing enormously as countries gear up for cyberwar. The full-time criminal crackers are another matter. For a while, in the 1990s, Eastern Europe was a paradise for mercenary hackers (who would wear black hats or white hats, depending on what they were paid to do). The East European governments were distracted by economic and political problems, and some of the governments were so corrupt that they provided protection, or even employment, for the renegade hackers. But while crime can pay, especially cybercrime, it is not popular with the major economic powers on the planet and this led to the start of a crackdown on these gangs early in the twenty-first century. Governments and businesses created computer-crime organizations that made criminal hacking a more dangerous occupation. Even with the increasing number of cyberpolice, cyberspace will get more and more dangerous. There will always be temptations for part-time black hats looking to make a quick buck. Indeed, it is suspected that most of the criminal hacking activity on the Internet is being done by part-timers. Cybercrime will increase, but some of the cybercriminals may find themselves practicing their skills for government-run cyberwar operations. Russia and China have also found it useful to make talented, captured cybercriminals an offer they can't refuse ("work for us or go to jail").

But there is an enormous pool of white-hat hackers as well, and it's a much larger number of people than the black-hat gang. Most people don't like to get hacked by some black hat, and many of the black hats who have been run to ground so far have been caught because angry civilian white hats got on the case. This has led to many police organizations (especially the FBI) getting to know talented white-hat hackers.

Because good programmers know they are good and are themselves picky about where they will go to work, they often avoid government or military jobs. Because white-hat hackers and police share a desire to catch black-hat hackers, the police are at least able to call in white-hat consultants, sometimes as volunteers, to crack cybercrime cases. It's not just the inability of the government to match the money the competent white hats are already getting, but that many white hats don't want to spend all their time chasing black hats. But the United States has an enormous pool of white-hat hackers. In any wartime situation, all this talent will prove to be a national military asset.

NSA No Geek Magnet

One of the major problems the NSA (National Security Agency) is having with the advances in Internet and cryptography (secret codes) technology is the NSA's own reluctance to hire many of the new generation of computer programmers. This was the result of a generation and culture gap. At the start of the NSA in the 1950s and 1960s, the agency hired programmers versed in traditional mainframe computer culture. The PC revolution bypassed the NSA and now they find themselves very much unequipped to deal with many of the new computer technologies that have evolved in the last two decades. The NSA always concentrated on specially made (to create and decipher secret codes) computers. As PCs became more powerful, the NSA missed the development of new software development tools and techniques created for these mass-produced computers. By the 1990s, it was possible to do cryptography on PCs, and do it a lot cheaper and with less effort. For this reason, young programmers saw the NSA as being retro and hostile to new ideas. The younger generation of programmers have been reluctant to sign on. This recruiting difficulty is common throughout government, with the commercial sector offering more appealing work (in terms of modern equipment, professional attitudes, and more money). As a result, the government has to use a lot of contractors. This brings in better programming talent (at great expense) in most cases, but doesn't solve the problem that programmers generally don't like dealing with the backward attitudes of government organizations toward software development. Ultimately, the NSA is having difficulties keeping on top of the computer and crypto technologies available to terrorists. The NSA has at least recognized the problem in the last few years. The needs of the war on terrorism (to crack codes used in terrorist's e-mail, for example) are creating a new atmosphere of innovation and enterprise in the NSA.

Clueless Criminal Management

Programmers have always had to deal with clueless management. This is slowly changing as managers with some programming experience climb the corporate ladder. However, the dot-com madness of the late '90s didn't help matters. In 2000, Kroll Associates, the corporate-security firm, ran checks on seventy executives and board members of Internet companies. It turned out that 39 percent of these Internet movers and shakers had previously been found guilty of fraud, had failed to reveal a recent bankruptcy, previously violated SEC rules, or had associated with organized criminal organizations. Such problems are not unusual in the ranks of business executives, but Kroll pointed out that the usual percentage in offline businesses is 10 percent. The dot-com field was so full of hype and people who didn't know what they were doing that the bad actors got the scent and moved right in. This had serious security implications for the Internet. New companies, for example, are the ones most prone to making mistakes in the security area. With so many issues to resolve before going—and staying—online security is not initially given prominence. This is especially true if a lot of the company management are hustlers without much knowledge about the Internet. Many dot-coms that died, and some that didn't, suffered embarrassing (and often expensive) break-ins as a result. The most damaging hacks were the ones that grabbed credit card and customer information. In some cases, hundreds of thousands of credit card numbers (and other information useful to crooks) was taken. The word quickly spread among the black-hat hackers about which sites were run by dweebs who didn't believe in security. As a result, the more vulnerable sites got more than their share of hack attempts.

Tell It to the Judge

The Department of Defense tries to catch and prosecute those who hack their sites. This is done largely to discourage others. Most of those caught are script kiddie–class hackers. Because they're more a nuisance than anything else, the military tries to at least recover the costs of catching the hacker and repairing the damage. These costs can run from $100,000 to several million bucks per incident. The American legal system often makes this difficult. One case demonstrates this. In 1999, the Department of Defense caught Chad D. Davis hacking a U.S. Army Web site. He pled guilty on January 5, 2000. The army wanted to recover damages. But the judge agreed to consider the defense's assertion that the army had failed to take reasonable steps to protect the server and to take that into account while determining the cost of restitution. It turned out that, while the Army had patched their Web servers to fix some known vulnerabilities, the specific server in question had not been patched. The army knew about the problem and had actually patched the server earlier. But when the Web site was moved to its current server, the sysadmin had neglected to install new patches. This enabled Davis to get in and replace the army material with a message announcing his hack. The judge held the army responsible for not protecting itself from a known problem.

Reserve Cyberwarriors

As the Department of Defense was losing trained cyberwarriors during the dot-com madness of the late 1990s, they also were trying to form cyberwarfare units. Training soldiers to protect, and attack, Internet sites, was expensive. But these troops could make a lot more money with those skills as civilians. Finally, in 2001, someone realized that this wasn't a unique problem. There had always been a shortage of professional and technical people in categories that were hot on the civilian job market (programmers and technicians of all sorts). Therefore, the solution, as developed over the last few decades, was to cover these shortages by forming reserve units for these specialties. Human nature being what it is, the military couldn't keep the hotshots from leaving, but it could play a guilt game with them and convince them to sign up with a reserve unit. Many troops went along with this. It was patriotic, they made a few extra bucks, and if there was ever a war, they would be in on it. This had particular appeal for the cyberwarriors. Peacetime practice of their craft was somewhat exciting, but in wartime they knew they would see even more intense action, often head-to-head with the best hackers of hostile nations.

There were other advantages to this approach as well. While the reservists would only be working for the army about one month a year, that would be sufficient to keep them up to date with what the active-duty army cyberwar units were up to. Moreover, the reservists would be able to bring with them the latest civilian Internet tools and techniques.

The military also had the option of hiring reservists as civilian contractors for some projects. This saved money because there was less time and money needed for training (on how the military did things) and security clearances. Without these reserve cyberwarriors, the military would have to call in civilian consultants in wartime. In the midst of dealing with a hot situation, the civilians, no matter how good they were, would have to learn what the military was doing. Aside from the time needed for this, there was also the hassles of background checks and security clearances.

The appeal to patriotism and professional pride worked as well. The reserve cyberwar units have had great success in recruiting. In addition to recruiting military cyberwarriors who are getting out, the word is out to all the young men and women in the Internet-security business. The Department of Defense is creating five reserve and National Guard units (with a total of 182 high-end cyberwarriors) and plans to increase the number to 600 by 2007. The September 11 attacks have helped recruiting as well.

Simulated Media

The U.S. Army rangers (2,200 in number) are considered the elite infantry force of the army. Training is intense, but it is no longer confined solely to combat. Over the last few years, more and more exercises have included the assumption that often the media will be on the battlefield as well. The rangers, therefore, learn how to deal with journalists who arrive in the middle of battle, or are already there when the rangers arrive. This has already happened on some peacekeeping missions. The younger ranger officers aren't crazy about this, but they all realize that the modern battlefield is often thick with media people and that the issue has to be dealt with. This aspect of Information War has become more crucial as media reporting has become more real-time. Journalists now go off to the most out-of-the-way places with satellite phones and related gear that allow them to report, in real-time, with Web-cam quality video. Combat officers have to know how to deal with this. Say the wrong thing at the wrong time, and add a misleading video, and you have a cyberwar defeat on your hands. Whatever gets on the TV news will spread over the Internet to every corner of the world within hours. The officer who made the gaffe may find the previously friendly locals now not so friendly and perhaps shooting at him as well. Cyberwar doesn't use bullets, but it can certainly conjure them up in a hurry.

The Dark Side of Military Web Use

The Department of Defense has always been concerned with OPSEC (Operations or sometimes Operational Security). This is, as the military puts it, "The process of denying to potential adversaries information about capabilities and/or intentions by identifying, controlling, and protecting generally unclassified evidence of the planning and execution of sensitive activities." What this means is that military information is highly controlled. When the World Wide Web showed up, the people in charge of OPSEC soon realized that they had a major problem on their hands.

The troops took to the Web enthusiastically, and they began establishing Web sites for their units. Pride has always been a principal means of building morale and keeping the troops (and their families) spirits up. The concept of a unit Web page, therefore, spread like wildfire. On these pages were posted names and biographical information about the troops in the unit, what the unit was up to at the moment, and all sorts of stuff of interest to the troops in the unit, as well terrorists and foreign nations that might be fighting these units some day. At this point, as the officers in charge of OPSEC discovered, good intentions had a dark side.

It wasn't long before counterintelligence agencies discovered that real, or potential, enemies began logging on to military Web sites. Here was a bonanza of information on the American military, regularly updated by their own, proud troops. The unit Web pages were so popular, however, that they simply couldn't be forbidden. Even if that was done, civilians (often at the urging of the troops) would reestablish them elsewhere. Moreover, much of the information on the unit Web pages was already available to anyone who wandered onto a military base and looked at bulletin boards and read the base newspaper. Still, such easy access saved the perpetrators time and travel expenses while creating massive headaches for the enforcers of OPSEC, who saw congressional representatives ahead and a free-speech confrontation brewing.

The military, therefore, responded as it usually does in such situations, it issued rules and guidelines for military Web pages (official and unofficial, as many of the unit Web pages were created by the troops on their own time and with their own resources). First, there would be no posting of information that was normally considered confidential or classified. This involved planned troop movements or operations that had not been officially announced. It was also made illegal to post detailed personal information (addresses and phone numbers of troops, for example). Even before September 11, 2001, such data was seen as useful to terrorists.

These restrictions did not raise tumult among the troops or their families. It made sense to people in the military. Most important, the military didn't try to mess with the troops' e-mail. In fact, e-mail was being encouraged. Even sailors, and especially the guys in submarines, had access to it. E-mail was an enormous morale booster for the troops, especially the ones, like sailors, who were separated from their families for months at a time. With more U.S. troops being sent to rough neighborhoods for peacekeeping, places where their families could not accompany them, e-mail was extremely popular. And the brass loved it as well because that improved moral translated into happier, more productive troops. This helped keep people in uniform, for it was an unfortunate fact of military life that more people got out every time more of them were sent on long cruises or isolated, peacekeeping missions.

But e-mail was not without its OPSEC problems either. While troops were warned not to discuss classified or sensitive information via e-mail, there was no easy way to enforce this. Those on ships or in isolated places where the military provided the Internet connections would have all their e-mail scanned automatically for sensitive information. Any suspicious e-mail would be held and looked at for OPSEC violations. If the e-mail was clean, it was released. If not, the author was contacted and given some counseling on OPSEC. Any .mil (i.e., military) e-mail account also got the scanning treatment. A lot of troops, however, had nonmilitary e-mail accounts. Some did so because they preferred, like many people in the civilian sector, to keep business and personal e-mail separate. Still others did it because the .mil e-mail sometimes became backed up due to the protective scanning process. Another reason, of course, was because a lot of the troops didn't want all their e-mail scanned. Even if it was software doing the scanning, well, this was America and Americans take their privacy more seriously than most other people of the world.

It gets worse. The OPSEC people initially overlooked military chat rooms. Others are used by dependents of military people. Everyone was talking shop, and often saying things that would give the OPSEC folks coronaries. In one case, a young sailor sysadmin, trying to find ways to make his ship's server more secure, was caught describing technical details of his server's security in a chat room. The sailor was only trying to get some free technical advice, but anyone could have been in that chat room taking notes. Law enforcement and counterintelligence agencies who have been monitoring chat rooms of all types stumble on lots of OPSEC violations like this. Not a lot can be done about it, except for those accessing chat rooms via military Internet accounts because the military has software to identify who is saying what. More OPSEC counseling is needed.

The navy is also worried about leaks, as ships now have access to the Internet. For protection and surprise, the navy relies on its ships remaining undetected while on the high seas. Some sailors have already been caught revealing location information in casual chat-room conversations.

One scenario the navy is worried about is terrorists getting the location of a sailor's family from a Web page, kidnapping a family member, and then pressuring a sailor to commit treason. While far fetched, everyone now realizes we are dealing with a ruthless and imaginative generation of terrorists. And the current crop of terrorists has already used the kidnapping angle to force soldiers to spy for them or see their wife or kids killed.

There are no easy solutions to all this. For the moment, the military has to balance the benefits of the Web with a host of new dangers.

Hacking Without a Computer

Some forms of hacking are highly dangerous and don't require any knowledge of programming. For example, one can obtain (with little difficulty, and about $500) a radio that operates on the frequencies used by airport flight controllers. Since these radios are portable, the hoaxer is usually in a car and keeps moving, making it difficult for even an alert police team to catch him. While the hacker in this case would not have to know computers, he would have to understand air-traffic control procedures. In this type of situation, it would be possible to direct two or more aircraft into a situation that would cause a midair collision. For whatever reason, this form of vandalism is more popular in Britain, where the number of such incidents went from three in 1998 to over twenty in 2000. There are one or two serious cases a year in the United States, and the culprits are often caught and jailed. The British activity is apparently the work of just three individuals and none of them appear to be terrorists. One possible reason for the greater incidence in Britain is the popular hobby of "plane spotting" (noting ID numbers of aircraft and an intense interest in airport operations). Two points should be made. First, to pull off an effective hack, technical information and equipment is needed. Second, the data and equipment is often easily available.

CHAPTER 8

The Cyberwarriors

NSA—The U.S. National Security Agency. A top-secret organization (during the Cold War, the government wouldn't even admit it existed) that develops secret codes (encryption) to keep American secret communications secret. The NSA also works on how to crack enemy codes (decryption). The growing use of encryption on the Internet has attracted a lot of attention from the NSA.

Red Attack (or Red Team or Tiger Team) is a group of friendly Internet experts who will hack your system to see how good your defenses are. This can be expensive (starts at $5,000 and quickly runs to six figures), depending on how big your system is.

SIPRNET is the Department of Defense's classified (secret) Internet that sends everything using encryption (coded) and is not connected to the Internet the rest of us use.

L et's get some of the basics out of the way.

Who are the cyberwarriors? Cyberwarriors are the troops that actually fight the battle for information. Not just any information, but data that plays a crucial part in deciding who will win, or lose. This means most combat troops. Warships, tanks and warplanes operate in groups, linked together in networks of information. Headquarters receive so much data that a major chore is sorting it all out fast enough to make it useful. But the cyberwarriors we will concentrate on most are those who defend the networks themselves, and attack those of the enemy. The major network is the Internet, but there are many other smaller ones.

Who has armies of cyberwarriors? The United States, China, Russia, Japan, South Korea, and most European nations have organized special units for attacking, and defending, the Internet and their smaller networks. Smaller nations see such efforts as a way to level the playing field if they face a larger foe. The U.S., in particular, is seen as particularly vulnerable to cyberwarrior attack because America makes the greatest use of the Internet.

Which of these forces are the most dangerous and who is getting better, or worse, at cyberwar? The United States has the most formidable cyberwarrior forces, but China has publicly said that it sees cyberwar as its most formidable weapon in any future war with America.

Why has the Internet become a battlefield? The idea of using the Internet as a battlefield is part of a larger concept called Information War. The basic idea is that it's not just the Internet, but information in general that is the key to making armed forces effective. There's a lot more information to be had these days, and whoever has the most, and knows what to do with it, will win any future war. Fighting it out on the Internet, or any other kind of network, is simply a part of this larger battle for information.

Will Cyberwar Work?

A lot of what can be done with cyberwar is speculative, partly because new equipment and technology is constantly appearing on the scene, and partly because it's only recently that military planners began looking at this angle as a new form of warfare. Think about it: the idea of computers all over the place is very recent. Computers were invented during World War II, and there were only a few of them. Computers had little to do with the Vietnam War during the 1960s. It wasn't until the 1991 Gulf War that the idea of "cyberwarriors" took hold. The 1990s saw a vast explosion in the use of personal computers and communications networks. Before the 1990s, most PCs were still the province of geeks and intrepid businessmen. The main network was the one the telephone companies owned. By the end of the 1990s, the world had changed. Everyone knew what a PC was, most of us had one and were connected to the Internet. So were most businesses, government agencies, and military units. Never before has a new, mass-communications system arrived on the scene so rapidly. It was quickly discovered that past experience was not very useful. Or was it?

Cyberwarriors can be found ensconced in headquarters filled with video displays and skilled technicians feeding commanders the latest data on who's (and what's) on and off the screen. This is actually the over-fifty-year-old story of radar and sonar operators playing their equipment to figure out where the enemy was and what he was up to. It's just writ larger with a lot more gear tied together electronically and run from the same place. The U.S. Navy introduced the use of this sort of thing sixty years ago. They called this setup a CIC (combat information center). Back then, all they had was radar, sonar, and lots of radios to communicate with other ships and aircraft. At the time it was pretty high tech. But the amount of electronic gear kept growing in quality and quantity. The army and air force adopted the navy's CIC approach. When the Internet arrived, it became obvious that every unit needed a CIC. Not just every unit, but often individual combat vehicles like attack aircraft and tanks. As we entered the twenty-first century, it wasn't just war anymore, it was cyberwar.

Information War Then and Now

Information War started out as one of those '90s buzzwords in the military and government. Basically it's a marketing scam. It's taking a lot of stuff that's been around for years and repackaging it so that it's easier to get more money from increasingly reluctant taxpayers. During the 1990s, hundreds of different military and government organizations recast their mission in life to include Information War. What Information War means is doing what you've always done, but doing it faster with computers and information networks (like cell phones and the Internet). In short, Information Warfare is nothing new. The basic ideas have been around for several thousand years, and the current high-tech version has been with us for nearly a century.

While Information War is a bunch of old notions mixed up in a new bottle, it has turned into a formidable new way of fighting: cyberwar. The terms "cyberwar" and "Information War" are often used interchangeably, and they both cover many distinct operations. These include:

Command and Control Warfare. Doing things that make it more difficult for your opponent to communicate with and control his combat forces This is an ancient principle of war. Yet this is perhaps the most potent military aspect of Information War. The key here is to be able to make decisions faster than your opponent, and then act on them. This is known as speeding up the decision cycle. Or, as the military likes to put it, "Getting inside the opponent's decision cycle." There should be nothing mysterious about the decision cycle, it's a fact of life. Everything we do is made up of decision cycles. The military has encapsulated the decision cycle in the acronym OODA (Observe something, Orient ourselves to what just happened, Decide how to respond, Act). Decision cycles are no different in civilian life. For example, if you see a hot, new job opening, but delay applying a little longer than someone else just as qualified for the job, then you're out of luck (and someone else has the job).

Information War can, however, prevent us from observing. Lacking that information, we are unable to properly orient ourselves, make a decision and, most important, act effectively. As an example, let us assume that some computer whiz got into one of the networks serving the U.S. intelligence-gathering operations.

The enemy hacker deleted some information and changed other data, in effect creating a false view of what was going on out there on the battlefield. This done, U.S. commanders would be observing a false version of reality and would end up making disastrous decisions. Like, say, bombing areas that were supposed to contain enemy ammunition dumps or vehicles, but actually contained refugee camps. Get the picture?

Operational Security. Called OPSEC (OPerational SECurity) by people in the military. It means preventing the enemy from getting useful information. The need for OPSEC generated such World War II slogans as "Loose lips sink ships," and "The enemy is listening." OPSEC is keeping an eye on secret information. Making sure your secret documents are locked up, or your electronic messages are in code, or not making them easily readable by the enemy. It also means training troops to keep important information to themselves.

Electronic Warfare. Using electronic means for playing the ancient game of deception. Beginning with the telegraph in the 1850s, electronic warfare came of age in World War II and is now a standard part of any professional warrior's arsenal. The development of electronic warfare reads like a history of technology for the past 150 years. Beginning with the telegraph in the 1850s, the telephone came along in the 1870s, then radio around 1900, sonar in 1906, and radar in the 1930s. World War II saw the development of most of the electronic weapons we take for granted today (smart bombs, electronic countermeasures, AWACS, CIC, computers, and battlefield networks). Basically, we have spent most of the last 60 years just improving the electronic weapons we invented during World War II.

Hardening. Means making electronic devices resistant to EMP (electromagnetic pulse). One of the side effects of nuclear war is the EMP. This is a wave of high energy that destroys or damages microelectronics (that make everything from military equipment to cell phones, TVs, and PCs work). Add 5 or 10 percent to a microchip's cost and you can insulate it from most EMP effects. Not completely EMP proof, but close enough for government work. And just because nuclear weapons are unlikely to be used doesn't mean you can ignore EMP, for there are an increasing number of devices that can generate a destructive EMP without a nuclear explosion. These EMP generators are seen as a potentially devastating weapon. Drive a truck (carrying an EMP generator) past the Pentagon or down Wall Street and let loose a blast of electromagnetic energy. Most PCs and other electronic devices within a hundred meters or so become junk. In addition, valuable data is lost and operations come to a halt until equipment can be replaced and all the damage sorted out. Most electronics in military equipment is hardened, but the vast majority of PCs used by the military and business aren't.

Hackers. These are the people who can get online and do lots of damage to the Internet with nothing more than their PC. This is guerilla war where just about anyone, anywhere in the world, can join in. All you need is a computer, a modem, and some determination. This is new, because only recently have we seen the introduction of international computer networks that just about anyone could get onto. The Internet is the best example of this. A lot of bored programmers and other people with time on their hands and malice in their hearts cruise the Net looking for trouble. This has been going on for decades. There's also a lot of mischief on nets within companies. Some crime, but a lot of mischief. Some attempts have been made, in the past decade or so, to turn the hacker problem into a military weapon. Hasn't been easy. Mischief is not always a useful weapon. But the payoff can be quite spectacular if you get one of your cyberwarriors into an enemy network during wartime. This has happened only in fiction so far, but many nations are working hard to make it real next time around.

Information Blockade. This is a variation on the ancient practice of blockading enemy territory from receiving shipments of goods. With data now so important, one can shut down the satellites, cable links, and microwave towers beaming data into enemy territory. Sometimes you can shut them down because you control them (the company providing long-distance telephone access to, say, Iraq, can be persuaded to turn off Iraqi access to the international telephone network). This will hurt after a while, especially in the more technical areas. International banking, the Internet, and communications of all sorts depends on these long-distance nets. Of course, nations can still use radio. But this is limited and no real replacement for communications satellites and fiber-optic cables.

Information-based Warfare. As radio and television became mass media, by the 1960s it was understood that the electronic mass media could have a decisive effect on public opinion and political decision making. Even before that, tyrants of all flavors (especially Nazis and Communists) realized how important it was to seize control of the media (print, especially) and direct it toward their own ends. By controlling the mass media, tyrants could get away with mass murder. As more people have become wise to the way the media works in collecting and distributing information, more people participate in shaping and influencing what passes for mass-media news. Pressure groups of all stripes realized that if they could generate a press release that catches the eye of radio and TV news directors, they can easily (and cheaply) get their message out. Excellent examples of information-based warfare were seen during the 1991 Gulf War and the 2001 Afghanistan War and, indeed, during every war in the past forty years. News is now considered a weapon, and is used as such.

Psychological Warfare. Long used, and nothing more than spreading demoralizing or misleading information among the enemy. Still used, and still works. It's a lot easier with the Internet, as well.

But there's another aspect to Information War that must be considered. Information War is largely defined by how you use information as a weapon against enemy troops. You can attack information, as you seek to keep the enemy in the dark (by destroying their radio and TV broadcasting facilities), or defend against it, as you try and eliminate false information the enemy is trying to feed you via computer, telephone, or camouflage. It is possible to seize control of an enemy control system with the right techniques and electronics. The technology needed for Information War ranges from jamming radars or radio broadcasts (by broadcasting lots of electronic "noise"), to the high-tech network intrusion (computer viruses or DDOS attacks that slow down parts of the Internet) that we read about in the news, and fear will become more common in the future. Information War is not new, we just have lots of new gear and techniques that increase our capabilities and the number of targets we can go after. The increase in capabilities and dependence on software and computer hardware have increased the need for commanders to consider Information War targets as part of their war plans. For if they don't, it is realized, the enemy might. Our growing dependence on electronic equipment and the Internet have moved Information War from being just one aspect of warfare, to the central one.

The Gulf War, the First Information War

The 1991 Persian Gulf War is often cited as the first Information War. Well, it was and it wasn't. That war saw more use of items considered as part of Information War. But at the same time, there was nothing done in the Gulf War that hadn't been done before.

The air campaign opened with an attack on enemy headquarters, communications, and utilities. Nothing new here. Except that in the Gulf War it was done more quickly and thoroughly than in the past. Nothing new there either. Since World War II, warfare by industrialized nations has been getting faster and more thorough. Learning from experience, as it were.

The Gulf War coalition waged a psychological warfare campaign on the Iraqis that was remarkably effective, at least if you go by the speed and extent to which the Iraqis surrendered when coalition ground forces appeared in their vicinity. Nothing new about this. It's happened several times in the last century. This was Information Warfare, insofar as the leaflets dropped on the Iraqi troops told them exactly how to surrender and emphasized the advantages of surrender (becoming honored guests of the Saudis and not getting killed by the Americans).

The Gulf War also saw an enormous amount of electronic warfare, using methods, albeit with newer equipment, that were invented half a century earlier in World War II. The media, for example, was used extensively by both sides to influence public opinion during the Gulf War. Again, this was a technique with an ancient (over four thousand years) pedigree.

Was what happened in the Gulf War really Information War? Yes, it was. And the success of high-tech weapons and equipment in that war, plus growing anxiety over computer hackers, led to the use, particularly by the military, of the term "Information War." There was another reason Information War became a buzzword. The Gulf War and Cold War ended at the same time. When wars end, military budgets are cut. To get more money, you needed a new war. When the World Wide Web burst upon the scene in the mid-1990s, it didn't take a marketing (or military) genius to see that there were dangers in this rapidly growing Internet phenomenon. The term "Information War" had been around for a long time, but when people in the Pentagon began using it to describe major aspects of the Gulf War, and what future wars would have more of, it caught on. All of a sudden when there was an agenda or budget situation that needed a little something extra to put it over the top, all you had to do was say "Information War," and the money was forthcoming. Each military service and department sought a definition of Information War that would serve their immediate needs and long-range goals.

But by the end of the 1990s, the generals began to realize that Information War was more of a threat than they thought it was. Meanwhile, it dawned on many Pentagon insiders that cyberwar was something that was fought during times of "peace." Indeed, Information War had turned into cyberwar. Suddenly, the military realized that they needed a lot of cyberwarriors, fast.

Peacetime Information War

Typical nonmilitary uses of Information War are industrial and economic spies who, whether as freelancers or as government agents, attempt to gain a competitive advantage for their side by revealing the enemy's secrets and protecting those of their employer. The Soviet Union did this for decades, and was quite successful at it. It wasn't called Information War then, but that's what it was. It can have a direct military effect if your infospies are going after military technology.

There was another insidious Information War angle that generally went unnoticed for decades. Consider the effect of bringing personal computers and police experts into a Third World nation. Computer experts put the names of those who are known to oppose the local dictator into a database. All of a sudden, the tyrant is a lot more effective in keeping dissidents under control. It's Information War. The most competent practitioners of police state Information War were the Communists, and they were the last ones to adopt the use of computers. The Soviet Union showed that you could still terrorize a large population with a primitive index-card database, and total control over all media. Classic Information War.

You don't need guns and bombs to wage Information War. Of course, violent weapons can be used. As we've seen, most of the tools of Information War have started out as being seen nonviolently—from writing press releases to collecting weather reports. It's just data. But warfare has a large data component to it. Even primitive tribal warriors, armed with nothing more than bows and spears, are acutely aware of the value of data; information on where the enemy is, how he fights, and the battlefield environment in general. Primitive man may not have had a lot of technology, but he needed and used a lot of data. I mean, how many bird calls (often used as signals by warriors) can you identify?

From primitive man to high-tech man, we see one of the major differences being how much more data is available and how dependent we are on so much data we don't understand and often don't even know we have. Do you know all the data being passed between components of your car? Automobiles now have microprocessors and data-storage systems. Without these, they cannot operate. Thieves have learned that your car radio and air bag are not as valuable as your car computer. So many a driver starts his or her car only to find out that someone has forced the hood open, unscrewed the car computer, and left the automobile without its brain and unable to even turn over the engine. One form of Information War is to use an electronic device that shorts out the circuits in a vehicle's computer, rendering the vehicle (civilian or military) useless without leaving any visible marks on it. So, whether stealing the car computer or zapping it, you are engaged in Information War.

But to make and use things like car-computer zappers, you need cyberwarriors.

One could say that Information Warfare is whatever you do to preserve the integrity of your own information systems from exploitation, corruption, or destruction, while at the same time exploiting, corrupting, or destroying an enemy's information systems and in the process achieving an information advantage if it comes to armed combat. Well, that's the Pentagon take on Information War. You don't have to use force as a follow-on to Information War. But you do need cyberwarriors, and at the dawn of the twenty-first century, the Pentagon realized it didn't have nearly enough of them.

But before recruiting a lot of new cyberwarriors, you needed a place to put them.

The United States Cyberwar Command

The Pentagon got a loud wake-up call during a wargame conducted in 1997. The exercise, called Eligible Receiver, used white-hat hackers from the National Security Agency to show how it was possible, given then-current conditions, to attack key aspects of the American economy. The hackers showed that the electrical power grid-control systems of some major cities were also vulnerable to similar penetration and disruption. The media also made much of how the exercise showed you could hack many 911 systems and shut them down. Actually, these NSA hackers didn't take down a 911 system via Internet access, they simply arranged for a lot of people to call 911 at the same time and shut down the system. This could be done automatically by using computers to keep dialing 911 and tying it up. But the fact that the story still circulates about "the guys who hacked a 911 system" is another example of Information War. Nevertheless, Eligible Receiver scared the hell out of the American military and political leadership. Information War was no longer just a Pentagon marketing scam and everyone wanted lots of cyberwarriors, fast.

Wargames also showed that satellite communications were at risk as well. It has long been recognized that satellites are vulnerable to hackers, for the only way to send commands to satellites is via radio. Most of these communications are done via coded messages, but, as we've seen, codes can be cracked, or spies can obtain the codes. In either case, you won't find out about it until there's a war, and all of a sudden someone else has either taken over your satellites, or disabled them. Having that happen is another example of why "surprise attacks" are so feared by military people. And it's not just the military satellites that are at risk. There are nearly 800 satellites up there, most of them are civilian, not military, and we know they are vulnerable. For example, in the 1980s, a hacker calling himself "Captain Midnight" took over a transponder (one of the several broadcast/receiver units on a satellite) used by HBO and substituted his own message. In 1999, there was an unconfirmed story about a hacker who took over a military communications satellite in an unsuccessful extortion attempt. By 1999, the military decided to set up a single headquarters to deal with cyberwar. The first job, of course, was defenses to deal with all these scary vulnerabilities.

The United States Space Command (USSC) was (and is) responsible for American military satellites and space operations. So in October 1999, it was put in charge of providing tools, procedures, and consultation for efforts to defend Department of Defense computer networks. It was to help prevent network attacks by hackers, terrorists, and criminals. What was really going on was some bureaucratic reshuffling. What USSC actually did was take over an existing organization: the Department of Defense Joint Task Force—Computer Network Defense (JTF-CND). In early 1999, JTF-CND was organized after, as the military put it, "exercises and real-world events demonstrated the need for a single coordinating agency with the authority to direct actions necessary for the defense of vital national computer networks. It was recognized then that JTF-CND was an interim solution and eventually would be assigned to a unified command."

Space Command's JTF-CND was set up in the headquarters of the Defense Information Systems Agency (DISA) and, with about a hundred personnel, operates a twenty-four/seven watch for major hack attacks. There was already a network of intrusion detection and reporting systems in place, and now someone was responsible for watching all of them and organizing a defense if there was a major attack. This is typical, and quite practical, military procedure. When faced with a new threat, the first thing you do is post lookouts to warn when the bad guys are moving in your direction.

Space Command set up four levels of alerts, based on how dangerous the cyberwar threat is. The lowest level of alert is "Infocom Alpha," the most serious is "Infocom Delta." When an Infocom Alpha is declared, Department of Defense sysadmins and users are told to change passwords (in case enemy cyberwarriors have stolen existing ones), restrict cell phone use (these are easy to hack into), update keys used to encrypt classified communication lines (in case the enemy has cracked the current keys and is grabbing all the stuff going over these lines), do an extra backup of important documents, urge military personnel to update virus protection on their home computers, review security checklists and, of course, report suspicious activity. During the Chinese-American "hacker war" of early 2001 (after the EP-3 incident), Space Command went to Infocom Alpha. Procedures for the other three levels of alert, up to Infocom Delta, are still classified. But based on what is known about the Infocom Alpha procedures, and all the technical work that has to be done, the drills for the more serious alert levels will require a lot more cyberwarriors. That may be why the details are kept secret, because it would be obvious that it will take years to recruit and train enough cyberwarriors to do the job.

Space Command uses two private internets. It conducts business over NIPRNET (Nonclassified Internet Protocol Router Network), which is the military network that has some connections to the Internet and has over 2 million servers. These attract the hundred or so intrusion attempts made each day. Most are script kiddies goofing around, but ten to twenty of these attempts are deemed serious enough to warrant further investigation. Although unclassified, NIPRNET contains a lot of logistics (supplies, including requests for things like fuel, ammunition and the like), and personnel matters (addresses, phone numbers, and even credit card numbers). After September 11, 2001, more restrictions were placed on nonmilitary access to NIPRNET. You could still send e-mail into and out of NIPRNET, but it was harder for nonmilitary users to get in.

Separate from NIPRNET is SIPRNET (Secure Internet Protocol Router Network). This net is not connected to the Internet (although it is run with Internet technology) and encrypts its data. This network is rarely attacked and penetrations are few, if any (all discussion of SIPR-NET attacks are classified). SIPRNET is used by the military for discussing anything that is secret. SIPRNET is available all over the world via the U.S. military communications network.

In October 2001, the Space Command took over responsibility for offensive computer warfare. This included developing highly classified computer-attack systems and tools. Space Command will develop, test, and "package" these offensive tools for use in future wars. This area is being set up in response to the acknowledgment that the only way to build an air-defense system in the age of cyberwarfare, or at least one that has any chance of slowing down U.S. air attacks, requires the use of computer networks. The same goes for command-and-control systems for ground and naval forces. Thus the emphasis on developing weapons that can disable similar computer systems. While this is less-destructive warfare, using electronic signals rather than bombs, it is also more effective. This is not meant to be "weaponless warfare," the civilian analog of the "paperless office." This form of cyberwar concentrates on Information War. By destroying or slowing down the opponent's ability to communicate or collect and analyze information, their weapons are much less effective. The air force has been doing this since World War II, with its use of electronic warfare to shut down enemy antiaircraft defenses. Blinding radars and jamming communications enables American bombers to get through to their targets with fewer losses. Cyberwar extends this form of fighting to include anything connected with the Internet, or any other electronic network.

As always, the key to effective network weapons is finding weaknesses before the enemy user does. As discussed, it's a constantly changing situation, as foreign network managers themselves discover their vulnerabilities and fix them. If a cyberwar attack fails because of this, then you use the bombs. But every American cyberwar attack that succeeds means that fewer U.S. warplanes and pilots are put at risk. And those smart bombs are expensive as well, so cyberwar can be cheaper.

Cyberwarfare Units Around the World

Military cyberwarfare (attacking Department of Defense computers via the Internet) has not produced any major damage, yet. On the civilian side, the costs of dealing with cyberattacks on commercial systems exceeds $50 billion a year. Cyberwar is still considered what happens when someone makes major attacks on the United States. This means the organized units of cyberwarriors unleashing their most powerful cyberweapons. There is still some debate among diplomats and Department of Defense lawyers about whether this would be considered an act of war. Why the uncertainty? If a nation can launch a major cyberwar attack without identifying themselves, who do you declare war on? Pulling this off isn't a sure thing because American cyberwarriors keep building better tools and techniques for tracing the origins of attacks and identifying the attackers. But an anonymous, major attack is still possible, in theory. It's unknown if a nation would risk such an action, because if the attack were successful, the United States would probably ignore the lawyers and just declare war anyway. That's what happened to Al Qaeda and the Taliban, even though both groups still deny responsibility for the September 11 attacks.

There have been some low-level cyberwars going on already. In East Asia, China, and Taiwan, cyberwarriors have been sparring for years. In fact, serious attacks have been attempted, although both sides deny it. Some major hacking of U.S. military sites has been traced back to Chinese cyberwarfare organizations.

Besides China and Taiwan, the two Koreas, Japan, and Singapore have also established cybewarfare units. South Korea has done it to protect South Korea's extensive electronic infrastructure from attacks by North Korea. For decades, North Korea has used terrorism, threats, and espionage to torment the south. The North Korean leader, Kim Jong Il, is known to be an avid personal-computer user, so one can imagine that there is enthusiasm for cyberwarfare at the very top. South Korea has a very computer-literate population, and discovered that they had far more cyberwarfare talent than they had first thought. The millions of South Koreans who became programmers (professional and amateur) over the last three decades, as South Korea became a major producer of PCs and computer components, naturally took to the Internet and discovered hacking. Once the southerners investigated what cybermischief the northerners could get into, they began organizing to defend themselves. Unfortunately, the north has very little electronic infrastructure to attack. But there's always China, Japan, and Russia. However, these are nations South Korea does a lot of business with, and maintains pretty good relations with. Yes, South Korea now realizes they have a formidable weapon. More so than any of their neighbors, with the possible exception of Japan, South Korea has more local talent who can carry out cyberwar attacks and, more important, defend the nation from such assaults.

Japan set up cyberwar units because it realized that it had the largest electronic exposure in their part of the world. Indeed, next to North America, there's probably no juicier cybertarget than Japan. Both nations have connected more of their economy to the Internet than any other country. The Japanese have concentrated on defense. They have a lot to protect, and for cultural reasons (they are very polite) and some lingering anxiety about their aggressive role in World War II, they have not done much to develop offensive methods.

Not so the Chinese, where a combination of growing use of the Internet, rapidly expanding technology industries, and a strong sense of nationalism have created a major cyberpower. The Chinese are also unique in that the government has tried, and succeeded to a large extent, in controlling the Internet within China. Of course, no nation can completely control the Internet. But the Chinese government has gone further than anyone else. This effort is aided by the thousands of capable, patriotic, and Internet-savvy Chinese who are eager to aid the government in this effort. These pro-government Chinese hackers outnumber those independent-minded black-hat hackers who scare governments and businesses in other nations.

As good as the Chinese hackers are, they have not been able to cover their tracks. Some of their efforts overseas have been traced back to China. We know what the Chinese, at least in general, are capable of. And we know that they are good. What we don't know is exactly how good and exactly what cyberweapons they could unleash during a wartime, or a near wartime, situation. This is the most frightening aspect of cyberwar. The best weapons are those that are kept secret until used. The victim hit by a new type of cyberattack has to first figure out what's going on before defenses can be devised and damage repaired. The larger and more capable a nation's cyberforce is, the more new unexpected attacks and tools they can develop.

Examples of Chinese cyberwar prowess have been seen in Internet battles between Chinese and Taiwanese hackers over the last few years. The dispute between China and Taiwan over Taiwan's independence has been fought most viciously on the Internet. The action has largely been minor, trashing each others' Web sites and the like. But there have been indications of more potent stuff. The most damaging Internet attacks require a lot of preparation and this usually involves quietly sneaking into the computers of potential victims to scout out defenses. The Cyberwarfare between Taiwanese and Chinese hackers had, by 2000, become something of a popular indoor sport. But that was only the most visible part of the battle. Programmers on both sides of the Taiwan Strait have, as a consequence of these constant attacks, developed some excellent new techniques for protecting Web pages. Less obvious is the regular attempts to break into critical government and military sites. In August 1999, over a thousand ATMs (automated teller machines) in Taiwan went offline because of one of the Chinese hack attacks. Both the Chinese and Taiwanese governments officially deplore all this hacking, but unofficially (and sometimes out loud) encourage it. None of the "patriotic hackers" have been prosecuted, although many of them have been debriefed by Internet security officials from their own governments. The mainland Chinese secret police have also kept a nervous eye on some of the "patriotic hackers" who are known to mouth off about things that are wrong with the Chinese government. While hundreds of Chinese cyberwarriors are in the military or on the government payroll, there are thousands of volunteers who are, like most people on the Internet, free spirits. It's these volunteers, whose identities are often unknown to the government, that frighten the officials. But the communist bureaucrats that run China are willing to live with this as long as the volunteers remain generally loyal to the government and capable of adding to the cyberwar effort.

In early 2001, Taiwan revealed that it had increased the size of its secret Information Warfare Task Force to battalion level (several hundred troops). The unit had also been given new equipment (the latest PCs and software tools) and pretty much a blank check to get what it needed in the future. Taiwan also did a little cyber–saber rattling, boasting that it had over a thousand computer viruses ready to unleash on China in the event of a war. Unless constructed to attack very specific targets, such viruses will spread all over the Net causing all manner of mayhem worldwide. During 2001, three computer viruses thought to be launched by the Taiwanese on China accounted for about half the cyber attacks around the world. Taiwan is tight lipped when asked for further information on such issues. China, however, is saying nothing about its offensive capabilities, and only talks about its defensive cyberwar units.

The Taiwanese and Chinese efforts are a reminder that most cyberweapons have a short shelf life, as they depend on software flaws that are constantly being discovered and fixed. But this is where China has an edge, for as the number of skilled Chinese software engineers and hackers increases, so does the ability of China to discover, and exploit, Internet flaws more rapidly than anyone else.

Worst of all, China has made no secret of favoring this kind of low-cost approach to warfare. While salaries (and very low ones, by U.S. standards) must be paid to some of China's cyberwarriors who staff the cyberwar headquarters, much of the work is done by patriotic volunteers among the ranks of China's growing number of software engineers and programmers. The eagerness of these cyberwarriors has been seen in the skirmishes with the Taiwanese, where volunteers jumped right in to defend the motherland. The only bright spot in all this is the Taiwanese, who are well aware of their position on the frontlines of the looming cyberwar. But should China unleash its cyberweapons, all of East Asia will suffer, just before the chaos hits the United States.

Aware of the potential surprise Internet attacks China could unleash, in 2000 the U.S. Air Force opened the Combined Aerospace Operations Center at Langley, Virginia. Its unique mission: to go out and find the latest civilian Internet and computer technology that would give the air force a needed edge in case of cyberwar attacks. A major problem with the military fighting an Information War is that, compared to civilian organizations, it takes far longer for the military to get new equipment certified for military use and actually delivered to the troops. Since civilians, and the troops, essentially have the same "weapons" in an Information War, the military has to make sure that they are not outgunned by the very population it is supposed to protect. The speed was noted, in the 1990s, with which the Chinese were able to get their troops the latest off-the-shelf computer equipment from civilian sources, and the U.S. is trying to accomplish the same end, acknowledging the fact that their Chinese counterparts now have more modern cyberwar equipment than they do. Much of this is due to the fact that air force computers, like elsewhere in the military, are only bought every few years. Specifically, with regard to the air force, equipment in the late 1990s was delayed by lawsuits from manufacturers who had lost out in the bidding to provide the newer technology. As the cases dragged on for months, more air force people noted that the PCs they had bought themselves for home use were much more powerful than the government ones they used on the job. Currently, the air force has changed its PC procurement policy somewhat so that in the future it will not fall behind potential foes who were buying the latest machines.

Later in 2000, the U.S. Air Force created the 527th Space Aggressor Squadron. This unit would provide realistic sparring partners for American cyberwarriors. This approach grew out of wargames in the late 1990s that showed the U.S. was becoming more dependent, in wartime, on its growing fleet of communications, reconnaissance, and navigation satellites However, no one had bothered to look at ways to attack America's extensive satellite network, and when the matter was looked into it was discovered that there were indeed many vulnerabilities. One of the major ones was the radio networks that controlled the satellites. This system, although encrypted, was as vulnerable as the Internet. And a lot of Internet traffic, especially military was dependent on those satellites for getting data from one part of the world to another. One of the four subunits of the 527th squadron specialized in "Red Attack" (figuring out the most effective enemy attack methods, preferably before the enemy does). It has already become common for Internet security firms to establish "Tiger Teams" of expert hackers who would test an organization's defenses by attacking them. The air force's "Red Attack" crew were just doing the same thing to the wireless network that controlled America's military satellites.

The United States also has hundreds of cyberwarriors in the FBI, where hackers involved in criminal acts are hunted down. But the FBI and the Department of Defense aren't the only ones going after the growing number of cybercriminals. The Treasury Department is responsible for going after counterfeiting, money laundering, and all manner of financial fraud. The Treasury Department's Secret Service also guards the president and key government officials. In 2000, the Treasury Department finally got the Internet religion and asked to increase the Secret Service strength by a hundred agents, all of them trained in the arcane arts of Internet crime.

Many of the hacking tools used by criminals are similar, often identical, to those used by cyberwarriors, so in wartime the FBI and Treasury Department would have cyberwar resources available as well.

Mysterious China Catches Up with Its Past

In late 2001, China graduated the first class of officers who had taken a one-year course in psychological warfare operations. The country had already organized several cyberwar units and is putting a lot of money into training Net-savvy engineers. A major motivator for this sort of program is the realization that the Internet and other mass media have become major military weapons. There's a great deal of irony in this, because for several thousand years, China was in the forefront of developing new psychological warfare operations. The Chinese interest in psychological warfare was what made the country seem so exotic to foreigners. For example, it was noted that there was extensive use of hostages in medieval China, a fact that was also not unknown in Europe. The king would demand that key (and potentially traitorous) nobles send one of their sons to the king's court. The official reason for this was so that the young man (often a child as young as eight or nine) could get to know the king, and vice versa. The real reason was that if the child's father turned on the king, the "hostage" would be killed. The Chinese, as you can see, were very practical in matters of loyalty. For example, a Chinese saying was, "the easiest way to take a fortress is with a donkey." That is, a donkey loaded down with gold or silver to bribe the garrison. Which is why the families of most fortress commanders lived elsewhere, in a place where the emperor's men could quickly kill them if daddy sold out the emperor's fortress.

In short, the Chinese have long recognized how important networks of information, reliability (of generals and commanders of key fortresses) and tools for influencing both, are when trying to run a government.

Ever resourceful, Chinese military sages wrote many books of advice on how to use psychological and Information War tricks to get the fortress commander to surrender anyway. How? Simple, arrange for a false report to reach the emperor that the fortress had fallen to a bribe. Then make sure the fortress commander found out about his late wife and kids (and often grandparents and siblings as well). If you could pull that off (it was not easy, but was done often enough), you could probably get the fortress at half price because the commander was angry that his family had been killed. False messages, well-placed rumors, and other Information War techniques that still work were all part of the Chinese way of war for centuries.

Why did all this Information War wisdom fall into disuse in China, only to be revived by the needs of cyberwar? Blame it on nuclear weapons. China has not fought a major war in half a century. What has kept the peace, more than anything else, has been nuclear weapons. In the past, the major nations were less reluctant to get into a major scrape because the downside wasn't all that dire. At worst, you would lose a chunk of the current military-age generation, a bunch of money (you could make the peasants pay for that), and maybe have a little civil disorder. But now that all the big guys have nukes, a major war risks everything. So when there's a long period of peace, as has happened before in China, the result is rot. The military virtues of the ancients are forgotten, only to be relearned at great cost when the next war comes around.

What we are seeing here is the Chinese recognition that another major war has already started, and that they are blessed because this new kind of war, cyberwar, is lifting off slowly. This gives the conservative Chinese military leadership sufficient time to get thoroughly terrified, recover their wits, and do something about it. The Chinese are doing a lot about it. China fully intends, by their own published statements, to be the cyberwar superpower. To the Chinese, this is a very practical approach. They cannot afford the trillions of dollars it would cost to build a conventional military force to match what America already has. But since cyberwar is new, and no one has a lot of weapons or knowledge of how to fight a cyberwar, China has an opportunity to become the planet's mightiest cyberwar power.

The FBI and the National Infrastructure Protection Center (NIPC)

Most Americans think that the government, in particular the FBI, is able to go after Internet criminals and catch them. In reality, the FBI is a latecomer to Internet crime. The businesses most vulnerable to Internet crime, particularly major banks and financial institutions, have long maintained their own crews of Internet experts to protect themselves from Internet crime and hunt down cybercriminals. Once identified, with evidence compiled, the banks would turn the case over to the FBI for prosecution. The FBI likes to keep this sort of thing quiet. But in the late 1990s, as the public became more aware of the threat of cyberwar and Internet crime, the FBI was forced to do something; to take charge. The result was the National Infrastructure Protection Center (NIPC).

Set up by the FBI in 1998, the NIPC was to be a clearinghouse for reporting cyberwar attacks and remedies for those attacks. Technically, the FBI isn't in the cyberwar business. The FBI's job is to go after domestic criminals (who commit federal, as opposed to local, crimes) and hunt for foreign spies. But most of what passes for cyberwar so far has been perpetrated by criminals or kids looking for some Internet thrills. It's the Department of Defense who became aware that foreign nations could mobilize all these hacking tools and make a major attack. Since the FBI is responsible for investigating the day-to-day criminal and disruptive activity on the Internet, they set up the NIPC to consolidate all available information on hacking. The Department of Defense works with the NIPC because a lot of this day-to-day mischief is, for all practical purposes, low-level cyberwar.

There was also a PR angle. While the NIPC was saying all the right things about protecting us all from cyberwar, the reality of this new organization was different. Since the NIPC was under the control of the FBI, its efforts, such as they were, focused on prosecuting hackers, not on "protecting the national computer infrastructure." Moreover, the

NIPC didn't really have the resources to go after many hackers. In 1998 it worked on 200 cases, and upped that to 800 in 1999. But not a lot was accomplished, as the NIPC budget was only about $20 million (and rising, but not by much). Cooperation with the commercial sector was also a problem. For example, while the NIPC posted software on its Web site to detect zombies and such, it also provided software that gave the FBI access to protected networks. This brought up another major disagreement between the FBI and the infrastructure it was trying to protect. The FBI wanted more control over encryption, something the people who ran and used the Internet did not want anyone to have. The FBI wants to be able to go anywhere on the Internet (at least in the United States) and be able to read any encrypted material sent and received by American firms. Although the FBI says it's just trying to protect everyone from Internet criminals, most Internet users (both individuals and businesses) see "Big Brother" instead.

The FBI did have one eager market for their software, and this was government agencies. The FBI IntraGuard system was software designed to protect networks (government or private) from cyberattacks. Its capabilities included being able to detect suspicious activity and record data for a subsequent investigation. But IntraGuard was basically a commercial product with the FBI seal of approval. This made it easy to sell to government agencies, but the FBI connection worked against sales to nongovernment organizations. Businesses did not like the FBI monitoring what they did on the Internet.

There were also problems of cooperation. There has always been this problem with the FBI and other government agencies. The FBI likes to take information, but does not like to give anything out. It's a longstanding problem. Many agencies had learned to work around the FBI's bad habits. However, in this case the other agencies, especially the CIA and the Department of Defense, felt they were better equipped to deal with Internet security problems and figured they could pretty much ignore the FBI altogether. Moreover, the NIPC can't go after cybercrime originating overseas, that's the CIA's turf. Internet attacks can easily be made to look like they are coming from overseas, or ones that are outside the United States can be made to appear as if they originated in North America. Fortunately, this type of spoofing has become easier to penetrate. But until the NIPC experts have gotten a good idea of where the attack came from, they aren't sure if the FBI will be able to even go after the case or not.

In 2000, to make matters more interesting, the Department of Defense tried to grab control of Information War operations by rearranging the military budget to include a separate organization that would do what the NIPC was already doing. The FBI fought this, and the NIPC survived. But when George Bush became president in 2001, the Department of Defense again made a move to lead the Information Warriors. The issue is still in doubt as of early 2002, and will probably continue that way as the battling bureaucracies fight each other for control of this new battlefield, and all the additional money that is being thrown at Information War.

It was also noted that, early on, most of the NIPC's resources went to train FBI agents in the mysteries of Internet investigation, or to otherwise support FBI investigations. While the FBI asserted that it was now one of the Internet-security players, the other government agencies didn't go along with that. The FBI was largely ignored, and efforts were made to move the "leadership" role for Internet security to the Department of Defense. The FBI doesn't like that idea at all, and since September 11, 2001, has shown a higher degree of cooperation and common sense. Contributing to this new attitude was, no doubt, an unflattering Government Accounting Office report in July 2001. About the same time, the NIPC's own techies managed to infect their internal network with the SirCam virus. This was highly embarrassing, for who is going to trust the FBI to protect them from Internet problems if the FBI can't even protect itself from a common Internet virus.

Commercial Internet-security firms were much put off by the FBI's lack of cooperation. The FBI would ask much and say little; not exactly a free flow of information. Moreover, the FBI and NIPC was very much outgunned by the hacker talent available to the commercial firms. One got the feeling that the FBI didn't say much because they didn't have much to say. This seemed to be confirmed by the fact that nearly all the NIPC's security alerts were for attacks that were already under way. The fact is, the NIPC started out in an world that already had organizations, particularly CERT (the Department of Defense's Computer Emergency Response Team organization) and several suppliers of antivirus software, that were already issuing alerts. CERT also had a much better relationship with commercial firms and government agencies.

Another problem was that most of the black-hat hackers that could be caught tended to be either underage Americans or foreigners in countries that didn't have laws to prosecute hackers. Most businesses had a pretty low opinion of the FBI's ability to catch hackers. For that reason, only about a third of hacker attacks are even reported. The business world has long realized that the government doesn't really have the resources to pursue investigations involving Internet crime. So those firms, like banks with big exposures in this area, have their own personnel to investigate intrusions and, if they locate the culprit, hand the case over to the FBI to make the arrest and prosecute. The FBI likes to play down the fact that they get cases like this handed to them with all the tough, investigative work already done. The firms involved are often content to go along with this, if only to stay on the good side of the feds.

The turf battles and aura of lackluster performance surrounding the NIPC and FBI are at least recognized as a problem in Washington. But for the moment, no one has a solution.

The Missing Cyberwarriors

The American armed forces has embraced the Internet, and with it the danger of getting hacked and penetrated. But as vulnerable as the troops are, they still face losing more and more of the computer experts they need to defend themselves.

Those soldiers with computer experience are leaving in droves. Part of this is because of better economic opportunities in the civilian economy. But another critical reason is the workload these cyberwarriors are burdened with. As the armed forces install more networks, they encounter more problems and more exposure to hacking. The basic problem is that the best defense against breaking into nets is well-trained systems administrators (sysadmins) to keep the software up to date and secure. Most Net penetrations are the result of software that was poorly installed or not updated with the latest patches and protections. The demand for good sysadmins makes young soldiers trained in these skills a hot item on the civilian market. The military had a hard time getting these troops to reenlist.

A more pressing reason for the cyberwarriors not staying is the strain of moving these troops around as new crises crop up. The military uses networks everywhere and are working on equipping the combat infantry and armored vehicles with them. When the troops are sent to places like Bosnia, local networks are set up (and linked worldwide with portable satellite dishes). There were problems with this in Bosnia; as a result, a lot of cyberwarriors found themselves back in Bosnia, often more than once. Network and computer problems in other places like Korea, Afghanistan, and the Persian Gulf also creates a demand for specialists to be sent there. This is not an ideal lifestyle for most people, especially married soldiers. And most soldiers today are married. Troops often have to choose between their military careers and their marriages. The marriages usually win.

When the Internet and the World Wide Web became widespread in the early 1990s, the military was already working on "networking" their ships, aircraft, and tanks. This would make it possible to pass target information and data on where friendly and enemy forces are. The easy-to-use technology of the Word Wide Web seemed an ideal solution. But there was a catch. The Internet and its World Wide Web component were created by thousands of independent programmers. The software was often created as "freeware" (to be given away) and continually updated by eager volunteers. When you change software a lot, you make some mistakes. The mistakes that are missed are the ones that don't affect operations, but rather compromise security. These trapdoors and loopholes are the cause of most network break-ins. The other major security hole was the inside job, or a stolen password. For government systems, some 95 percentage of the illegal hacks into the system are inside jobs, usually involving a stolen password. The best defense against all of these problems was competent sysadmins who stayed on top of all the software changes and kept their systems up to date. But there were never enough sysadmins to go around, and when the military greatly expanded their inventory of networks, they found that they had a cyberwarrior shortage. Hiring much more expensive civilian contractors, often former cyberwarriors, helps somewhat. But Congress does not like the much higher price the civilians charge.

The military is trying to adapt by using more automation for the upgrades and updates needed to keep Web software up to date. Corporations, with the same types of personnel shortages, are going in the same direction. But the civilian outfits have a higher proportion of Web hotshots to back up the automated systems. That makes a big difference. So the military tries to compensate by severely restricting how military servers can be set up and modified. While that policy is frustrating to the troops, it does pay off in better security. But none of this does much for the fact that the military is having a real bad time holding on to skilled Web technical staff. If it comes to a cyberwar, this shortcoming will be mentioned a lot as a reason for this or that particular defeat.

Web Risk Assessment Team

Recognizing that the military Web-security personnel cannot match the skills of civilian practitioners, the Department of Defense used the time-honored technique of rounding up reservists with the special skills needed and turning them loose. In early 2000, the Department of Defense established a reserve unit full of Internet experts that would spend one weekend a month checking military Web sites for sensitive or classified information (that was not supposed to be there). This unit, known as the Web Risk Assessment Team (or WRAT, as the unit is called) is typical of the new approach of the Department of Defense to computer security. After going over 800 major Department of Defense Web sites, the unit found 1300 Web pages with security problems. They found ten sites where details of U.S. war plans (normally top secret) were posted. WRAT is also assigned to improve the security of DoD (Department of Defense) sites, and are using various proven techniques (developed by commercial firms to protect their own secrets) to do it.

The Cybermilitia

Before the United States had an army, it had local militias. This was mainly a matter of money. Full-time soldiers are expensive. The militia idea, which is actually an ancient one, simply uses civilians trained and equipped to fight as an army. When there is a threat, the militia gets called up.

Well, we're still in the Age of Militias when it comes to troops who can fight a cyberwar. The only problem is, no one has actually organized this militia. Except for the Web Risk Assessment Team (described above), the idea is still just another proposal rattling around the Pentagon.

The proposals themselves vary. One resulted in the Web Risk Assessment Team. Others have actually identified talented hackers among people already in reserve intelligence and electronic-warfare units. Another proposal is to form a special security force for policing the Internet. The main problem with a full-time Internet police force is that there is such a (trained, not to mention talented) manpower shortage right now (and in the foreseeable future) that it would be difficult to staff such a force at government pay levels. One solution would be to try and organize and reward the pro-bono cybersecurity efforts that have been going on for some time. A lot of talented white hats just get pissed off and go after bad guys on their own nickel. An example is the HoneyNet project (the voluntary network of "Honey Pot" servers set up to attract, analyze, and document black-hat activities and techniques).

The military is already establishing cyberwar reserve units, if only because the military already had over a million people in reserve units.

Thousands of these people are qualified Internet experts, mostly by virtue of their civilian jobs. Many more could be brought up to cyber-cop level with additional training. Such training could be provided by the government, and few of the troops in question would turn it down as it would enhance their current careers.

Like many National Guard and reserve units, the cyberwar companies and battalions can be called out in a national emergency. In this case, it wouldn't be for hurricanes or forest fires, but for times when there is an upsurge in Internet vandalism or actual cyberwarfare. In early 2001, there was just such an event when Chinese hackers went after America's Internet infrastructure because of the EP-3 aircraft incident. Later that year, the reservists with Internet expertise were called out again to help with the war on terrorism. The one downside of the Internet warfare reserve units is that many members have day jobs in Internet related fields, and they are particularly missed when called up during an Internet emergency. But their employers know this and can plan accordingly.

Another government option would be to set up a cybercorps as a government-controlled company, find a few really good people to run it, give them a lot of money, and turn them loose. A cybercorps could pay market rates for the right people, and still have a close working relationship with government agencies and commercial firms that spend a lot on Net security (banks and brokerages, for example). As a separate corporation, with clearly defined goals, the cybercorps would not get tangled up in the office politics to which operations like the NIPC fall prey.

Most of the successful criminal activity comes from the victim being careless. Cybercops won't be able to do much about that. But a lot of the malicious mischief on the Internet could be eliminated if the cyber-cops were good enough to hunt down and document what a lot of the black-hat vandals are doing. These guys don't steal as much as disrupt. But to a business that has to pay millions of dollars in additional personnel costs to fix the damage, it's not much different than an outright theft. The FBI would still be able to prosecute, and wouldn't have to worry about attracting top, hacker talent with paltry, civil-service pay scales.

The traditional solution for this sort of problem is to issue lots of contracts for the "beltway bandits" (the defense consulting firms in the Washington, D.C. area) to go after the problem. This is what the army special forces did in early 2000. Fourteen programs were identified, mostly having to do with researching better ways to defend computers from hackers. The intentions here were good. The government was looking to develop software that would track activity inside a server and sound an alert if any user did something that appeared to be a hacker trying to gain control over the server. The other major research area was the development of software that wouldn't just sound an alarm and wait for human intervention, but would automatically shut down parts of the system to foil any hacker activity. Worthy efforts, these, to be sure. But there were several problems with the way the Department of Defense was going about it. First, while the defense consultants had excellent people, they were not as good as the folks in the Internet security industry, where software like this is always being developed for the civilian market. But the Pentagon can control their beltway bandits in ways they cannot control commercial firms. There is a cozy relationship between the Department of Defense and these consultants. If the Pentagon needs a study to show that a Pentagon screwup was actually a brilliant move, there's a defense consultant who can make it happen. These guys do a lot of useful work, but because they live or die depending on how many contracts they get, doing some dirty work from time to time is just the cost of doing business. The Pentagon has had success in contracting consultants or university researchers to look into exotic areas. That's how the Internet itself got started. But in a fast-moving technological environment, like where the Internet is now, studies are obsolete before they are finished.

The freewheeling structure, and atmosphere, of the Internet is very popular with a new generation of hackers. You can't change this, and if the government and military is going to get the manpower it needs, other than during a major war and national mobilization, some innovative recruiting and organization ideas are going to be needed.

What Cyberwar Will Look Like

Actually, few Internet attacks will directly kill people. That, however, isn't what worries the military. Because the Internet is now the core of a much larger information network, the armed forces can be less effective if the Internet is successfully attacked. This would mean more American troops getting killed while resulting in less damage to the enemy.

For example:

- False e-mail messages are easy to send. Kids can do it, and sometimes do. A bunch of false and misleading messages, sent by someone who has a list of commanders who would be sending them, and knowledge of what a legitimate message would look like, could do a lot of damage before we caught on. If you bother to look at all that incomprehensible text that accompanies an Internet e-mail message, and you know what to look for, you can quickly tell what a bogus message looks like. But before anyone noticed that the messages were not real, thousands of fraudulent messages would already have screwed up the deployment of our forces, sending ships, aircraft, supplies, satellites, and ground units off in the wrong directions. This would mean chaos for days, if not weeks. Plus, the enemy (who sent the false messages) would know where our guys were going, providing better attack possibilities for them. The enemy would do all this by patiently infiltrating our computer networks in peacetime. This sort of thing is going on right now. The problem is, no one has yet invented tools to insure that all the snoops are caught, or even detected. We do it, too.

- Another crucial Internet attack in the early stages of a war would be one that corrupts military databases. Actually, you don't want to corrupt (randomly scramble data) these databases in the traditional sense, as this would generate an error message when our troops and planners went to use those systems. No, the way you do it is to make changes in those databases that insure that the wrong supplies and spare parts are sent out by the automatic resupply systems. You want to change the targeting databases so that our missiles and smart bombs miss their targets, or so that our electronic-warfare equipment has a harder time detecting and jamming the enemy's radars.

- Sleeper programs are software planted in a computer on a warship. When these are activated, the ship's computers and databases can be crippled or disabled in any number of ways. You could also plant sleeper programs in the computers of air force and army units. Activation of the sleeper programs can be via a command sent in on the Internet, or when the victim's computer does certain things, like running the kinds of programs that would indicate that a war is underway. Planting these sleeper programs are what keep cyberwar units busy in peacetime (looking for sleeper programs). Planting sleeper programs is hard to do, but not impossible. And when you find one of these sleepers, you want to keep it a secret. Like a booby-trap operated by remote control, you want to disable the sleeper programs, but make the enemy think that the sleeper is still intact and ready to go.

- Internet mischief can also directly trash some equipment. Military equipment is called, with good reason, "high performance." This means that it can perform safely most of the time at the limits of its performance specifications. It also means that it is more liable to failure if a vital component is knocked out. Operators of military equipment (aircraft, weapons, and electronics) are trained carefully so that they know when they are pushing their equipment toward the breaking point. This potentially unsafe situation is allowed in military equipment because in combat you often have a choice between definitely getting killed, and maybe getting zapped if you push the gear beyond safe operating limits. The best example are jet fighters. In wartime, pilots can push the engines, and some of the electronic gear, a little further. This means the engine might have to be junked real soon, but the extra speed you squeezed out of it can save your life in combat. These days, a lot of this risky military equipment is controlled, or partially controlled, by software. A further improvement of the latest stuff is the ability to easily modify the software to make the equipment more effective against newly discovered enemy capabilities. Sometimes the changes are made via a network, in most cases the changes are made on a networked PC, and the new software then manually carried to the equipment and loaded. You can see the possibilities here for someone who knows something about your software and has gained access to your networks.
- There is a particular kind of sleeper program called a "sniffer." This program will copy messages and data and send it off to the bad guys. A sniffer could even analyze messages and data being sent. If the sniffer program identified something as important, the sniffer would randomly waylay the transmission. By not stopping all messages that fit the profile, you would still do damage and it would take longer for the user to figure out that they have hostile software on their system. People still expect things to go wrong with their computers from time to time. As long as you have the user looking for a bug, and not a sniffer, your sniffer can continue doing its damage for a longer time.
- All the damage doesn't have to be against strictly military targets. Your sleepers and sniffers, or straight-out Net attacks, can go after payroll and benefits databases for military and Department of Defense civilians. This will cause morale problems and tie up computer experts who might be working on more militarily critical jobs.

That's what individual cyberwar attacks can do. To really make a difference, attacks deployed together have to be directed at larger targets that will cripple, or seriously injure, our ability to defend ourselves. There are several specific target areas that an enemy would direct their cyberattacks at. Spread the individual attacks over too many of these areas and the overall damage is less effective. You want to do a lot of damage in one class of targets to have a decisive effect. There are three areas the attacks can be concentrated against:

Deploying Forces. These are the ships, ground combat units, and aircraft being sent to a combat zone. If these can be slowed or disabled, if only for a while, they will have an effect on the battle. All American combat units depend on Internet access for their peacetime, and, to a lesser extent, their wartime operations. Each warship has its own internal Internet network, as well as other networks. Warships, and support ships, are the most vulnerable to an Internet attack. Air force units spend most of their time with logistics (dealing with supplies) and maintenance of warplanes heading into combat. Perhaps the most vulnerable air force targets, at least in the U.S. Air Force, are the hundreds of transports. The warplanes cannot fight overseas without the hardworking freighter aircraft flying in spare parts, weapons, and other supplies. A concentrated, and massive, attack on the air-transport units would really screw up any deployment of U.S. forces overseas. This would, of course, also delay deployment of, say, an American airborne division.

Mission-critical Facilities. The military uses the term "mission critical" to mean something that, if missing, would prevent a military operation from succeeding. At the top of the list would be anything dealing with transportation and communications. Military and civilian airports are highly dependent on computers and networks. A cyberattack on them could shut them down for days and reduce their capabilities for longer than that. Satellite-control centers are also very vulnerable. Here, the damage could be even worse. If the cyberattack were powerful enough, it could knock several satellites

Mission-critical Systems. Here we mean specific computers or groups of computers that control a specific military function. While the Department of Defense has thousands of different computer networks, a small percentage are considered mission critical. Of course, these are the best-protected systems and the hardest ones to get into, which makes a successful cyberattack here all the more useful.

Examples of mission-critical computer systems are those that control the movement of supplies, access to spy satellites, air and sea transports (what's on them, where they are, and where they are headed), details on electronic warfare, the setup of communications networks, and so on. You get the idea. Some government computer systems can also have military repercussions if they are trashed, such as those dealing with paying firms that supply military material (from boots to bombs). The Justice Department is always on the lookout for spies and saboteurs. If the enemy can get into the Justice Department computers that contain information on what the U.S. thinks it knows about foreign spies, much damage can be done.

The Internet has proved enormously useful for the military, but with that has come a potentially huge vulnerability. It's a lot easier for the troops to get access to the Internet, and obtain benefits from it, than it is to build defenses against cyberattack. SIPRNET (the encrypted version of the Internet that is not connected with the regular Internet), while more secure, is also far less useful than the regular Internet.

We won't know who has won the race to use the Internet as a military weapon until there is a war and we discover who is more vulnerable, and who has the more-powerful Internet weapons. The world's cyberwarriors are getting ready for this war, and they are justifiably nervous about who will win when the first cyberwar occurs.

CHAPTER 9

The Cyberwarrior's Weapons and Tools

175

known or typical passwords to gain illegal entry into a password-protected Web site or server. All you need is a user name. These tools are not as useful as they used to be because more and more sites are shutting out a user name if too many incorrect passwords (three to ten, for example) are entered one after another. The site then tells the user to try again in five minutes or so. This is okay for a real user, but long enough to make password guessing ineffective. It would take days to grind through hundreds of thousands of possible passwords. Without the delay, the guessing tool could be in within minutes or, at most, an hour or so.

The military, especially in the United States, took to the Internet quickly and enthusiastically. Since combat is not the kind of environment we think of when the Internet comes to mind, the troops had to use some imagination to make it all work. The American military has been working on how to use the Internet as a combat tool through most of the 1990s. After all that time, a lot of "Internet-powered" military weapons are showing up.

One unusual aspect of creating military tools for the Internet is that most of the best tools were first made by civilians. So the troops had to adapt a lot of civilian hacking tools for military use.

The Cyberwarrior's Toolbox

From the cyberwarriors' viewpoint, the best thing about his job is that his weapons are cheap and easy to obtain. There's nothing to carry around, actually. All the principal weapons are available on the Internet, or can be stored there. Why, some cyberwarrior might be storing their toolbox on your home or office PC.

Moreover, you can train a basic cyberwar foot soldier in a few weeks. Most of the basic tools are found on the Net, or as the basic equipment of any Internet-ready PC. One could easily train thousands of basic cybersoldiers in a short time. The fear is that this is what a country like China will do. While many experienced hackers will automate a lot of their work, there are still some things that work better if there's a bit of human judgment involved.

The hacker underground has never been very well hidden. Get online, go to a search engine (like Google.com) and type in "hacker tools" (with the quotes). You'll get over 10,000 hits. What's on the first page of hits is more than enough to get anyone going.

The guys (it's overwhelmingly guys) who create hacker tools do it, naturally enough, to make their hacking easier. Why make them available for anyone to download? Largely because the only reward for most hackers is a little ego stroking. They get that by creating the most effective tools. There once was a time, not too many years ago, when hackers would brag about what they had done with their tools. But that is less common these days. The feds are coming down harder, and getting pretty good at identifying anyone mouthing off too loudly about their cracker exploits. And the police are more likely to send hackers to jail rather than giving them probation and a fine.

But there's another reason why a lot of these tools exist. People who protect the Internet use this stuff to make sure their servers are safe. By using hacker tools, especially the ones that, well, "probe" the millions of computers connected to the Internet, looking for unprotected machines that will allow for further mischief, you can at least see what you're up against.

The basic tools are security probes, network scanners, and packet sniffers. These items are used to find vulnerable servers, or even PCs connected to the Internet. If you're going to hack a system, the first thing you have to do is find one you can get into. Scanners are often automated and then just allowed to run and run, reporting back when vulnerable systems are found. This automated approach might also turn loose a probe program, although this is more effectively done with some human supervision. A probe goes deeper into a vulnerable system, obtaining more detail about how the system is set up and just how vulnerable it is. Packet sniffers literally grab data going into or out of a system in order to try and obtain passwords or simply look at what unencrypted stuff is passing by. There are thousands of programs out there that do the probing, scanning, or sniffing. You will also find tools and advice for defeating the probes, scanners, and sniffers. That's why there's so much activity building these tools. There's a war going on and no one gains an edge that is anymore than momentary. So new weapons and defenses are conjured up daily.

In the late 1990s, you could probe and scan with impunity because not many sites were watching out for this activity. No more. People are getting caught probing and prosecutions, or at least detections, are on the rise. So you also have to learn how to hide your tracks. This is the case with cyberwarriors as well, although not all the troops are as careful as they should be. An increasing number of probes and penetrations are being traced back to suspicious locations in places like Russia and China. We're talking about government-controlled institutions, not just Chinese and Russian universities.

Probing and scanning is what you do as a form of basic training for your new cyberwarriors. The serious stuff of penetrating a vulnerable site requires a lot more skill and experience. The big difference between most of the thousands of hacking attempts that take place every day, and cyberwar, is that most attempts to get into other people's computers are done by amateurs. This sort of thing is a hobby for a lot of kids, and not a few adults. Cyberwarriors, those trained to make military-grade attacks on the Net, operate differently, although the tools they use are similar to the ones wielded by your everyday script kiddie or professional hacker.

The military hackers tool kit will be more standardized because any serious military cyberwar operation will involve hundreds, or even thousands, of people. Standardized tools make it easier to train people and compare results between people on the team. Standardization also makes it easier to upgrade everyone's tools, something that has to be done frequently. The Internet's inner workings are constantly changing, and this means the tools to crack it must change as well. Moreover, the toolmakers constantly find better ways to make their tools work.

Another thing to keep in mind. Details of exactly how cyberwarriors actually operate is a big-time secret. One thing everyone involved in this new form of warfare quickly realized was that secrecy was one of the most powerful weapons in your cyberarsenal. The more the other guy knows about how you operate, the less successful you will be. So what I am describing is, in general terms, how any cyberwarfare organization would have to organize and operate. Enough has leaked out over the last few years to allow that much to be known.

Even if information on an enemy network is obtained (by having a spy or traitor e-mail, mail, or hand carry it to you), you still have to scan and probe to confirm that the information is real, and not some kind of trap.

The scanning and probing are the easiest part of developing a cyber-attack. The entire drill for an attack can be summed up with the acronym SPAA (scan, probe, analyze, attack). There are often additional steps if you are going after a network that is not publicly available. A good example would be the private military Internet networks (SIPR-NET, Intellink, NIPRNET, and the proposed GOVNET). Just getting access to these networks is a major operation, and would use more of the traditional techniques for espionage and wiretapping. During the Cold War, the U.S. used a nuclear submarine to tap into a secret Russian military communications system. That was only because part of the cable ran underwater to a Russian submarine base on an island. That achievement was later betrayed by an American traitor, and the same sort of treachery is in play with cyberwar as well. It's a dirty business.

The cyberwarriors would leave it to others (spies, foreign agents, traitors) to gain access to private networks, and this would have to be done to do really serious damage to military targets. But a lot is still connected to the Internet we all have access to. And this is where most cyberwarriors would devote their efforts and apply their tools.

Tools and Techniques of SPAA (Scan, Probe, Analyze, Attack)

Scanning can best be described as drawing (and updating) maps of an ever-changing Internet. These aren't really maps, in most cases, but huge lists of Internet locations and what exactly is there (from a technical point of view). A lot of this is probably done with widely available tools, most of them automated. You literally just turn these automated scanners loose on all, or a part of, the Internet, and you get reports back of what is found. The Internet is a huge beast, with over 50 million servers and over 2 billion Web pages. Technically, scanning means mapping a particular portion of the Internet, but for American military purposes you need a constantly updated map of the entire Net, with additional detail on military and government areas. The "map" is stored in a database, and this database is a major, military asset. The database would also be a primary tool for your cyberwarriors and some of your off-the-shelf tools would be modified to work with this database. The amount of scanning on the Internet is huge according to the scanning detectors placed on a sample of servers out there. If you stay on the Internet for more than a few hours, you will probably be scanned. Put a new server on the Internet, and within hours it will start getting scanned. A lot of people like to make Internet maps. Actually, a lot of this scanning comes from purely commercial endeavors (like marketing maps of the Internet, or checking for automatic updates of the software on your PC). But a lot of it is script kiddies and others looking for mischief or a victim. The cyberwarrior wants to identify military and government servers, and discover how good their security is. In some cases, certain types of military/government organizations are automatically given further attention after they have been identified during a scan. Otherwise, only sites that are very vulnerable get visited again, or for use as possible sites for zombie, attack programs.

Scanning takes advantage of the fact that any computer on the Internet must be able to automatically provide certain technical information if another computer asks for it. These automatic questions and responses take care of a lot of the Internet housekeeping that makes the Web work. But a hacker uses this system to obtain a lot of useful information on who is out there and how their systems are set up. Probing is a more detailed sort of scan, where the hacker will deceive the automated system (in ways too technical to explain here) to obtain more information about how a server or local network is set up. With the increasing security on the Internet, probing is coming to mean a more thorough examination of a server. Sometimes this is done with an automated tool. Often the target being probed is a network itself that is connected to the Internet. If your scans and probes find a really valuable site, you'll send a skilled hacker to check it out rather than an automated probe. When probing, you have to be careful not to be detected. A live hacker is less likely than an automated probe to do something that will set off an intrusion alarm. From about 2000 on, the use of intrusion-detection software became increasingly common. This software was designed to catch hackers in the act, but not let them know they were being watched. The sysadmin for the server would be alerted and a game of cat and mouse would commence, with the hacker playing the role of the mouse. All of this activity would be captured in a log for later reference and analysis. Naturally, the most competent hackers are usually skillful enough to recognize a server equipped with an intrusion detector. But no one is perfect at knowing they have triggered an intrusion detector and are now being stalked. It is always possible to get past an intrusion detector, just as it is possible to get past most building-alarm systems. First you find out what kind of intrusion-detection system is being used (there are all manner of telltale signs, but some of these are very faint and subtle). If you are good enough to figure out what kind of intrusion detector you are up against, you take advantage of that system's weaknesses to get past it. This is not as easy as it appears in the movies. And this is where the cyberarmy with the largest tool kit has an advantage. Moreover, American security experts and military cyberwarfare people have an edge because so much of the Internet software is created in the United States. This gives Americans better access to the inner secrets of this software. If such an advantage is not squandered (by not using it), it can be decisive in a cyberwar. But sometimes an old trick like "frequent false alarms" can cause an annoyed sysadmin to disable an intrusion-detection system. This angle has long been used by professional burglars to get past alarm systems (the security people get tired of rushing over to find no burglary in progress and eventually decide there's something wrong with the alarm and turn it off until the technicians can check it out in the morning). It's been used to hack into well-protected servers as well. A savvy sysadmin will recognize the trick, but not all sysadmins are so astute.

But sometimes you have to take chances when probing, especially when, for example, it looks like one of your password-guessing tools might get you in as a "legal user." Unlike many other cyberwar tools and weapons, which are kept secret until a war starts, the probing tools have to be used in peacetime, and all the players are constantly picking up information on how the other side functions. This, in turn, provides some insight on how each nation's cybertroops operate.

Analyzing enemy sites and networks can take a long time. What you are trying to do is figure out how the site is run and what hardware and software is being used to do that. There are thousands of different programs and computer components that can be used in a server, and all the combinations will react a little differently if you are trying to hack your way in. If you can get root access (the ability to actually run any of the programs on the site), your job is a lot easier. But in today's well-protected sites, your analysis must use a combination of constant probing, sneaking around if you do get inside, and even picking up information from Net gossip, the open press, and other sites. Actually, for the really important sites, analysis goes on constantly. This is because Web servers that keep Web sites up and running are constantly being upgraded. This means the site you probed and analyzed so thoroughly last month will be a substantially different site in a few months. And that means that the attack plans based on your existing analyses will become less effective.

Attacking sites actually takes place in two phases. For sites that you have been able to get into, you can leave behind several useful bits of software to monitor the site and report to you about that. But there is a risk that such stay behind software will later be discovered. So you have to balance the risk versus the benefit. For DDOS (distributed denial of service) attacks, you need programs that will transmit lots of junk at the server you want to shut down. The best place to leave these is on PCs that are always connected to the Internet via high-speed connections. This means home PCs with cable modem or DSL connections. For sites that you want to maintain access to, especially during wartime, you would place a very stealthy program that just observes what's going on and, of course, keep your access to the site easily available. This is extremely valuable, as it allows you to not only grab passwords, but overcome the problem of well-run sites constantly changing their passwords.

Keeping a stay-behind program alive is tough to do because the most critical sites are constantly being scanned and analyzed by their owners looking for just such enemy programs. But even if you don't leave anything behind, the analysis of target sites gives you a better idea of what weapons will bring it down at a crucial moment. These "warloads" are programs sent to the penetrated sites just before war breaks out. Sometimes the warloads will do the same thing stay-behind programs do, plus more immediate tasks like corrupting or destroying data. There are also computer viruses that can be unleashed as part of the main cyberattack. These viruses are designed to trash enemy sites and not yours, or those of your friends and allies. There are enormous quantities of tools available on the Web for building viruses and a large portion of any nation's cyberwarriors will spend most of their time building and modifying viruses. Most nations with an active cyberwar program have arsenals of dozens, or hundreds, of these special wartime viruses.

Those nations with cyberforces, and most major nations now have them, must also guard their tool kits and arsenals. While the arsenals (containing viruses and other warloads) are kept on networks not connected to the Internet, the cybertroops do have to be online much of the time with their own scanning, probing, and analyzing tools. And whenever they are out there, they can be observed and analyzed. Think of it as a large chess game, but one in which you can design your own chess pieces and variations of the rules.

SIPRNET and the Threat

In 1994, just in time for the explosion of Internet use because of the arrival of the World Wide Web, the Department of Defense established SIPRNET. This is a network using Internet technology and tools, but is entirely separate from *the* Internet. SIPRNET was built to carry top-secret messages and documents. At the same time, the government set up INTELINK (a separate Internet for the FBI, CIA, DEA, and NSA to exchange classified information) and NIPRNET (a separate, unclassified Internet for the military).

SIPRNET was also encrypted (all data was sent using a secret code) and thought to be invulnerable. Or was it? By late 1999, some network experts in the Department of Defense had become a little worried. The National Security Agency, and other organizations, had set up Red Teams of hackers to attack Department of Defense networks with widely available hacking tools. Naturally, they got into some places and not others. But the scariest thing learned was that the Department of Defense systems didn't even detect 99 percent of the attempts (successful or not). This got people to thinking about just how secure SIPRNET was. Insiders knew that it was, in theory, possible to hack SIPRNET. It would take considerable resources, or some inside help. As more post–Cold War spies were caught, and it was realized that many unknown agents might never be caught, the prospect of an insider helping to crack SIPRNET became more of a possibility. The collapse of the Soviet Union in 1991 sent many (now unemployed) Soviet spymasters and spies to the United States looking for work. These fellows had been a lot more effective than we had thought and one could never again assume that an inside job was unlikely. By the end of the 1990s, it was realized that the Soviets had bought, bribed, or blackmailed so many people working inside the U.S. government that there were few big secrets the Soviets didn't have.

The Department of Defense had already experienced embarrassing accidents with viruses and such somehow moving over from the Internet to the separate networks (there are several, but SIPRNET is the most well-guarded and the only top-secret network). The story is usually the same, users pick up a virus on the Internet, move it via a floppy to their SIPRNET computer, and it spreads. Another way, although less frequent, is when a server that was hooked up to the Internet is physically moved to a new building, where someone says, "Hey, we need another server for our SIPRNET stuff, and there's an unused server right there . . ." Naturally, the "new" server most probably has picked up some nasty viruses when it was hooked up to the Internet and promptly spreads them throughout SIPRNET.

Both of these problems are supposed to be solved by now, but another problem with SIPRNET is that everything about it is so secret that few people are even authorized to check its security. And then there's the ever-present possibility of an insider betraying SIPRNET. In the commercial world, it's long been acknowledged that the major cause of serious (as opposed to just hacking around) penetrations is an insider providing passwords and other essential information needed to get into a heavily protected system.

Once the Y2K problem was taken care of, the Department of Defense proceeded to spend billions to beef up the security of its networks. This included SIPRNET, which got the same kind of constant scrutiny the unclassified networks received. This effort was thought necessary as more locations around the world were given access to SIPR-NET (which has always used its own separate network of satellite link, ground lines, and undersea cables).

The "success" of SIPRNET has led to a call for the establishment of GOVNET, a separate Internet for the entire government. Actually, this is a pretty good idea, but not for the reasons most people would imagine. The biggest problems with the Internet are not the small number of creeps and crazies who send viruses. No, the major problems are anonymity and the ability to freely design their Web spaces if need be. GOVNET, which is private, would make every user accountable. No one would be anonymous. There would be no tools vital to hackers available on GOVNET, which would be, literally, government property. The only software available on GOVNET would be stuff that was needed to transact government business. The other cause of most Internet insecurity, badly written Web site software, could be controlled on GOVNET. Only approved software would be allowed to run on GOVNET Web sites. Okay, GOVNET might not be as flashy as most commercial sites, but it would be safer. What more do you expect from the government? You want flash, you go to Hollywood.

Actually, there's not a lot of enthusiasm in the government for GOV-NET. For one thing, it will cost billions to install and actually to make more work for government employees' use. Since it will be a parallel cyberspace, you won't be able to get to the same sites as on the Internet. Every government office will, of course, have one or more PCs attached to the regular Internet. An unspoken reason for resisting GOVNET will be the inability to cruise the Net for unrelated work activities. And those few machines connected to the Internet will probably be in a common area where you can't surf for fun without being observed. Moreover, the main reason each government office will have a regular Internet connection is because the government will still maintain Web sites as a public service, and they will have to handle e-mail from citizens and non-government organizations that do not have access to GOVNET. You can have PCs set up to access GOVNET and the Internet, but this means viruses from the Internet will get into the same computer that connects to GOVNET. There are ways you can prevent the movement of viruses from the Internet to GOVNET in theory. But in practice, it won't be 100 percent, or even 50 percent secure.

We already have an example of this with INTELINK (the private Internet for U.S. intelligence organizations), which simply didn't get used much. Until after September 11, 2001, when everyone in the intel business got religion and began using INTELINK; for a while. But as the

Internet demonstrated, if you build something that works with human nature, they will come. Do it the other way, to keep people from going to all sorts of strange places, and they will stay away. The private internets keep the crazies and hackers out, but they don't appeal much to their users.

There's also the money issue. The U.S. government spends nearly $50 billion a year on its computers and networks. Half of that is for the defense department and most of the top-secret affairs are handled with the Department of Defense networks. There is more urgency about increasing the security of the really critical (top secret) stuff, than to protecting a lot of government agencies that could get their Internet sites zapped by viruses and malicious hackers without getting people killed.

Data Mining, OLAP, and Brushing

This growing ocean of electronic documents is providing some unique Information War opportunities, like data mining. This was invented to help marketing departments move products. The idea behind data mining is pretty simple. Using computers and statistical programs, you can plow through huge amounts of data looking for useful relationships between groups of people (especially wealthy people) and certain products. Marketing professionals look for buying and product-preference patterns so that successful new products can be developed and existing ones improved. Who buys what? Or, more importantly, who wants to buy something that does not exist yet. Manufacturers and retailers have long collected data on consumer preferences, but "mining" this data manually has not always been cost effective. With computer-driven data mining, it is.

Commercial data mining came of age in the 1990s, as the computers became cheap and powerful enough to make sense of the masses of data being collected by retailers and manufacturers. Traditional data mining just applied the usual statistical tools for matching up different bits of data. But the approach to data mining changed in the 1990s as new software, and more powerful PCs, allowed marketing people, not just statisticians or other geek-type people, to do the analysis. The marketing folks couldn't care less how the analysis was done as long as they were able to extract some useful information to make a buck off of. Once people began to make money off data mining, more money went into new data-mining systems and statisticians and programmers became more interested. This led to things like On-Line Analytic Processing (OLAP, also known in geek speak as Fast Analysis of Shared Multidimensional Information, or FASMI). On Wall Street, OLAP is done with the constant mass of data on the financial markets, but what made it special was that OLAP has some of the characteristics of a video game. The user of the data-mining program could ask a question about what a stock or bond was doing and get the results graphically. This could be the familiar distribution plot (lots of little dots scattered around a line going from the lower left of the screen to the upper right). You could get any visual you wanted (pie charts, bar charts, and even 3-D graphics). All this new stuff naturally led to some new techniques, and new words to describe. Thus we have "brushing," which enables the user to click on any bit of data that is visually shown and remove it, or add another element, or generally muck with the data until you find what you are looking for, or at least find something useful. This interactive approach, which does not require skilled statisticians or computer experts, is naturally very popular with business people and intelligence analysts.

Commercial firms, and no doubt the CIA as well, will not spend most of their time OLAPing, but will be working offline using information from the data warehouse. This is another new term, and means the terabytes (thousands of gigabytes) of data held on hard drives for instant analysis. But for cyberwarriors, OLAP will serve as one of the more powerful tools. Not exactly a weapon, but rather a large searchlight that can not only spot stuff, but also describe what might be hiding in plain sight and looking like something else. Analyzing millions of attacks on computer systems is a typical job for OLAP. Going through all the data manually would be, for all practical terms, impossible. With OLAP you can do it in minutes.

Most businesses use OLAP on large databases of who and when people purchased their products over months or years. The important thing was you didn't have to be a computer expert to run the OLAP software. If you knew your business (selling perfume or motorcycles), you would quickly fund useful sales patterns using OLAP.

Data mining has also been found to have military uses. Intelligence agencies, especially since the advent of spy satellites and electronic reconnaissance, have collected far more information than they could sort through. It's a dirty little secret of the intelligence business, but there are warehouses full of data tapes that have never been examined. Satellite photos, electronic signals, and messages have been collected in far larger quantities than could be examined.

Naturally, the intelligence agencies have been the first ones to see these opportunities. Letting computer software sort through all this would find important things about foreign armed forces; where they are, how they operate. You could never hire, train, and pay enough human analysts to do this. There was simply too much data and too little useful information in it. Data-mining technology changed all that. In 2000, it leaked out that the CIA was hitting up Congress for a large chunk of money to buy a bunch of new computers in order to examine, well, the entire Internet. All the time. In excruciating detail, including chat rooms (well, some of then anyway, many are password protected, although that can be overcome as well). As part of this project, the CIA wants to build a separate Internet-based network so that CIA employees can more safely exchange information. The CIA also wants to buy new computer and networking equipment to enhance its current efforts to hack into companies and organizations suspected of supporting organizations hostile to the United States.

This was not the first CIA foray into data mining. In the early 1980s they bought a lot of the new computer workstations. Custom software was designed to enable analysts to plow through the gigabytes of data the agency had in its existing files. It was useful, but keep in mind that today's off-the-shelf PCs (one to two gigahertz CPUs) are over a hundred times faster (and much cheaper) than the workstations of twenty years ago. You can do some serious, and fast, data mining these days. The success in hunting down many of the terrorists in the 1990s was due, in part, to these data-mining efforts.

Now the CIA wants to ratchet up the data-mining game and go after all the nuggets buried in the billions of Web pages, Usenet messages, and chat-room conversations plus, quite likely, a lot of e-mail traffic. This is classic information analysis, but on an unheard-of scale. With so many people on the Internet, there are many involved in murderous terrorist plots who will drop tiny bits of information at different times and in different places. To the terrorists (or whomever) on the Net, the information they leave behind would not appear to be of any intelligence value. Get enough of these small bits and quickly connect them and you can discover useful things like who is doing, or planning to do, what, with whom, to whom, when, and with what.

Put another way, if you have several hundred million people constantly communicating on the Internet, there's no such thing as useless information. It helps to be able to read other people's electronic messages, and the CIA has been doing that for decades. But even more useful is the ability to scrutinize the mighty river of data the Internet represents. This sort of thing will reveal secrets people didn't even know they had. Unfortunately, because of the secret nature of the CIA, we'll never find out exactly what they did, and how they did it, at least not until this work is declassified decades from now. We do know, from what commercial users of data mining have done, and are planning to do, what an intelligence agency can get out of the Internet. In short, intelligence organizations can pull a lot of useful information out of huge (billions of messages) amounts of data. For example, if hundreds of terrorists around the world mention, in vague and offhand terms, a certain kind of operation, and others mention a certain key individual (even using different names), all these bits of data can be pieced together like a jigsaw puzzle. Pretty soon you see a pattern for a particular operation, and who is involved in it.

Wiretaps and Information Warfare

When the first electronic communications arrived in the 1850s, it wasn't too long before someone figured out how to tap the wire (climb a telegraph poll and attach your own telegraph key, via a wire, to the telegraph wire) and listen in on what was being tapped out by telegraph operators using the line. The telegraph key was a simple device that looked like a typewriter with one key. Press the key and you interrupt the electric current and cause a click on a telegraph key at the other end of the wire. This pattern of clicks (Morse code) only started disappearing from military use in the 1990s.

Wiretaps have long been a valuable tool for catching criminals, spies, and terrorists. In 2000, there were 1,190 court-authorized wiretaps in the United States, few of them for espionage and terrorism investigations; the exact number is secret, probably no more than a few dozen. Most wiretaps were for drug cases. The FBI had already realized that the best information on espionage and terrorism cases would come from overseas, and the United States had (and still has) a vast information-gathering network of satellites, ground stations, and ships. The U.S. has a free hand collecting information overseas, but many legal restrictions apply within the United States. The government has also realized that spies and terrorists were taking advantage of the Internet. So in late 1999, the FBI came up with the idea of tapping into Internet traffic to look for messages to and from terrorists. The "tap" is done by getting a court order for an ISP (like AOL) to allow the FBI computers to check all the ISP's incoming and outgoing messages. This capability was called Carnivore. In the Summer of 2000, the FBI asserted that Carnivore was the single biggest factor in detecting and aborting as many as six terrorist attacks by Al Qaeda (the Osama bin Laden organization). All the Internet tap does is look for a list of words that, say, Islamic terrorists are known to use in their e-mail. You look for e-mail messages that have, for example, "Allah," "destroy" and "infidel" (non-Muslims) in them. You can also look for messages to or from certain e-mail addresses and, along with the messages containing the suspicious words, grab them for later analysis. If the messages are encrypted, you have to decide if it's worth the effort to decrypt (break the code used) them. Even after September 11, 2001, this kind of "wiretap" proved useful in tracking down terrorists.

Word got out about Carnivore, which was not unexpected (too many computer professionals outside the FBI were involved to keep it a secret) and Al Qaeda began to use more-encrypted e-mail or other means of communicating. However, news of Carnivore caused a big stink in the U.S. when its existence became publicly known in 2000. Even though the technique was nothing more than a modern version of the wiretap, applied to the Internet, a lot of people began yelling about "Big Brother" reading all of their e-mails. The FBI explained Carnivore to Congress, and the American public, in the following testimony:

> Service providers and their personnel are also subject to the electronic surveillance laws, meaning that unauthorized electronic surveillance of their customers (or anyone else) is forbidden, and criminal and civil liability may be assessed for violations. Not only are unauthorized interceptions proscribed, but so also is the use or disclosure of the contents of communications that have been illegally intercepted. It is for this reason, among others, that service providers typically take great care in providing assistance to law enforcement in carrying out electronic surveillance pursuant to court order. In some instances, service providers opt to provide "full" service, essentially carrying out the interception for law enforcement and providing the final interception product, but, in many cases, service providers are inclined only to provide the level of assistance necessary to allow the law enforcement agency to conduct the interception.
>
> In recent years, it has become increasingly common for the FBI to seek, and for judges to issue, orders for Title III interceptions, which are much more detailed than older orders that were directed against "plain old telephone services." These detailed to be successfully implemented require more sophisticated techniques to ensure that only messages for which there is court authorization to intercept are, in fact, intercepted. The increased detail in court orders responds to two facts.
>
> First, the complexity of modern communications networks, like the Internet, and the complexity of modern users' communications demand better discrimination than older analog communications. For example,

Internet users frequently use electronic messaging services, like e-mail, to communicate with other individuals in a manner reminiscent of a telephone call, only with text instead of voice. Such messages are often the targets of court-ordered interception. Users also use services, like the World Wide Web, which looks more like print media than a phone call. Similarly, some Internet services, like streaming video, have more in common with broadcast media like television, than with telephone calls. These types of communications are less commonly the targets of an interception order.

Second, for many Internet services, users share communications channels, addresses, etc. These factors make the interception of messages for which law enforcement has court authorization, to the exclusion of all others, very difficult. Court orders, therefore, increasingly include detailed instructions to preclude the interception of communications that lie outside the scope of the order.

In response to a critical need for tools to implement complex court orders, the FBI developed a number of capabilities, including the software program called "Carnivore." Carnivore is a very specialized network analyzer, or "sniffer," which runs as an application program on a normal personal computer under the Microsoft Windows operating system. It works by "sniffing" the proper portions of network packets and copying and storing only those packets that match a finely defined filter set programmed in conformity with the court order. This filter set can be extremely complex, and this provides the FBI with an ability to collect transmissions that comply with pen register court orders, trap and trace court orders, Title III interception orders, etc.

It is important to distinguish now what is meant by "sniffing." The problem of discriminating between users' messages on the Internet is a complex one. However, this is exactly what Carnivore does. It does *not* search through the contents of every message and collect those that contain certain key words like "bomb" or "drugs." It selects messages based on criteria expressly set out in the court order; for example, messages transmitted to or from a particular account or to or from a particular user. If the device is placed at some point on the network where it cannot discriminate messages as set out in the court order, it simply lets all such messages pass by unrecorded.

One might ask, why use Carnivore at all? In many instances, ISPs, particularly the larger ones, maintain capabilities that allow them to comply, or partially comply, with lawful orders. For example, many ISPs have the capability to "clone" or intercept, when lawfully ordered to do so, e-mail to and from specified user accounts. In such cases, these abilities are satisfactory and allow full compliance with a court order. However, in most cases, ISPs do not have such capabilities or cannot employ them in a secure manner. Also, most systems devised by service providers or purchased "off the shelf" lack the ability to properly discriminate between messages in a fashion that complies with the court order. Also, many court orders go beyond e-mail, specifying other protocols to be intercepted such as instant messaging. In these cases, a cloned mailbox is not sufficient to comply with the order of the court.

Now, I think it is important that you understand how Carnivore is used in practice. First, there is the issue of scale. Carnivore is a small-scale device intended for use only when and where it is needed. In fact, each Carnivore device is maintained at the FBI Laboratory in Quantico until it is actually needed on an active case. It is then deployed to satisfy the needs of a single case or court order, and afterward, upon expiration of the order, the device is removed and returned to Quantico.

The second issue is one of network interference. Carnivore is safe to operate on IP networks. It is connected as a passive collection device and does not have any ability to transmit anything onto the network. In fact, we go to great lengths to ensure that our system is satisfactorily isolated from the network to which it is attached. Also, Carnivore is only attached to the network after consultation with, and with the agreement of, technical personnel from the ISP.

This, in fact, raises the third issue—that of ISP cooperation. To date, Carnivore has, to my knowledge, never been installed onto an ISP's network without assistance from the ISP's technical personnel. The Internet is a highly complex and heterogeneous environment in which to conduct such operations, and I can assure you that without the technical knowledge of the ISP's personnel, it would be very difficult, and in some instances impossible, for law enforcement agencies to successfully implement, and comply with, the strict language of an interception order. The FBI also depends upon the ISP personnel to understand the protocols and architecture of their particular networks.

Another primary consideration for using the Carnivore system is data integrity. As you know, Rule 901 of the Federal Rules of Evidence requires authentication of evidence as a precondition for its admissibility. The use of the Carnivore system by the FBI to intercept and store communications provides for an undisturbed chain of custody by providing a witness who can testify to the retrieval of the evidence and the process by which it was recorded. Performance is another key reason for preferring this system to commercial sniffers. Unlike commercial software sniffers, Carnivore is designed to intercept and record the selected communications comprehensively, without "dropped packets."

In conclusion, I would like to say that over the last five years or more, we have witnessed a continuing steady growth in instances of computer-related crimes, including traditional crimes and terrorist activities that have been planned or carried out, in part, using the Internet. The ability of the law-enforcement community to effectively investigate and prevent these crimes is, in part, dependent upon our ability to lawfully collect vital evidence of wrongdoing. As the Internet becomes more complex, so do the challenges placed on us to keep pace. We could not do so without the continued cooperation of our industry partners and innovations such as the Carnivore software. I want to stress that the FBI does not conduct interceptions, install and operate pen registers, or use trap and trace devices, without lawful authorization from a court.

—*July 24, 2000 testimony before Congress by Donald M. Kerr, Director,
Lab Division, Federal Bureau of Investigation*

The FBI is already going beyond Carnivore with a sniffer for packet networks that can plug into larger data sources, rather than individual ISPs. The FBI believes that it has made a convincing case to the courts regarding the legality of "sniffing" as the Internet equivalent of a wiretap on a single phone line. The FBI also points out that nearly two-thirds of wiretaps are for wireless devices (mostly phones, but also pagers and the like) and can justify asking for a wiretap on a person (and all the communications that person uses).

The FBI is miffed at the flack they take from civil liberties groups about wiretaps (which are few) and things like Carnivore (which is looking for messages from certain individuals, not everyone's e-mail). The FBI knows that, as a practical matter, it doesn't have the resources (people or equipment) to check a lot of e-mail. And, legally, they can only look at e-mail from people the court allows them to check on. Moreover, when there are cases of FBI access being abused, it's almost always by some low-level clerk selling the info to crooks. Said clerk usually gets convicted and sent away for a long time. Meanwhile, without things like Carnivore, more crimes get committed. But it's long been fashionable to rant about Big Brother and that's not going to change anytime soon.

The Faster Cyberwarrior Wins

The U.S. Air Force, like the army, is implementing what it likes to call high-speed Information War capabilities. For a long time, one of the major air force challenges has been quickly detecting, pinpointing, and attacking enemy air defenses. If the air force can do this faster than the enemy can use these weapons, fewer aircraft will be knocked down, or forced to abort their attacks. For decades, special aircraft were used to detect and attack enemy air-defense radars. This meant a large number, often the majority, of the aircraft sent out to attack enemy targets were there just for dealing with enemy air defenses.

But technology marches on, and now the air force is going to make every fighter and bomber in the attacking unit capable of detecting enemy radars, and doing it with more accuracy. This is done by installing several dozen sensors in all aircraft (including tankers, transports, and electronic warfare planes). Each sensor detects every radar signal that hits it, as well as its frequency, direction, and the precise time. This information, along with the precise location of the aircraft when each signal was received, is instantly transmitted (often via a communications satellite) to an aircraft or ground station with a command computer that can take all the information and compute where each signal was coming from (to within fifty feet) and what kind of radar it is. The command computer can then order an aircraft carrying missiles or bombs to hit the target. Since the radar signals will usually be picked up before the aircraft is within range of enemy antiaircraft missiles, the command computer may advise an aircraft with long-range missiles to launch one at the radar. The army also has long-range (160- and 300-kilometer) missiles that can do the job as well. Even artillery can be used, if it's within range. And in many situations, artillery may be in range (and be the weapon that could respond first).

Many potential enemies have noted the effectiveness of American attacks on antiaircraft defenses, and know to turn on their radars only at the last minute. This technique was used with some success by the Serbs in 1999 and is well known to any other potential foe. Doing this, the U.S. aircraft can be pinpointed and a missile launched before any American defensive moves can be made. But with the new system, which we won't see used for another five years or so, American aircraft can nail the enemy radar before the antiaircraft missiles can be given a target. This is a good example of how Information War is applied to the use of weapons. Speed kills, especially in Information War.

The Battlefield Internet

When the World Wide Web appeared in the early 1990s, lots of people saw clever uses for this new technology. This included the U.S. Army, which developed the idea of a battlefield internet. They called it "digitalization" (of the battlefield), a concept that included putting computer displays in most combat and command vehicles. Individual soldiers would also have body computers and information displayed on goggles or a goggles-like device. The body computer is down the road a few years, but the flat-panel displays in armored vehicles, aircraft, and headquarters are already here, as well as better communications.

In combat, information about the location of friendly and enemy troops, as well as the position of minefields and obstacles, is a matter of life and death. The new digitalization equipment allows the troops to more easily communicate with one another. Now that you can see where everyone is, you don't hear endless messages like "where are you?" Because this is the army, and there is a battle going on, the communications are rather more disciplined than your usual Internet chat room. Even with that, the troops took eagerly to the increased amount of computer and communications gear they were getting. Throughout the late 1990s, the army experimented with installing computer equipment in vehicles and aircraft, and making the battlefield Internet work.

In March 2001, the U.S. Army sent 7,500 troops from the 4th Infantry Division to the National Training Center to test the latest digitalization equipment. The troops now had digital communications gear that allowed them to instantly exchange video, voice, and text data between armored vehicles, artillery, aircraft, infantry, and headquarters. The idea was to have a combat force that can react more rapidly than the enemy. By bringing firepower onto targets more quickly, the enemy is put at an enormous disadvantage. For as long as soldiers have been fighting, getting information about the enemy to your commander has always been a problem. The digitalized force solves that. The commander always knows where his own troops are and obtains better information about the enemy faster. The impact will be similar to what happened when police cars got radios some fifty years ago. All of a sudden, crimes like bank robbery got a whole lot more dangerous. Once a crime was reported, the police could rapidly use radio to rally their people, and quickly receive information from witnesses or, say, police on foot who saw the robbers speed by. Radio alone did not revolutionize warfare as much because battles are a much more complex and chaotic process. Digitalization and the use of computers, plus soldiers who have years of Internet experience, will make a big difference. But another reason the army was eager to test digitalized units under combat conditions was to discover those things they hadn't thought of yet. New forms of warfare tend to create opportunities, and pitfalls, that no one foresees. Just as many armies stumbled into blitzkrieg warfare in the late 1930s and early 1940s with uneven results, the same is expected to happen again with digitalization when this technology actually hits the battlefield.

The army makes a big thing about not making the same mistakes encountered in the past when radical new technology was introduced. The idea of giving the troops Internet-like capability right on the battlefield could be a major breakthrough, or a large disaster. At the National Training Center, where very realistic combat exercises take place, some of the digitalization weak spots were found. As the computer displays filled up with symbols, the troops tended to believe they knew where everything was and concentrated on running a fast break on the enemy. In theory, this is good. The digitalization gives the user an information advantage. While the enemy is still trying to figure out who is where, the digital force knows where everyone is and is executing a crushing attack. In reality, not all the information on the displays was accurate or up to date, and this has led to some embarrassing friendly fire accidents at the National Training Center. This happened when the computer screen said there was an enemy tank over there, but instead it was a friendly vehicle. Troops also had problems wandering into minefields or roadblocks no one had managed to get into the digital database. This can be characterized as growing pains with the new technology. But it also points out that the digitalization technology works best, if it works at all, only with trained and disciplined troops. Just like experience on the Internet enables you to do things more quickly (like use a search engine or set up a chat room), troops will have to spend a lot of time actually using their battlefield Internet technology so they can use it effectively. Most of today's troops grew up with video and computer games. And this taught the troops one dangerous lesson. Computer games almost always show unambiguous information. What you see is what you have to deal with. On the battlefield, things aren't so clear cut. In fact, dealing with ambiguous information (what you see on the computer screen isn't always what is actually out there) is one of those skills required for survival in combat. So the Nintendo generation must lose some bad habits before they can take full of battlefield digitalization.

The Afghanistan War gave a partial test to digitalization, mainly because not all the digitalization equipment was there. But a lot of it was, and the results were pretty spectacular. The air force was also working through the 1990s on its own version of digitalization (which already hooks up with part of the army's digitalization). The air force's goal was to be able to hit targets within ten minutes of spotting them. Why ten minutes? Because during the 1991 Gulf War, the futile attempt to find and hit Iraqi scud missile launchers needed, it turned out, a reaction time of ten minutes (between spotting the launcher and getting a bomb or missile on it). It took the Iraqis at least ten minutes to get out of the way, so hit them in less than ten minutes and you'll destroy them.

Otherwise, there's nothing magical about ten minutes, it's just a number based on what is needed to hit one type of target. Small groups of tanks or trucks can clear an area in a few minutes if they know they've been spotted. But it gave the air force a goal.

In Afghanistan, air-force digitalization used reconnaissance systems (satellites, aircraft, JSTARS, and drones) to find targets, a command aircraft (carrying a guy who can authorize any attacks, cutting out the lawyers and politicians who slowed things down in Kosovo and the Gulf War) and bombers nearby ready to release a smart bomb that can hit a target. First, this approach was used in Afghanistan to destroy moving military vehicles. That worked pretty well, and pretty soon the Taliban were staying off roads when they thought American bombers might be around. Then came the support of the ground war. This used American special forces troops and air-force ground controllers to communicate directly with the bombers overhead. The guys on the ground used a laser to "light up" the target for a bomb, or used GPS satellite navigation to precisely locate the target and transmit those coordinates to the bomber overhead, where the coordinates went into a bomb's GPS navigation system, and the bomb was released. Initially, the air force thought they could get bombs on target in eleven minutes. By the end of 2001, they were doing it in less than ten minutes.

Some of the spotting and communication systems used in Afghanistan were improvised. More easy-to-use stuff was built, bought or otherwise put into the hands of the troops in 2002. This gear combined binoculars and a laser range finder that captured the exact location of the target and transmitted it directly to the bomber overhead, where the coordinates were put into the GPS guided bomb. The bomber crew has computer displays that can show the location of the target spotters on the ground and the place where the bomb is being sent. The aircraft computer can also quickly calculate if the bomb is going too close to friendly troops. Sometimes this can't be helped, and the guys on the ground have to let the bomber crew know that this is going to be a close shot.

The Afghanistan experience demonstrated another aspect of how the military uses technology. On the battlefield, the troops will improvise. They call it "field expedients," and with your life at stake, you tend to get really creative with what you've got. For the last two decades, more troops have been taking their personal computers and other electronic gadgets on combat or training operations. The Department of Defense is depending on this; that the troops will improvise when the shooting starts and make the battlefield Internet work. Based on past experience, this is probably how it will play out.

The battlefield Internet technology is not just for the combat troops. The same technology is being introduced throughout the military, just as it has spread throughout corporations, from factory floors to the CEO's executive jet. In late 2000, the U.S. Army had military police test a new "Digital MP" system. This consists of a wearable computer and special eyeglasses containing a Webcam that sends a constant video stream of what the MP (military police) is looking at. Inside one of the eyeglasses is a computer display (of the same type available commercially for games or "eyeglass computer displays"). The eyeglass display can bring up data or pictures, basically anything you can view on a computer screen (although the resolution isn't as good, about 480 by 640). For example, an MP could call up, using voice commands or an ID entered on a portable keypad (worn on the arm, as they are now for space suits), photos of people who are wanted or the file photo when you suspect someone is trying to get in with false ID. The Digital MP system is designed to give military police access to more information, which in the last century has proved to be the major asset added to the policeman's arsenal. This is particularly true for counterterrorism operations, where false ID is widely used to get the bad guys into places they aren't supposed to be. The Digital MP ensemble also includes a "digital book" the size of a PDA that contains additional documents the MP might need. This gear was also designed for infantrymen, but durability and battery-life problems prevent it from being practical for this work. But for MPs, who don't bounce around as much as the infantry, and tend to be closer to a fresh supply of batteries, the system works, and the MPs will work out the kinks so that a more reliable system will be ready for the infantry in the future.

But these wireless-battlefield Internet devices all have one major vulnerability: being hacked. Fortunately, there is also a need for Net security in the growing number of wireless Internet gear civilians are using. This includes cell phones, PDAs, and e-mail devices (like the Blackberry). Sure enough, when these items were first sold, the manufacturers said they were secure from hackers. They were wrong, and now wireless-network security is a big business. The military will buy a version of the most robust wireless security available (using some form of encryption). But they will still be vulnerable, and an opponent will have to work harder to hack these systems. The biggest problem the troops will have to worry about is jamming (a wireless version of the DDOS Internet attack) that will drown out wireless messages with electronic noise.

While the United States is in the lead with the digitalization technology, other nations are adopting it as well. In 2000, the French Army adopted a digital-information system for reconnaissance vehicles, tanks and antitank vehicles. Sweden demonstrated another aspect of digitalization. They began developing digitalization technology back in the 1970s for their air force, but kept it secret. The Swedes noticed that no one else was working on this and realized that if they were the only ones with it, they would have a much more effective air force than their likely opponent, the Russians. This spotlights another aspect of new military technology. If you have something new, and the enemy knows about it, countermeasures can be developed. Or, in the case of digitalization of air combat, they can build the same systems for their own aircraft and eliminate your advantage. So, if you can get away with it, keep the new stuff secret. The Russians used this approach effectively before World War II, unleashing new weapons the Germans knew nothing about, and to great effect. The United States did the same thing with its stealth aircraft, keeping them secret until they entered service. When the Cold War ended, it was eventually revealed that the Russians had developed several weapons (high-speed torpedoes, missiles, and the like) that no one in the West had known anything about.

Even the Canadians, who have long been tight with military spending, ordered a new Military Message Handling System for $26 million and have been enthusiastic adopters of Internet technology for military use. Countries like Canada, and China, which don't like (or simply can't afford) to spend on new military technology, have found it much cheaper, and quite effective, to adapt off-the-shelf Internet technology for military use. Personal computers and the Internet are proving to be, for the military, the most potent off-the-shelf technology they have ever encountered.

For most nations, digitalization gear costs more than they like to spend on peacetime forces. This is changing as they see U.S. forces perform far more effectively as digitalized forces. During the 1999 Kosovo War, there was a glaring difference in effectiveness between U.S. air forces and the Europeans. The American smart bombs and superior electronics gear were far more effective than what the Europeans had. It was no secret that the Europeans didn't have the same smart weapons and other high-tech gear the U.S. warplanes used, but for over a decade, the Europeans had gotten around this by convincing themselves that all these Yankee gadgets were overrated and not worth the expense. Oops.

It's true that being first with new weapons and equipment means you are going to pay more, and suffer more teething problems. Anyone who has rushed out and bought a new type of electronic gadget knows the feeling. A new type of computer, camera, or wireless networking will cost more, and be less reliable than if you wait a year or so. But waiting can be fatal when it comes to military equipment. Our European allies found this out during the 1999 Kosovo bombing campaign. We were there to take out the targets that the lower-tech European warplanes would have been at great risk going after. The Europeans don't like to say out loud that American military technology saved the lives of many of their pilots, but that's what happened. It happened again in Afghanistan. Russian veterans of their 1980s war there initially said that the Afghans would beat up on American troops and prove formidable adversaries. After seeing how the new digitalization worked, with the special forces troops on the ground with their special radios, laser range finders, and GPS gear, and the air force with their GPS bombs, the Russian vets tended to remark wistfully, "If only we had had that stuff."

Full Color and Guided by Satellite

One of the major advances of Information War has been the ability to give the troops technology that has become cheaper and more powerful because of the large number of civilians using the same equipment. Case in point: computer displays. In the last few years, PC users have noted, with some pleasure, that computer displays are getting larger, lighter, and cheaper. Well, the lower-weight option (flat panel) will cost you extra. But even the flat-panel gear is getting cheaper.

The troops need this stuff. Consider this: there are more troops who go into battle looking at a computer display than there are infantrymen. Welcome to the twenty-first century.

No one in the Department of Defense will say if troop complaints about the many dinky, monochrome displays still installed in tanks, warplanes, ships, and command posts had anything to do with it. But there are a lot more equipment upgrades involving installing color displays, and often larger ones at that, in military equipment. The real reason is that the military has done a lot of "human engineering" research over the years, and they are finding that the generation of troops raised on PCs and video games are a lot more effective if they have a larger, color, computer display. With the larger quantities of information generated by satellites, UAVs, Webcams, and many other sensors, it's easy to miss something when it all comes flooding onto a trooper's computer display. Often, too much information just confuses, becoming counterproductive. But as Wall Street learned in the 1980s, if you carefully design how stuff is thrown on the screen, you become much more effective.

However, there's one critical element that soldiers have to worry about, and Wall Street traders don't: where am I? The GPS satellite-based navigation system was just coming online when the 1991 Gulf War broke out. Receivers cost thousands of dollars. Despite the high price, and spotty performance, the GPS was wildly successful with the troops. This love affair has continued. The units are so cheap now (off-the-shelf ones go for under $100) that troops will often buy an extra one in case the government issue one goes bust. It was also noticed that the troops would often go out on training exercises with a laptop equipped with GPS and a mapping system using CD-ROMs. This caught the eye of the brass. Naturally, it was lower-ranking troops who first thought to use this unofficial navigation method. Of course, the laptop-GPS combo is a commercial innovation from the mid-1990s. But it's gotten so cheap that most new cars will have it in a few years (it's optional equipment now). The system is very common in Japanese automobiles (in Japan, where street numbers are usually given out according to who builds first on a street, not just going from one end of the street to another).

The military mapping systems are a little different, as they can also show the location of friendly vehicles. This is done by having each vehicle constantly transmitting its location (according to the GPS) to nearby vehicles. There's also a version in the works that would show the latest reported position of enemy vehicles. There have also been tests of systems that allow this information to be transmitted to headquarters and warplanes overhead. This makes the tanks and warplanes a lot more lethal, and cuts down on friendly fire losses.

The U.S. Navy caught on to the color display Information War tool via the many fans of *Star Trek* who eventually became admirals. These admirals don't always like to talk about that angle, although it has leaked out from time to time. But watching how much more easily a fictional starship was commanded via a roomful of visual displays, many different designs have been developed during the last two decades. The most recent effort is a command ship equipped with a "knowledge wall." This is an array of monitors showing the status of task-force ships, aircraft, and amphibious forces. In addition to the maps and data, the system can also support teleconferencing. With the prices coming down for the larger displays, these are being installed. Going to flat-panel displays, even though they are more expensive, actually saves money. Using lots of conventional CRTs generates too much heat for the air-conditioning on the ships. Upgrading the air-conditioning costs too much, so the flat-panel displays, which throw off less heat, as well as drawing less power, allows for more displays without major upgrades to the air-conditioning systems.

More displays and larger displays are essential because of the larger amount of information coming into a carrier task force. Satellites and UAVs and recon aircraft can now send back real-time video and other electronic information. E-mail from ships and subs has become standard, with all sailors now being issued an e-mail address when they join. The navy is also using cell phones and wireless-equipped PDAs on board. All these devices can send information to the command center and the knowledge wall. Here's where you get Information War as a group exercise. Facing the knowledge wall are over a dozen officers and technical experts. As the information shows up, opportunities, problems, and potential solutions appear. The group acts together, bouncing ideas off one another and rapidly solving problems and exploiting opportunities. These information systems are now considered so vital that damage-control exercises today include dealing with attacks on the ship's information systems. Yes, even in the middle of the ocean, the navy is concerned about a malicious hacker doing them some damage. But more important is practicing how to function after a missile hits the ship and parts of the Information Warfare systems are damaged.

The navy was actually the first to develop the concept of a multimedia setup for headquarters. During World War II, the combat information center was developed. There were no TV-type displays; television was too crude back then. But large displays were updated (with position of aircraft and ships) manually and audio and other information was piped in. The British used a similar system to direct the Battle of Britain in 1940. This campaign often saw over a thousand aircraft in action at one time. Every headquarters now has computers and most of them have a graphics program to show what's happening out there. During the Gulf War, a Department of Defense wargame was used just for its ability to display the tactical situation (there was less confidence in the predictive capability of the wargame itself).

Not only is more information coming to the commanders, but the detail is increasing (quality being added to the quantity). One of the big fans of HDTV (high definition TV, soon to be a national standard) is the military. Unlike HDTV, the TV cameras currently used in recon aircraft, UAVs, and even ground troops, are rather blurry. HDTV adds more detail and sharpness. This allows computers to better see through deceptions and calculate things like the speed of vehicles or aircraft that show up in the picture.

In late 2000, the U.S. Navy began modifying the USS *Coronado*, the flagship of the 3rd Fleet, to equip it with a lot of the new Information War toys. This ship went on to serve as the "battle lab" for testing all this new combat-information management stuff before the rest of the ships in the fleet received it.

It's all about information, not just having it, but displaying it so the troops can still make sense of it when they are under a lot of stress. It *is* like a computer game. But if you lose, you die for real. For this reason, one of the design considerations for these systems is making them hacker proof. As was discovered with the Internet, potential hacks (discussed during the early days of the Internet) eventually became real. On the battlefield, a hack of the troops' information network can quickly turn fatal.

AirNet and Information from Above

The U.S. Army has embraced Information War on the battlefield, but is having problems getting all the needed (or, as it sometimes turns out, unneeded) equipment to fit. In late 2000, they cut the purchase of A2C2S (Army Airborne Command and Control System) helicopters from 207 to 119. The army also put off the introduction of these modified UH-60 choppers from 2000 to 2004. These helicopters are to be used as flying command posts for brigade and division commanders. Ever since Vietnam, the troops have dreaded the sight of a brigade or division commander flying overhead in a helicopter because it usually meant that the old man was likely to be viewing the battlefield with binoculars and second-guessing the NCOs and officers on the ground. Next thing you know, you got a general on the radio telling you to move a little more to the north and asking you to hurry through the woods. The general, of course, doesn't know that the woods contain a mini-swamp and no trails at all. But, hey, it all looks so clear and simple from up there. This is the dark side of too much of the wrong information. Even the generation of officers who were on the receiving end of this micromanagement during Vietnam seemed to forget all that once they became generals, they got a helicopter, and could treat their troops like toy soldiers in a sandbox. This is Information War at its worst. Recognizing the problem, and realizing that generals all grew up on *Star Trek* reruns, the army decided to take advantage of all the new electronic goodies and tried stuffing them all into a Black Hawk (UH-60) helicopter. This would allow the commander to gather information from a wide variety of sources (satellites, recon aircraft, and ground troops) as well as knowing where all his troops are at all times. Putting the stuff in a UH-60, along with the chopper crew and a small staff, allowed the commander to be more mobile and less likely to get killed. Headquarters have been increasingly vulnerable to missile or air attack because of the high volume of electronic messages being sent. All that broadcasting has led to headquarters being called "missile magnets." Having half a dozen or so A2C2S helicopters per division made headquarters a more difficult target. This approach also made it easier for the commander to get around and visit his subordinate units personally, which is always a good thing and needed even more so because of the increasing dependence on electronic information from subordinates.

But war isn't a video game, and the human element has to be attended to, which is best done in person. Pulling off this ambitious delivery schedule depended on some contractors having some new equipment ready, or available in lighter versions, in time. No doubt blaming it on Y2K, the contractors missed their deadlines. When finally in service, the A2C2S will have five computer workstations. Flat-screen displays and more powerful microprocessors make this possible. The A2C2S is another component in the army's digitalization program, which will enable combat vehicles and commanders to instantly exchange information on where they are and what information they have on the enemy. This speeds up the ability of American troops to find and fight the enemy. This has always been a major advantage for the faster force, except for the backlash items like micromanagement. No one is sure how all this is going to work out in combat, but few generals on the planet want to be the last ones with access to a battlefield internet.

Military Chat

In late 2001, for exercises in the Persian Gulf, the British Royal Navy put together its largest force of warships since the 1982 Falklands War. Forces included an aircraft carrier, two destroyers, four frigates, two nuclear submarines, two amphibious ships, five minesweepers, and eleven support ships. Aircraft embarked included fifteen Harriers and twenty-five helicopters. Some 8,500 sailors were involved. What really made this exercise different was the extensive use of the Internet. Each ship had its own intranet (an internet network that can operate without access to anything outside the ship) as well as encrypted internet connections between ships. Instead of using radio for communications, extensive use was made of private chat rooms. But unlike the usual free-for-all in public chat rooms, the navy used the usual "net discipline" (which predates the Internet by over half a century) so that important messages don't get lost in a lot of chatter. A task force of warships requires a lot of communications between ships to keep the operation going. The vast majority of this stuff isn't seen in movies of naval operations because it really doesn't mean anything except to a sailor. It's a lot of technical material, and a lot of it is in jargon. Most of it doesn't have to be sent out in a great hurry, so there's plenty of time for sailors in each ship to just type it in using the new chat rooms. This has the additional advantage of leaving a record of who said what and when (these chat rooms have logging turned on, so everything is saved to a file, and time is displayed with each person's message). The radio is still available for emergency messages. In fact, the radio is even more useful for urgent messages, since most of the stuff is being typed. If a sailor hears a radio message coming in, he knows it's very important, and not some administrative stuff like "close to three kilometers and reduce speed to fifteen knots." Moreover, once all the bugs are worked out of this ship-to-ship use of an internet, you can easily add the transmission of other digital data, like maps and information on enemy forces.

Moreover, the Internet is a valuable military communications technology because just about every recruit is already familiar with it. It's cheap, the security is pretty good (although most civilian users don't bother with this), and it's very flexible. And warships are usually far enough way from the enemy to make if difficult to jam or hack the ship-to-ship Internet traffic.

Missile Masters on the Battlefield Internet

The idea of using the Internet on the battlefield began before there even was an Internet. When telephones and radio got their first workout during World War I (1914–18), the more thoughtful military men noticed how these new electronic gadgets allowed information to travel a lot faster across the chaos of the modern battlefield. But all this was theoretical because telephone lines were often cut on the World War I battlefields, and the radios of the day weren't very portable. But by the time World War II (1939–45) came along, there were a lot of portable radios.

Even before that, in the 1930s, American artillery officers figured out a way to get a radio or telephone message from anywhere along miles of frontline from someone wanting a lot of firepower applied to one target and, within an hour, have the fire from hundreds of artillery guns hitting that target. This 1940s-era marvel scared the hell out of the Germans, but it required a lot of work. There were no computers to do all the calculations required, and the guy up front could make a fatal error when reporting the position of the target.

Fast forward to 2001 and the barren hills of northern Afghanistan. The troops have better radios and other electronic gadgets for pinpointing the location of targets. Our Afghan allies are awed at how the Americans can talk into a radio, press a few buttons and then, within minutes, the ridge a mile or so in the distance disappears in a roar and cloud of dust. The enemy was there, but isn't there anymore; unless you count the body parts scattered around the large crater.

And this wasn't even exactly what the bright guys were thinking about during the 1990s. That idea, called NetFires, is still in the works. This system was designed by the army, and doesn't depend on the air force. But it does depend on a battlefield internet that will make all the good guys aware of where all the bad guys are. That part is seen as easy, because Internet technology keeps improving and the stuff is quickly debugged by millions of eager users. Weapons that could take advantage of all this information are another matter. Even with Internet speed, valuable targets, like tanks, can keep moving. Therefore, for a battlefield internet to work, you have to be able to hit targets almost as soon as you spot them.

To do the killing, two new missiles were developed. The main one is PAM (precision attack missile). PAM is a 178 mm–diameter missile that weighs a hundred pounds and has a range of fifty kilometers. PAM attacks from above, with a twenty-eight-pound warhead. This enables it to kill any tank by hitting the thinner top armor. PAMs are vertically launched from what looks like a four by six by four foot (wide by deep by high) cargo container. Actually, it *is* a cargo container. The missiles are shipped from the factory in this sealed container. Each one-ton container holds fifteen missiles and can be carried on the back of a truck or Humvee. Once you plug a PAM container into the wireless battlefield internet, the missiles are ready to fire. Depending on how many enemy targets you expect to come your way, officers are assigned areas of the battlefield and given passwords for PAM containers in the area. These guys become the "missile masters" and are authorized to send one or more PAMs against any enemy vehicle that shows up on their screen (which could be anything from a rugged "battlefield laptop" to a larger flat-screen in a headquarters tent, vehicle, or bunker). The battlefield Internet is using aircraft, UAVs, satellites, and ground sensors to pick up targets. When the missile master sees a target he wants to kill, a point and click will send the coordinates of the target to a nearby PAM container, launch a PAM to the approximate location, where the missile's own sensor will pick up the target and home in on it. The sensors will, most of the time, pick up the vehicle as destroyed and adjust the missile masters screen accordingly.

Recognizing that there will be situations, like where there are a lot of woods or jungles, that will prevent sensors from spotting a lot of targets, there's a second missile, the LAM (loitering attack missile), same weight and all of the PAM, except it is actually a mini–cruise missile and can fly around an assigned area for forty-five minutes looking for a target. If one is not found, it just crashes and explodes. If a target is detected with the built-in radar (laser radar, or LADAR, actually) and the built-in software recognizes the vehicle as an enemy, the missile attacks from above. Alas, the LAM warhead isn't large enough to take out most tanks, but anything else would likely be toast.

The major elements of this system have already been tested, and the whole thing gets a workout in 2003. No one has any illusions about NetFires version 1.0 working all that well. So many things can go wrong with the target identification, missile reliability, and the battlefield Internet itself. Once all those problems are solved (probably by version 3.0 or so), you still have to worry about what the enemy will do to defeat NetFires. Given the heavy dependence on wireless communications, NetFires will have to worry about getting hacked, jammed, and generally messed with.

When you bring the Internet to the battlefield, you have to expect the hackers to be there as well.

CHAPTER 10

The Enemy: Black Hats, Script Kiddies, and Crackers

Technical Terms You Might Not Recognize in This Chapter

A complete glossary, including the terms defined below, can be found at the back of the book.

Security Software—These are programs that make your personal computer less liable to be damaged by attacks over the Internet (viruses, in particular). The most common security software is antivirus software (which monitors your PC for the presence of viruses and eliminates them when found) and firewall software (which keeps bad stuff from getting into your PC in the first place).

There are at least thirty magazines and nearly 500 bulletin boards, thousands of chat rooms, and several hundred thousand Web sites devoted to crackers, black-hat hacking, and all manner of misbehavior on the Web. The names of some of these hacker Web sites makes it pretty clear what is going on here: hackers.com, securityfocus.com, rootshell.com, insecure.org, piracy.com, and the granddaddy of them all, 2600.com. But even with all this help, only about 10 percent of the self-professed hackers really know what they are doing. The rest just download hacking tools and go play with them on the Web. The result is over a million Net crimes a year, plus many millions more in attempts at illegal actions on the Net. If you ever get burned by any of these Net criminals, it's likely to be some antisocial teenager who found criminal tools and encouragement on the Net.

Black-Hat Hackers

Black-hat hackers, the computer pros who like to do the real damage on the Internet, are not a large group. They are good guys who have, for a variety of reasons, gone over the line and used their skills to inflict damage on other Internet users. One reason for the wayward inclinations of these people may be the nature of the Net itself.

The Internet (and especially World Wide Web) has become an extremely useful tool for many people, including the military. Although in use since 1969, the Internet spread quickly when it became a commercial operation in 1991, and really took off a few years later as the World Wide Web appeared. Unfortunately, the simplicity and efficiency of the Internet was achieved by using many tools and techniques put together by volunteers in an atmosphere of openness and trust. However, as more people got onto the Net, it became increasingly common that you could not trust everyone. But the deed was already done, the software needed to keep the Internet going could not be recalled and beefed up with a lot of security features. And so we have an increasing number of hackers (people playing at going where they should not be) and crackers (those doing it with evil intent) making life miserable (or worse) for Internet users.

The basic vulnerability of the Net is the numerous ports that allow information to get in, and out, of a server (a PC making Web pages available to the Internet). Think of the "ports" as separate telephone lines opened up by your PC to allow different jobs to be done, simultaneously, on the Internet. It's this capability that allows you to download a file while going from Web page to Web page. Depending on how powerful your PC is, you could be downloading over a dozen files at once while looking at two or more different Web pages. Each Internet location (or page on the World Wide Web) runs on a computer (called a server) that is permanently attached to the Internet via a telephone or network connection. The Internet works because any user can quickly find a Web page, file to download, or whatever. A lot of the fancy stuff you can do on the Web (shopping, games, or simply flashy graphics on a Web page) involve additional programs on the server that make it happen, and open the server up to illegal entry to those who know how the new software works. There are often several different programs running on the server to support one Web page, and any one of these programs may have an intentional, or unintentional, opening (port) for a Web user to get inside the server. This is the hack (or crack).

In the early days of the Web, hacking was a harmless sport. But less-honest crackers (also known as black-hat hackers) know that once on the server they can often take it over and cause all sorts of mischief. There are networks other than the Internet, and these can also be penetrated, but it is a lot harder. No network is perfect, thus none are completely invulnerable to attack. But some are very well protected. This level of security requires time, money, and talent to implement, and there's never enough of that to go around, especially in large organizations like the Department of Defense. A well-protected server is also often more time consuming for a legal user to get into and use. What happened through the 1990s was the development of two quite different types of security on the Internet. Large organizations, and computer-savvy users, have well-protected servers and Internet-capable PCs. But the majority of users, and most Web sites, are not as well protected. The well-guarded Web sites are attacked by the most capable black-hat hackers for the challenge, or because there's something worth the effort to steal. The less well-protected sites and users get hit by both talented hackers (for practice, for an easy score, boredom, etc.) and the millions of amateurs (who make no real impression on the more secure sites).

The black-hat hackers developed a growing arsenal of weapons to use against military and commercial sites. The more nasty types of attacks, and defenses against them, are:

DDOS (distributed denial of service) attacks disrupt service on a local network. Web servers in military headquarters or organizations take care of all the e-mail coming in or out. A DDOS attack will flood that server with so many incoming messages that the server can do nothing else but try and deal with the flood. Since 1999, there has been a lot of new software that will protect servers from a DDOS attack, but in 1999 there weren't many DDOS attacks, or much off-the-shelf security software to deal with it. So at first, the military set up separate, and better protected, lines for the most critical messages (about 5 percent of the total). With this approach, the noncritical traffic could be DDOSed to death, but the important stuff would still move. Eventually, software capable of quickly detecting and defeating DDOS attacks was installed for sites that could afford it. But the Department of Defense is worried about how sophisticated these DDOS attacks are becoming. It's been noted that someone has been carefully "footprinting" (analyzing) Department of Defense and commercial sites. Moreover, there are now DDOS attacks that go after different parts of large sites with different kinds of DDOS weapons. With this approach, it's possible to keep hitting a site from different directions, and avoid counter-measures, so that the site is out of action for days. It's also been discovered recently that routers (the specialized PCs that direct traffic around the Net) can also be attacked. Many DDOS defenses are based on adjusting routers to deflect the massive amounts of traffic DDOS attacks throw at a site. Since developing these more-sophisticated DDOS attacks takes a lot of time and effort, it's thought that some governments have black hats on the payroll to create this kind of weapon. So, while DDOS is not the fearsome weapon it was in 1999, it is still a threat if used by capable programmers who know what they are doing.

"Vampire" programs like the 1980s Morris worm are still seen as a threat. A vampire program gets onto your server and does two things: First, it starts running. It doesn't actually do anything, it just consumes your processing power. Then the vampire starts replicating itself. Pretty soon (within minutes), your server is so busy running hundreds of copies of the vampire that it can do nothing else. Some programs like this also try and use the server's e-mail capabilities to send itself to other servers. Vampires are indeed still a threat as more flaws are found in Internet software, providing more opportunities for a vampire to install itself on vulnerable systems. For a military server, getting disabled like this could mean life and death for troops who depend on the server for information or other services. The military came up with several antivampire solutions. These included changes to the operating system that prevented more than a few copies of any one program from running at once, and limits to how much processing power one program could use. Detection systems were also installed to look for patterns that indicated the presence of a vampire. Many of these protection ideas have now been included in off-the-shelf security software. But the military can't wait for the commercial sector to do it, and tried to solve these problems as soon as possible. This is one reason the Department of Defense spends over $20 billion a year on its computer systems.

A common type of hack attack is to sneak onto a military server and copy files so they can be released to the public. Sometimes the hackers are just trying to score political points by revealing Department of Defense secrets. Black-hat hackers of this type are commonly called "hacktivists." Other times, the files don't get made public, but find their way to a hostile government. The best solution so far for this has been to leave a lot of juicy-looking, but actually worthless, "bait" files for the hacker to easily find. The real goodies are made to look like something not worth bothering with. This concept has since been expanded to the installation of Honey Pot servers to attract hackers. The Honey Pots are equipped with a lot of intrusion detection and tracing software to help track down the hackers.

Another of the 1980s-era hacks is a program that gets onto a system, looks for spreadsheet and data files, and then randomly changes numbers. The program than erases itself and any evidence that it was there. This is a very nasty kind of hack because it may be awhile before it is realized that data has been corrupted. By then, you may have no good backups left (the corrupted files having been backed up several times over the good backups). This is bad enough for a business, which can lose a lot of money after a hack like this. But for military files, it can get people killed. The only real defense for this kind of hack, aside from preventing it in the first place, is software that generates a checksum (a unique number created from the data in the file) and stores it on another file. Before backup copies are made (once a day or more), new checksums are generated and compared to the stored ones. The system will ignore files that have been edited (and such edits can be confirmed by checking if an authorized user was on the system to do it recently), but will expect the same checksum for the many files that don't get changed every day. If one of the checksums is different, the sysadmin is alerted and the hack damage can be repaired by using good backup files. Alas, the checksum system is rarely used, mainly because there are not that many black-hat hackers depraved enough to keep making this kind of attack. But the idea, and the techniques, exist to keep this kind of hack in wide circulation. Moreover, a really skilled black-hat hacker can get past the checksum protection (by making sure the changes made are such that the checksum is not changed). On the defensive side, recent operating systems come with built-in encryption for selected files or folders. Even a really dedicated black hat would have a hard time secretly changing data on encrypted files.

Another nightmare hack for military systems is one that leaves a backdoor on the server. This allows the hacker to easily get back on the server to do whatever he wants. You do this by hacking into a computer and just leaving a small program that allows you easy, and undetected, access to the server whenever you want it in the future. This technique would be used if a hostile government were planning a Pearl Harbor–type attack. If a lot of U.S. servers could be infiltrated like this, a lot of major damage could be done in a short time once hostilities began. The best defense against backdoors is to constantly monitor servers for unusual activity on the communications ports that would indicate a backdoor.

A variation on the backdoor program is one that sits on a server and activates (usually with destructive results) on a certain date or when certain events occur on the server (like activity indicating performance of a vital function, such as getting ready for a major military operation). One defense is to periodically copy everything off a server and then change dates or run patterns that might trigger the hack. Not a great solution, but for the truly paranoid, or extremely careful sysadmin, it'll do.

All of these techniques show that the black-hat hacker community (and it is that, a lot of them communicate with one another) certainly has a lot of skill in it. Black hats who have gone straight also point out that a lot of what motivates black hats is a "can you top this" attitude and the desire to show off one's technical skills without any moral restraints.

Patterns of Attack

Riptech, a computer security company with 300 clients in twenty-five countries, maintains event logs on its clients' networks (among many other computer security-related services). That's a pretty common security measure. While Riptech doesn't cover a large chunk of Internet activity, it does monitor a representative slice. It released a study of the 128,000 attacks that showed up in 5.5 billion log entries in the last six months of 2001. This was an increase of 80 percent over the first six months of the year.

Not surprisingly, 30 percent of the attacks came from the United States. This is not surprising because this is the nation with the highest concentration of Internet servers and users. But the U.S. only provided 3.5 attacks per 10,000 Web users. The highest proportion of attacks came from Israel, with twenty-six attacks per 10,000 users. In terms of being the origin of raw numbers of attacks, the United States was followed by South Korea, China, Germany, France, Canada, Taiwan, Italy, Great Britain, and Japan. Most of the attacks were low grade, but 43 percent of Riptech's customers reported at least one serious attack. Most of the attacks appeared to be random, but 39 percent appeared to be deliberate. The Code Red and Nimba viruses accounted for 63 percent of all attacks, but were excluded from the study because they would skew the results. Public companies were twice as likely to be attacked than private or nonprofit organizations.

Black Hats and Honey Pots

Unlike earlier commercial networks, the Internet is wide open. A malicious and knowledgeable user can go anywhere and do a lot of mischief; just about anything short of bringing down the entire Net (and maybe even that). Wandering around the cyberscape, snooping and vandalizing as they go, has become a favorite indoor sport. There is a "black-hat (hacker) underground" dedicated to getting into places they shouldn't be and doing as they please. The white-hat hackers have been outnumbered and outgunned. But that is changing. A little.

The biggest advantage the black hats have is sheer numbers. There are several million script kiddies who use hacking tools to play their noxious games on the Web. They do it for fun, in the same spirit that prompts many adolescent pranks. But the script kiddies find Net vandalism more entertaining because the damage done is greater, the chances of getting caught less, and there is no need to ever go face-to-face with your cohorts or your victims. Most communication is in chat rooms, where that favorite adolescent game, building an alternate persona, can be indulged. You don't even have to be very bright. The term "script kiddies" comes from the easy-to-use tools black-hat hackers create and make easily available on the Web. These tools are often point and click, and, well, provide easy-to-use scripts for the black-hat wannabes.

The black hats themselves are far fewer, only a few thousand (or few hundred, if you count just the really talented hackers who have gone over to the dark side). Most of the script kiddies are under eighteen, and thus are unlikely to get busted and jailed. Although white hats that find a script kiddie becoming really bothersome, and worth the effort to track down, discover that a phone call to the kid's parents often gets results. The black hats prefer to stay further in the background, for they are old enough to get arrested and prosecuted; and more of them are.

But the most worrisome black hats are the true criminals. Some of these black hats work for governments and use their skills to indulge in espionage and theft of technology from foreign governments. The criminal black hats go for the money.

The Internet's criminal underground shares a lot of information. Technical tips and newly found Net vulnerabilities are traded in password-protected chat rooms and encrypted e-mail groups. The script kiddies play a major role in providing a lot of this information. Numbers count, and the kiddies have lots of time to wander the Net knocking on doors and making risky moves the older black hats avoid. The kids like to brag, and the black hats listen and take notes about what new defenses the script kiddies have encountered.

When the black hats see a particularly promising new vulnerability, they go in themselves. They proceed very carefully. The criminal black hats plan their operations as thoroughly as a professional heist. Nothing is left to chance, for getting caught can be fatal (in China, they sometimes execute black hats caught committing crimes). A skilled black-hat hacker will carefully and methodically probe his target site for weaknesses and defenses. This process might go on for days or weeks, with breaks to research unfamiliar defenses or a possible weakness in the site's software. When the black hat hacks his way into the site, he may just collect information and leave. More time will be spent studying what he found. Finally, after perhaps hundreds of hours of work, the black hat will make his move and go in to steal something, or simply damage the site.

Until recently, the only way you found out about a successful black-hat operation was after it was too late. And sometimes not even then. The black hats covered their tracks carefully. To them, a successful operation was one that was never discovered. The main method for covering your tracks is to find the server's logs, which record everything that happens on the site (who enters the server and what they do) and erase entries that would identify the penetration. This is often very difficult to do as the logs are often encrypted or protected by intrusion detection or antitampering software. But it's the mark of a skilled black-hat hacker to leave no evidence behind.

Then the white hats came up with the concept of Honey Pots.

A Honey Pot is an Internet server (a PC a Web site is running on) that looks real, but is carefully monitored to record everything the black hat does. This way, the white hats can collect information on the black hats and have a better chance of hunting them down. Because of the expense and skilled manpower required, it's not practical to put the monitoring software on every site. Bank and high-security government servers have substantial defenses that monitor any (well, nearly any) penetration and shut down if any unauthorized entry is detected. This doesn't help to identify the black hats, but all these sites want to do is remain secure, not play cop.

The Honey Pots have proved a useful tool in finding out what tools and techniques the black hats have. For example, Honey Pots can show how black hats cover their tracks (by altering logs or other new tricks no one has heard of yet). This makes it possible to build better defenses. Honey Pots also make the black hats uncomfortable and less confident that any server they are hacking into is not rigged to catch them. Once word got around that Honey Pots existed, black-hat hackers now had to spend more time trying to find out if the server they were hacking into was really a Honey Pot. This was not easy and it makes the white hats happy.

However, the black hats now know the Honey Pots are out there, and the technological war of wits has commenced. The white hats keep making the Honey Pots more convincing. As a bonus, they add elements to non–Honey Pot servers to make a knowledgeable black hat think it's a Honey Pot. This keeps some of the black hats away. An electronic scarecrow, so to speak, and a bonus, as it were.

All of this goes on out of sight. Thousands of server administrators have illegal software planted on their systems for various acts of Web vandalism (especially denial of service, or DDOS, attacks). The U.S. government has detected several penetrations of military sites, and theft of information. What worries them is the penetrations they have not detected. Although you don't hear much about it, for obvious reasons, the Honey Pot has become a military weapon. In wartime, the militarized black hats could take out Department of Defense servers more quickly than a missile. At that point, some of the script kiddies may realize they are potential traitors. But until then, the kids are just trying to have some fun.

Cybercrimes and Cyberterrorism

Once the world appeared to have survived the Y2K scare relatively unscathed, attention turned to other potential computer disasters. Indeed, one of the bonuses coming out of the massive audits and reprogramming the Y2K project (to make sure programs did not crash because the year date was stored as two numbers and computers might not read "00" as "1900" instead of "2000") entailed was the massive number of flaws found in communications programs. The Y2K project required that a lot of software be scrutinized in a way that would have never happened had there not been the danger of Y2K mishaps. Before that, the common attitude toward software was, "if it ain't broke, don't fix it." But a lot of software that appeared to be working fine did have problems that had nothing to do with Y2K. There was a lot of thirty-year-old software out there that few programmers really understood anymore. If this stuff broke, an expensive consultant was hired to fix it, but no one bothered to have someone check to see if there were major problems festering beneath the surface. Because of the billions of dollars spent on fixing the Y2K problems, the many potential problems with this older software became known. All of a sudden, unseen software problems became important. This, coupled with the increasing possibility of computers being attacked via Internet connections, made more business and government leaders aware of a previously ignored threat.

As the world began finding out in the 1990s, there were a lot of malicious creeps on the Internet who loved to exploit communications software bugs to go where they weren't supposed to go and do what wasn't supposed to be done. Governments and military organizations were most concerned about these attacks being used like a military weapon. Some nations, particularly the United States, had already spent money on cyberwar and were becoming aware of some major potential vulnerabilities. It was dawning on people that this was a threat right up there with nuclear weapons, chemical warfare, and the use of biological weapons. As the twenty-first century dawned, a list of the likely types of attacks began to emerge. Most of these have to do with the penetration of computer systems via the Internet (or any other network that allowed access via the telephone system).

The most feared attacks are:

> Electrical systems are shut down, momentarily or for days. While there is no standardization in the electrical generation or distributions system, it is common to control systems remotely via the Net or a telephone connection. Security also varies, but an ambitious hacker could penetrate several systems, figure out how they worked, and do considerable damage. The military usefulness of this is obvious. U.S. military hackers are thought to see this particular kind

of attack as very useful, at least in nations advanced enough to have remote access in their electric-power industry.

Criminal groups, or governments, stealing from bank accounts. This is something that is an ongoing problem. A highly organized and massive attack of this type, however, could make a terrorist organization even more formidable. Rogue states like North Korea and Iraq have long used illegal scams to provide cash flow for their dictators. Kim Jong Il, the dictator of North Korea is known to be a PC enthusiast, so an attack of this sort may already be in the works from that country. Or attacks may have already been made, for the ideal hack of this sort would involve draining accounts in such a way that it looked like an internal flaw in the bank's computer system. One military use of such access would be to cause enough disruption (by destroying or altering records) to cripple banks and the banking system. This could disrupt segments of the economy that have the most military impact. Or you could just try to disrupt as many major segments of the economy as possible and inflict a lower capability on the entire nation.

Some lower-tech nations, like Iraq or North Korea, might find it advantageous to bring down the entire Internet. Since the larger nations (like the United States) are much more dependent on the Net, this would be an overall advantage to a nation like Iraq or North Korea (or even China).

Assassination via tampering with hospital records. Most state-of-the-art hospitals now have computerized systems that keep track of what drugs are to be administered to patients, when, and in what quantities. These records also explain what a patient is allergic to. You can figure this one out yourself. While a really big shot (senior politician or military leader) would have medical personnel manually double-checking medication and such, mid-level people (military, espionage, or diplomatic types, or just someone who was getting in your way) could be killed. Again, the ideal way to do it is subtly, so the fact that it was a cyberattack was not revealed. That way, you can do it again. Maybe someone's already doing it that way.

The military uses a lot of computers to take care of mundane tasks like logistics, transportation, assignments, training schedules, and so on. These computers do not get the industrial-strength security (which is expensive and requires more specialized people to maintain) that more important tasks (war plans, communications with combat units, nuclear weapons, research, and so on) get. Thus, it's easier to get into these systems and enough damage can be done to have an impact on military operations. This can be done two ways: At the beginning of a war or military operation, in a massive way, to disrupt enemy operations as much as possible. The other approach is to do as much undetected mayhem as possible.

Another target that can hurt military operations would be the mass deletion of government records. This would make government operations more difficult, and in wartime, the government provides many vital operations for the military. In particular, the government hires contractors and makes deals to arrange transportation and housing for troops. If government payrolls or contracts can be disrupted, a government's troops will be much less effective.

Police departments and intelligence agencies usually have high-grade security on their main headquarters. But there are lots of "branch offices" that have lowered security. Intelligence agencies often work with local police departments, and the electronic records here are even easier to get at. This kind of crime is also of great interest to criminal organizations, and some hacking has apparently already taken place along these lines (to find out the names of witnesses or if some gangster is being investigated or wiretapped).

Another area with some military impact, and a lot of benefit for terrorists, is hacking and disrupting the court and prison computer systems. Operations like this are already of great interest to criminal gangs, who will often sell their access to anyone with enough cash. Playing with the court and prison system computers makes it possible to get your low- and mid-level people out of jail (and out of the country before they can be rearrested).

Immigration and customs computer systems. Cracking these can enable saboteurs and spies to get into (or out of) an enemy country more easily. Customs service computers that have been hacked could allow the smuggling of bombs and stolen technology.

Air-defense systems have long been tied together by computers. The U.S. did it first in the 1950s (leading to the design and manufacture of the first modems). Hacking these systems can start a system crash or enable false reports to be put on enemy radar screens.

The air-traffic control systems are linked by a network. Ironically, the best defense the American air-traffic control system has are the ancient computers that run it. This makes it more difficult (but not impossible) for cyberwarriors or terrorists to get in there and commit some mass murder (or just subtly interfere with air operations so as to hinder the war effort). The older computers were not designed with Internet access in mind and most hackers would be unfamiliar with computers made so long ago. Military air-traffic control systems, which use more modern computers, are better protected, but still vulnerable.

Another transportation system that is vulnerable are the waterways. This is particularly true of those rivers and canals that are dependent on dams to regulate water levels for safe barge and ship traffic. Gaining access to those dam systems (at least the ones that have a Net connection) via the Internet would also provide an opportunity to damage some irrigation and water-supply systems.

Industrial facilities (nuclear and conventional power plants, chemical plants, refineries, or other industrial facilities) are vulnerable to tampering via Net connections. This could cause thousands of civilians to be injured or killed, not to mention damage to, or destruction of, the facilities.

Something to keep in mind: a lot of the above systems may have been successfully hacked already, but not noticed because there are so many problems with computers that are obviously (or thought to be) the result of human error. Most of the troubles with computer systems have always been due to human errors (either in the design or maintenance of hardware or software). Indeed, there have been so many human-error problems, compared to obvious hacks of systems, that it is very difficult to find a good hack among all the problems caused by people's ineptitude.

Cybercriminals

Criminal activity on the Web is increasing along with the number of vulnerable commercial operations coming onto it. There have always been techies who have fallen in with the criminal element and gotten rich (or imprisoned) using their skills illegally. Late in the Cold War, the Soviets recruited teams of hackers in Western Europe to crack NATO military and government systems. Secret information was the goal, and we only know about the jobs pulled off by hackers that were caught and prosecuted. Criminal hackers are generally open to offers from anyone (with the right amount of money) to do anything.

Particularly worrisome is the increased amount of cybercriminals operating in post–Cold War Russia and Eastern Europe. These groups are very skillful and have been going after banks and other well-protected sites. There are three main reasons for such a concentration of hacking talent in this area. First was the Communist-era educational system that produced more engineers and scientists than jobs. Then there was the longtime scarcity of decent computer hardware in the Communist countries. What was available tended to be rather primitive computer technology compared to what was found in the United States, which required local programmers to work harder with less. Moreover, the Communist nations could not afford to buy newer, better, and more powerful computers every year or two, so the local programmers had to get the most out of older and more-limited hardware. These ragged, socialist economies produced many underemployed programmers with excellent skills. Lastly, during the Communist period, there was no way for a skillful programmer to create a new product and profit from it. Indeed, there was a culture of theft, with Western software seen as something to steal, or to take apart (ignoring copyright and patent protections) for the development of new products. Taking apart someone else's software and basically doing whatever you wanted without regard to intellectual (or any) property rights became part of the local culture. This also produced superior hacking skills. While many programmers in this region have gone straight, many remained on the dark side of the art. These skills became available for criminal, military, or terrorist operations on the Net and Eastern Europe became a paradise for the local cybercriminals. The more conventional gangsters were quicker to learn how to pull off scams on the Net. The East European criminal gangs were also more trigger happy than their Western counterparts and knew how to motivate their hackers with terror, as well as money. And the price for failure to pull off a hack was often death. Not the sort of motivational skills taught in Western business schools, but effective up to a point.

As the twenty-first century dawned, Russia and Eastern European nations, under pressure from America and European nations, began to crack down on the cybercriminals in their midst. But given the degree of corruption in Eastern Europe (especially Russia), government officials sometimes got in on the scams. Occasionally this was done officially, as when hackers went on the government payroll to do military or industrial espionage. While many of the criminals are patriots of a sort, there are others (like the many Chechen gangs in Russia) who will work with terrorists. Like most criminals, hackers will sell to anyone. For Western antiterrorism agencies, this is a major problem when it comes to the illegal encryption tools sold by hackers in Eastern Europe. Most nations regulate what kind of encryption tools can be sold openly, and East European criminals saw powerful (and illegal) encryption as just another lucrative racket (along with drugs, prostitution, extortion, and so on). Terrorists, as well as common criminals, used the high-powered encryption to keep their communications secret.

It's more difficult for terrorists to obtain cyberwar services that might hurt the countrymen of the hackers, however. For example, few East European criminal hackers would help crack the air-traffic control system, or a nuclear plant's communications system in those nations. But they may become more mercenary in the future. For example, the (Muslim, and often pro Al Qaeda) Chechen gangs are developing their own hacking crews, so such sensitivity may not be a problem for terrorists in the future.

Criminal hackers in the West, and emerging software superpowers like India and China, are providing enough legitimate, and more lucrative (and safe) jobs for those who might be temped to go rogue. This has always been the case in the West, where even a convicted hacker can usually find a good job after doing time. However, the temptations are always there. Many Indian and Chinese programmers spend lots of their spare time learning the intricacies of the Internet. This leads to playful manipulation of the Net at first. It then often leads, as it has so many times before, to schemes to beat the system and steal (credit card fraud, usually). Young programmers tend to develop a sense of invincibility and this leads these kids to attempt, and often pull off, brazen acts of larceny on the Net. This is made worse by the reluctance of large financial organizations to report these thefts. This is changing as the losses mount and businesses, and police forces, develop better skills at hunting down and catching the cybercriminals. But at least for the first decade of the twenty-first century, the struggling economies of Eastern Europe, and especially Russia, will remain a prime breeding ground for Net crimes.

Common Internet Fraud Schemes

Most Internet crime is low tech. And most of it is perpetuated via e-mail. Anyone who uses e-mail knows all about "spam" (unsolicited e-mail), and that's how most Internet criminals do their business. Despite the low-tech nature of these crimes, it's important to know about it because even the high-tech scams take advantage of human nature. Remember, most illegal system entries are via stolen passwords.

Below is a list of the most common crimes committed via the Internet. So if you ever feel tempted to fall for any of these, don't. Now you definitely know better.

The Business Opportunity (often some kind of "Work at Home" offer like data entry on your PC or answering e-mail for a business). This works by pitching an attractive, can't lose, "no obligation" opportunity. However, there's a small administration fee. In pre–e-mail days, the fee was higher to cover the cost of ads or mailings by regular mail. But spam does not require envelopes, stamps, or printed material, and is much cheaper. Sending spam costs almost nothing. This allows the criminals to ask for a lower, and more likely to be paid, "processing fee"; often as low as ten or twenty bucks. The crook gets away with it by taking advantage of the speed of the Internet. They spam millions of people, collect the money at a post office box (rented under a false name), deposit the checks (to an account opened with false ID), and clean out that account and disappear before anyone expects to get any of the promised services. These criminals know enough about how the Internet works to use suitably impressive forged sender ID for their spam. The only crooks who get caught doing this sort of thing are the newbies who haven't got the timing down and hang around long enough to get nailed.

Credit card theft is rampant. The most common item stolen when a business Web site is hacked into is credit card information. Hang around the black-hat hacker and script kiddie sites and develop some contacts and you will soon have access to stolen credit card numbers (for a price or because someone is feeling generous). Using the purloined plastic can be tricky, as the trillion-dollar credit card industry can afford some heavy-duty technology and talent to keep after these scamsters. Again, the old pros usually get away with it for a long time, and the teenage wannabes get nabbed first time out. Some of the script kiddies go looking for an e-business site with credit card information, and for a while in the late 1990s, they were able to get past the flimsy, or sloppy, Web security so common back then and grab credit card information. These days, they are as likely to wander into a Honey Pot, followed by a visit from the FBI (credit card fraud is a federal offense, and the feds like to hang a kid out to dry from time to time as a warning to the others).

The Official Information Request. This fake pitch can come from a company or government agency the recipient does business with. A popular hustle is to spam customers of an ISP (like AOL or Earthlink) with phony (but official looking) requests for new credit card information. ". . . because there is a problem with your existing credit card." After years of warnings from ISPs, people still fall for this one. One fake government spam pretended to be from the IRS and demanded that the recipient fill out a questionnaire within forty-eight hours "or else." The spam demanded information like social security numbers and bank account data. This one continues to show up every year in the two-month period before income taxes are due on April 15.

Financial institution fraud is for professionals only. The hacker would have to know how banks and financial institutions work. In many of these organizations it is common for some transactions to be authorized by an e-mail from a known source. To pull off this kind of crime you have to find out who can be deceived into approving a loan, money transfer, or whatever. This sort of thing can sometimes involve a bit of industrial-strength hacking, and rarely involves spam.

Investment fraud is another spam favorite. The most popular one involves someone (the sender of the spam) who is looking for a partner (the victim) with a bank account to facilitate moving illegal (or quasi-legal) money out of a foreign bank account. The usual result is that your bank account is cleaned out. Another investment fraud is selling overpriced securities, or phantom (fake) securities, via the Internet. This kind of scheme used to be done face-to-face, but now gets done much more efficiently via the Internet. As always, if you want to do anything faster and more efficiently, use a computer.

Nondelivery of goods or services is often a result of incompetence, not fraud, but the result is the same. Again, the speed of the Internet enables more frauds like this to succeed. Spam ads, often artfully done with HTML graphics, are made to look legit. These scams often take credit cards, which requires more work on the part of the criminals (the credit card companies are alert to crimes like this). Sometimes services are offered, like help in getting a job or a loan. A purely Internet variation on this used the very popular on-line auctions. Despite strenuous efforts by outfits like eBay, there is still some fraud (people sell items they haven't got) in this area. As always, buyer beware.

Ponzi (or pyramid) schemes have gained a new life on the Internet. People are convinced to invest in some surefire deal (currency trading, foreign home mortgages, or whatever), and the early investors get generous returns on their investment. The people running the scam don't invest the money, however. They just pay out some of the invested money as "dividends" in order to build up a buzz and get more people to invest. When it appears, to the crooks, that the flow of new investments has peaked, they take off with the money. This is an ancient swindle, made famous in the 1920s by a Mr. Charles Ponzi, who pulled off a spectacular scam of this sort right after World War I.

The Year of the DDOS Zombie

In the summer of 1999, there was the first outbreak of DDOS attacks. DDOS, or distributed denial of service attacks, take advantage of security weaknesses in Internet software. Many of the basic-control commands the Internet uses for servers to communicate with one another can easily be forged (or "spoofed"). By sending certain spoofed commands to several servers, you can trick the servers into sending a huge quantity of control messages to a specific server. No matter how much capacity a server (or, sometimes, group of servers) has, if you can throw enough of these control commands at it, you can shut it down. Well, not exactly shut it down, but the server ends up spending all its time dealing with the false messages and has little time to do anything else. Sort of what happens when too many people log onto the Victoria's Secret site to see the lingerie show. What made the 1999 DDOS attacks unique was that they used zombies: programs secretly planted on hundreds of servers in order to launch an even more intense DDOS attack. The 1999 attack on a university server shut down that Web site for two days by using an army of 227 zombie programs. The use of the zombie programs indicated several things:

First, the black-hat hackers are really getting into the dark side to pull this off. It took some effort to create the zombie program and get it distributed. The hackers actually have their own, malevolent, Open Source movement going, and they even maintain the zombieware; the one used in 1999 was the first in a line that has been constantly patched and "improved" to the present. The Evil Open Source angle is pretty scary, because it means that dozens (if not hundreds) of skilled programmers are cooperating over the Web in secret to create tools for attacking the Internet.

Second, there are two reasons to develop zombie programs. The obvious one is that you can generate a larger data stream, and thus shut down larger sites. But the zombies also make it harder to catch the culprit. With the older techniques, sending false control messages from one location meant you had to stay online while you were doing it. Thus a clever and hardworking hacker could catch you in the act. No such luck with zombies, unless you catch the hacker while he's installing one of the zombie programs.

Third, there are many poorly supervised servers out there on which the black hats can install thousands of zombies. That done, they can launch DDOS attacks capable of bringing down any of the major sites on the Internet. While white-hat hackers and many software firms are hard at work developing tools to defeat DDOS, it would be months before these began to appear, and years before solid anti-DDOS stuff is widely available. What has actually happened is that an arms race has developed with the evil DDOS programmers coming up with new attack software as fast as the Internet security companies can develop new DDOS defenses.

Fourth, and most shocking to the FBI, is that there appears to be this vast, black-hat hacker underground that they didn't really know about. Oops.

On February 7, 2000, the other shoe dropped. A massive DDOS attack hit the most popular single site on the Web: yahoo.com, making it unavailable for several hours. Over the next few days, there were similar DDOS attacks on major sites like Amazon.com, CNN.com, ETrade, and eBay. By February 9, 2000, the Internet, clogged with the extra traffic from these DDOS attacks, took 26 percent longer (on average) to do anything (like load a Web page or download a file).

One fifteen-year-old Canadian student was caught and prosecuted for launching the DDOS attacks. Although he was responsible for some of them (and pleaded guilty in early 2001, having been caught because he had bragged about it), later investigation revealed that there were thousands of script kiddies and black-hat hackers out there who had access to DDOS tools and knew how to use them. By late 2001 it was estimated that one or two DDOS attacks a week were committed on major sites, with many more on smaller ones. The vast majority were a time-consuming nuisance for those sites. But except for a few attacks, like the one on Microsoft in early 2001, there was never a DDOS holocaust. In fact, as often as DDOS attacks are made, they only hit about one Web site in 10,000 every week. Not only that, but the average length of a DDOS attack is ten minutes. You only hear about the attacks that shut down sites for days (or, in at least one case, for good).

There was talk in black-hat circles (the law was now monitoring some of their "secret" discussions) of taking out the Internet access in entire countries (like China or Egypt) with DDOS attacks. Mention was also made of carefully planned attacks on key routers, to try and knock out Internet access for portions of the United States or major Web sites. The threats were credible, for there was now a number of different zombies available, and many different types of attacks that could be carried out.

It appears that a major disincentive for DDOS problems were the realizations in black-hat circles that there were a lot of cops on their cases. The FBI alone had six investigations going by early 2001. Perhaps more frightening were the number of very capable white-hat hackers who were poking around. The one thing the black hats and script kiddies really fear is a white hat who is mad—and also a good hacker. This is how most black hats get caught, convicted, and sent to prison.

One of the things they don't like to talk a lot about in the black-hat community is that, when it comes to quantity and quality of hacking skills, the white-hat crowd has an enormous advantage. There are simply many more white-hat hackers and the best Internet hackers tend to be white hats (or, at worst, gray hats: guys who have been naughty in the past but have gone straight). The black hats are tolerated as long as they don't annoy the white hats too much. But some white hats get really, really irritated and they will come after you. And most of the time they will catch you. And if you are lucky, they will just humiliate you and chew you out. And if you are smart, you will just sit there and take the abuse as gracefully as possible. Because the alternative is a visit from the FBI. Some white hats want to nail an annoying black hat, but aren't willing to spend all the time it will take to assist the FBI. So what black hats fear the most is an angry white hat with time on his hands.

It was these DDOS attacks on Yahoo in early 2001 that really brought the U.S. government into the cyberwar game. Before that, the FBI was slowly gaining expertise in computer and Internet security, as well as a better understanding of what hacking was all about. The FBI normally treated computer crime the same way they did other forms of criminal activity. That is, big cases that were interstate (to make it a federal matter) would get the FBI's attention. Everything else would be referred to the local police. But that was a major part of the FBI's problem. When the Internet was involved, it was not, by any stretch of the imagination, a local case. And most local police (including state police) departments were as unprepared regarding computer and Internet security as the FBI was. Even reporting an Internet crime was difficult. Many people went to their local police. In most cases, the community police knew that this was a federal case. The FBI quickly learned to pass most cases to the federal prosecutor, or simply state (in so many words) that they couldn't handle it. For most of the late 1990s, the FBI was hustling to figure out how to manage the growing avalanche of Internet crime. Meanwhile, companies, or wealthy individuals, had to pay for investigation of these crimes. The local federal attorney would then prosecute if it looked like a winnable case. This has only recently begun to change in the last few years as the FBI, IRS, and the entire federal justice system established offices victims could report Internet crimes to and investigators to go after the cybercrooks.

There were federal agencies that were Net savvy, however. The National Science Foundation (NSF), which had handled the transition from ARPANET to Internet, knew all about the Net. But it wasn't a police agency. The CIA, and its secretive little brother the NSA (National Security Agency), also knew a lot about the Internet, a lot more than the FBI, but the CIA cannot, by law, operate within the United States. And the NSA's job is to create (encrypt) and crack (decrypt) secret codes. Nevertheless, the CIA has always been in the vanguard of PC and Internet technology.

Although most people think of the CIA as a bunch of secret agents, the truth is that the majority of the people in the CIA are geeks of one flavor or another. The CIA has long been hiring white-hat hackers, and will interview black hats who are willing to renounce the dark side (and take a lie detector test to prove it). The CIA has lots of people who study foreign banking systems, and out of this came the agency's ability to "hack banks." This first came up in the 1990s when it was leaked out that the CIA was available to hack (or already had hacked) Saddam Hussein's foreign banks accounts, or those of Serb strongman Slobodan Milosevic, or Osama bin Laden. This capability has gone largely unnoticed (although it has been reported). After all, we're talking about foreigners in possession of a lot of illegally obtained money. Moreover, the banks that get hit by the CIA cybertroopers are reluctant to complain out loud, although there are usually some protests via diplomatic channels. Naturally, if you develop the hacking skills to get into foreign banks (which are not as well protected against this as U.S. banks), you have people who know a bit about Internet crime.

Fortunately, the CIA and FBI, which had not gotten along well for decades, started working closely together during the 1990s. This was important to the FBI in the cyberwar area because the CIA has much larger cyberwar resources, and the FBI has large needs. Unfortunately, there are never enough good technical people to go around. The FBI is still primarily a "people" (not a technical) organization and geeks looking for a government gig are likely to favor the more geek-friendly CIA (which has lots of technical jobs). The armed services also have some hospitable places for Internet experts, but few of them are for civilians. So if you want to be a government cyberwarrior without going through boot camp, the CIA was, and is, the place to go.

Meanwhile, the Year of the Zombie is still with us. Many government geeks have gotten into the institutional paranoia thing and are waiting for another wave of big DDOS attacks. Alas, that's one of the problems in working for the government. You lose touch. The major commercial sites have, as they are prone to do, gotten all over the DDOS problem. Sure, the DDOS threat is still out there. But if the black hats want to do a major DDOS on someone, they are largely wasting their time trying to use it on the (now) well-protected commercial sites. Unless they come up with a really new and surprising version of a DDOS attack. This is possible, although the defense is constantly working on countermeasures for yet unused types of DDOS attack. The one real fear about DDOS is use of a nasty new version as a weapon in a cyberwar.

Any old DDOS technique is still a good tool for tormenting someone with a low-budget site, and that's where most of the DDOS attacks are being felt these days. To paraphrase the old saying, "the rich get better protected from DDOS while the poor get more attention from the black hats."

The Feds Get on the Case

Since the Internet is a national network, any crime committed on it is a federal, not a state or local, offense. That means the FBI has to deal with it. But the FBI has historically been slow to take on new forms of interstate crime. Like everyone else associated with the Internet, however, even the FBI eventually had to pay attention. By the late 1990s, the feds (FBI, Secret Service, CIA, DEA, and ATF) were scrambling to catch up with a growing Internet crime wave. Naturally, the FBI could not expect to go after all the Internet criminals. There were simply too many of them. But the FBI did, as is their custom, go after high-profile cases.

A perfect example of this kind of case involved an American billionaire, Russian hackers, a highly visible U.S. company, extortion, and international intrigue. In a word, everything the FBI likes in a case. Below is the government statement from when the culprits were caught. Note that as of early 2002, the two Russian hackers are still trying, without much success, to avoid extradition to the United States. Mr. Bloomberg (currently the billionaire mayor of New York City) and his company stand ready to aid the prosecution of the two Russians, who will probably be back in the U.S.A. by the end of 2002.

August 14, 2000 United States Attorney
Southern District of New York

MARY JO WHITE, the United States Attorney for the Southern District of New York, and BARRY W. MAWN, the Assistant Director in Charge of the New York Office of the Federal Bureau of Investigation jointly announced that OLEG ZEZOV, a/k/a "Oleg Zezev," a/k/a "Oleg Dzezev," a/k/a "Alex," and IGOR YARIMAKA, who are citizens of Kazakhstan, were arrested on August 10, 2000 in London, England for allegedly breaking into Bloomberg L.P.'s ("Bloomberg") computer system in Manhattan in an attempt to extort money from Bloomberg.

ZEZOV and YARIMAKA are charged in separate three-count Complaints unsealed today. They are each charged with one count of interfering with commerce by using extortion; one count of extortion of a corporation using threatening communications; and one count of unauthorized computer intrusion.

According to the Complaints, ZEZOV gained unauthorized access to the internal Bloomberg Computer System from computers located in Almaty, Kazakhstan. In or about the Spring of 1999, Bloomberg provided database services, via a system known as the "Open Bloomberg," to Kazkommerts Securities ("Kazkommerts") located in Almaty, Kazakhstan. ZEZOV is employed by Kazkommerts and is one of four individuals at Kazkommerts's associated with Kazkommerts's contract with Bloomberg.

In addition, according to the Complaints, ZEZOV sent a number of e-mails to Michael Bloomberg, the founder and owner of Bloomberg, using the name "Alex," demanding that Bloomberg pay him $200,000 in exchange for providing information to Bloomberg concerning how ZEZOV was able to infiltrate Bloomberg's computer system.

As described in the Complaints, Michael Bloomberg sent an e-mail to ZEZOV suggesting that they meet. ZEZOV allegedly demanded that Michael Bloomberg deposit $200,000 into an offshore account. Bloomberg established an account at Deutsche Bank in London and deposited $200,000 into the account. According to the Complaint, Michael Bloomberg suggested that they resolve the matter in London and ZEZOV agreed.

As described in the Complaint against YARIMAKA, on August 6, 2000, YARIMAKA and ZEZOV flew from Kazakhstan to London. On August 10, 2000, YARIMAKA and ZEZOV met with officials from Bloomberg L.P., including Michael Bloomberg, and two London Metropolitan police officers, one posing as a Bloomberg L.P. executive and the other serving as a translator. At the meeting, YARIMAKA allegedly claimed that he was a former Kazakhstan prosecutor and explained that he represented "Alex" and would handle the terms of payment. According to the Complaint, YARIMAKA and ZEZOV reiterated their demands at the meeting. Shortly after the meeting YARIMAKA and ZEZOV were arrested.

On August 11, 2000, YARIMAKA and ZEZOV were presented to a British Magistrate in Magistrate's Court in London, where they were held without bail. The United States will seek their extradition.

If convicted, YARIMAKA and ZEZOV each face up to 20 years in prison on the interference with commerce by using extortion charge; 2 years in prison for the extortion of a corporation using threatening communications charge; and 1 year in prison for the unauthorized computer intrusion charge. Each defendant faces a fine of the greatest of $250,000, twice the gross pecuniary gain derived from the offense, or twice the gross pecuniary loss to persons other than the defendant resulting from the offense, for each count.

Ms. WHITE praised the investigative efforts of the Federal Bureau of Investigation, the Metropolitan Police of the New Scotland Yard and the Kazakhstan authorities. Ms. WHITE expressed her appreciation to Michael Bloomberg and Bloomberg L.P. for their cooperation. The investigation is continuing.

Ms. WHITE stated: "The Internet is not a safe haven for criminals. As this case demonstrates, through the cooperation of foreign law enforcement officials and American businesses, hackers who use the Internet to extort American businesses, and gain access to restricted computer systems, will be apprehended and dealt with vigorously no matter where in the world they are located."

Mr. MAWN stated: "This investigation and these charges should dispel the notion that using a computer to commit criminal acts literally a world away from one's victim provides a zone of safety from law enforcement scrutiny. In fact, the growth of computer-related crime in recent years has resulted in a closer coordination among law enforcement agencies around the world. This investigation demonstrates the cooperation of both American business entities and our international law enforcement partners to address twenty-first-century crime."

OLEG ZEZOV, 27, and IGOR YARIMAKA, 37, live in Almaty, Kazakhstan.

Assistant United States Attorneys PAUL B. RADVANY and JOSEPH V. De MARCO are in charge of the prosecution. The charges contained in the Complaints are merely accusations, and the defendants are presumed innocent unless and until proven guilty.

In addition to individual cases, the FBI likes to go after a large number of cases that can be pursued, and prosecuted, together. The FBI loves racketeering and conspiracies. They snag headlines and, if prosecution is successful, put a lot of bad people away at once.

In May of 2001, the FBI announced the successful conclusion of "Operation Cyber Loss." This was an investigation that nailed some ninety individuals and companies that had defrauded over 56,000 people on the Internet and fleeced these people of over $117 million. Like most major operations of this sort, there were more than the FBI involved. The National White Collar Crime Center and the FBI's new (founded in early 2000) Internet Fraud Complaint Center also participated.

"Operation Cyber Loss" was an attempt to put the fear of the law into the thousands of cybercriminals who operated on the Internet. The Internet Fraud Complaint Center was meant be a central place where victims of Internet crime could report their losses. This was meant to allow all Internet users to participate in a "cyber–community watch" program. By collecting all those reports, the FBI could more easily detect who the major scamsters were. Like in any other area of crime, a small number of criminals account for a disproportionate amount of the illicit acts. This allows the FBI to identify and go after the major offenders, and spare the greatest number of people from getting bilked in the future.

This was a very big operation.

The nationwide final phase of the operation, which rounded up the culprits, involved twenty-seven FBI Field Divisions (Boston, Charlotte, Chicago, Cleveland, Dallas, Denver, Detroit, El Paso, Houston, Las Vegas, Little Rock, Miami, Minneapolis, Mobile, Norfolk, New Haven,

Newark, New York, Phoenix, Pittsburgh, Portland, Sacramento, St. Louis, San Diego, San Francisco, Seattle, and Washington, D.C.).

There were sixty-one separate cases involving a verified loss of $117,577,000. Actual losses were greater because not all the victims could be found. But it was estimated that there were 56,170 victims involved. In the final phase of the investigation, there were twenty-seven search or seizure operations that resulted in fifty-seven arrests, plea bargains, or convictions, and ninety indictments. These indictments included people being charged with 110 counts, including mail fraud, wire fraud, conspiracy to commit fraud, money laundering, bank fraud, telemarketing fraud, intellectual property rights (software piracy), and interstate transfer of stolen property.

Because these cases covered such a wide area of law breaking, a large number of law enforcement organizations were involved. These included the United States Postal Inspectors Service; Internal Revenue Service—Criminal Investigative Division; Securities and Exchange Commission; United States Secret Service; United States Customs Service; and numerous state and local, law-enforcement organizations including the New York City Police Department; New Jersey State Police; Salt Lake City Police Department; Springville Police Department; Oregon High-Tech Team; Oregon State Attorneys General Office; College Station, Texas Police Department; Seattle Police Department; Monroe, Washington Police Department; Boca Raton, Florida Police Department; Florida State Comptroller's Office; Connecticut State Police; Chula Vista, California Police Department; El Paso, Texas Police Department; and the San Diego, California Police Department.

One unsettling aspect of this case is that in its first year of operation, the Internet Fraud Complaint Center got 36,410 complaints, and 82 percent turned out to be valid. Now a lot of people who get victimized on the Internet don't even know where to complain. Interestingly enough, the victims of Internet frauds tend to be the same people who get hit with non-Internet scams. The 18–34-year-olds are the largest age group online (some 39 percent of the Internet population). But the fifty years and older folks are the fastest-growing age group online. In addition, the fifty-plus-year-old Web users, probably because a lot of them are retired, spend 19 percent more time on the Web than all other Web users. Older Web users also have more assets than younger ones. This means more money for investments, or any of the tempting scams seen on the Internet. It turns out that the same people who used to run telemarketing scams on older Americans are now doing it to the same age group via the Internet.

While a lot of the Internet scams are being run by the same people who were trying to steal money before the Internet came along, the most common crime on the Internet is unique to the Internet. Namely, not paying for goods bought in online auctions. Some 22 percent of the complaints the FBI received were of this type. The money isn't big, but we are looking at a lot of angry people. A distant second and third was credit card fraud and investment fraud (each with about 5 percent of the total complaints). By the late 1990s, American organized-crime groups began to show up running Internet hustles. Criminal gangs overseas (especially in Eastern Europe) had a head start of several years over their American counterparts.

The FTC (Federal Trade Commission) actually got into the Internet consumer complaint business several years before the FBI. While the FTC is a regulatory agency, dealing with consumer issues, it is not a police operation like the FBI. But it was the FTC that first noted the speed angle to Internet crime. Many Internet scams rely on speed. Getting information quickly and using it quickly. Sometimes the criminals don't fully understand this themselves. Many credit card and identity thieves get caught because their timing is off. While they gleefully charge on someone else's plastic, they forget that this crime will not pay unless they can convert their purchases to cash and disappear. Credit card purchases leave a trail, and even the cops know enough to not have the cards cancelled (which tends to give most crooks a wake up and get out of town call) until they can raid the hotel room the felons are living in and make the arrest.

The FBI, the FTC, and other federal agencies are developing new techniques to identify, locate, and arrest Internet criminals as quickly as possible. This not only catches more of them, but discourages the amateurs who now often (to their regret) think Internet crime is easy money. This is important, because the Internet has proved to be tremendously popular with crooks. Look at the numbers. In 1997, the FTC received only about a thousand Internet-crime complaints. But by 2000, the number of complaints had risen to over 25,000. Worse still, this was a quarter of all fraud complaints the FTC received, and at that point, the Internet accounted for only a few percent of nationwide commerce.

In 2001 and 2002, the faster and smarter cybercops piled up hundreds of arrests and indictments and scared off an increasing number of the amateur Internet criminals. But the prospects are still pretty grim as more professional crooks discover the Internet. Worldwide Internet crime was a $1.6 billion business in 2000, and is expected to grow to $15 billion by 2005.

As a result of the crackdowns on the simple Internet scams, the cybercrooks are now more and more likely to be professionals. Worse yet, they are often professionals operating overseas. This requires getting the State Department and Justice Department involved more frequently. However, many foreign nations don't even have laws against many of these Internet crimes. It gets still worse. Foreign crooks who don't speak good English (necessary for many scams) or with criminal records that would make it difficult to get into the U.S. legally, no longer have to worry about all that. They can operate anywhere in the world, as long as there's an Internet connection. The only thing that's prevented all this from producing an enormous cybercrime wave is that American credit card companies are eating a lot of these losses. The credit card companies, who have their own considerable antifraud forces, analyzed credit card transactions for signs of fraud and cut off the use of many American credit cards overseas. Sure, you can still walk into a car dealer in Manila and buy a new car with your plastic, but expect to answer questions with someone on the phone (from the credit card company) first. Most credit cards can no longer be used for Internet gambling, and any online operation that has an odor of fraud about it finds itself unable to use credit cards. Banks are also paying closer attention to wire transfers of money, which is another favorite means for crooks to remove money from victims.

For the past 150 years, each new form of electronic communication (telegraph, telephone, and Internet) was quickly adopted by criminals to carry out ancient scams. When the Internet came along, telephone fraud was still seen as a growing threat. No longer, as potential victims and inventive criminals both went online in a big way. It will take a few years before Internet users become wise and wary enough to keep much of the criminal activity down to "normal" levels. But that will only be the traditional scams. The mischief that involves Internet software and hardware will not be so easily tamed. This is another war altogether.

Rampaging Vulnerabilities

As the Internet population grew, along with the number of people probing the Net for vulnerabilities, the number of opportunities for mischief grew enormously. This happened because the number of key software programs available for hacking did not grow much at all. In fact, the different types of Internet software available for hacking shrank considerably as competition drove out a lot of competitors during the

1990s. This explains why Internet software gets combed over so thoroughly for defects by hackers. Find a flaw and you can make a lot of money exploiting it. It comes down to this: there's not much software to be had, currently. There's the server software that sits on millions of PCs and serves up the Web pages, but only two different programs power nearly 90 percent of the world's web servers. Apache has 56 percent of the market and Microsoft IIS has 30 percent. Then there are the PC operating systems and browsers that are used to contact the servers. Microsoft operating systems are on some 90 percent of PCs and Microsoft's Internet Explorer browser controls 80 percent of the market.

When you have several million software professionals working with a handful of programs, flaws can't help but be found. The hundreds of millions of users are also more likely to uncover flaws in the software, but they usually won't know exactly what they've stumbled across. And because of the nature of the Internet, information travels fast. People talk. From the beginning of the Internet, it was customary to be helpful. For the cybercrooks, this turned out to be paradise. There was all that open, and often detailed, talk about software flaws on the Internet, free for the taking. During the 1980s, hackers were exploiting known flaws in server and operating system software. Dangerous programs that took advantage of the flaws were being written as innocent exercises to see what could be done. These were classic "hacks." Then the Morris Worm got loose in 1988 and did a whole lot of damage. That particular "attack" was actually an accident. By the 1990s, black-hat hackers, who exploited software flaws just for the hell of it, or to steal, became common. Their malicious hacks were no accidents.

It's not just that there are a lot more programmers around looking for trouble, but there's a lot more for black hats to work with. In addition to lots of people picking apart fewer programs, the Internet server and browser software is larger and more complex. Make anything larger and more complex and you automatically get more things that can go wrong. There you have it, an unholy combination of more people scrutinizing fewer flavors of more buggy software, which continues to introduce more flaws as it is updated.

From one angle, all this is for the good. The vast majority of software professionals poking around in the server, operating system, and browser software are just trying to get these programs to work reliably and efficiently. When they find a flaw, they report it. And with a lot of bug reports, the software publisher will fix the damn thing quickly. Well, not always. Software publishers make money by creating new software, not repairing the old. Microsoft, in particular, is vulnerable here. Microsoft not only produces new software, but comes out with new versions of existing product so frequently that there are always a lot of older programs still in use. The older versions are even less likely to be patched. Ironically, the two best-maintained (bug free and quickly patched) bits of Internet software (Apache server software and the Linux operating system) are the Open Source software. In effect, no one owns them, but a coalition of users and volunteers maintains them. Sounds weird, but it works. Linux is no threat to Microsoft in the operating system area, but Apache actually has a majority of its market.

Microsoft software is not Open Source and they don't like fixing all those bugs (it's expensive). The longer the time between a new bug getting discovered and a patch being sent out, the more opportunity the criminals will have to figure out how to exploit the bug and set loose some nasty program on the Internet to take advantage of the bug. Malicious mischief like that cause over half the hacker attacks you hear about.

Microsoft's solution to the problem is to push for a law that makes it illegal to report a bug to anyone but the government or the publisher. Post it openly, and you're toast; FBI at the door and indictment to follow. Microsoft's logic is that when these bugs are announced publicly, the bad guys have time to concoct a criminal way to exploit the problem. That makes sense, but often the worst flaws are discovered by several different people or groups at about the same time. This worries most users because they believe that without the pressure generated by the publicity that their bugs get, Microsoft will drag its feet in getting a fix out. People see that more than they see any downside to public announcement.

Make no mistake about it, there are a lot of bugs. In 2000, 1,090 flaws in Internet software were found, of which 4 percent of them could be used for serious hacking (and serious damage). In 2001, 2,437 flaws were found, of which 13 percent could be exploited by hackers. You could say that the age of cyberwar was created by growing quantities of flawed software and malicious hackers.

The U.S. government is not happy with this situation. In early 2002, the U.S. Air Force, which generally takes the lead in cyberwar matters, warned Microsoft to improve the security of their software real fast or risk losing their biggest customer: the U.S. government. Microsoft software sales to the U.S. government (directly, and indirectly through software installed in hardware) amounts to billions of dollars a year. The government has long bought Microsoft software because it was the cheapest and easiest to install (if not the easiest to use). But as more people find their jobs dependent on the Internet, the security and reliability of Microsoft software has become an issue. And the threat is not an empty one. There is a lot of enthusiasm within the air force for the cheaper and more reliable Linux operating system. While Linux cannot run many of the games that are so popular on PCs using Microsoft operating systems, the air force sees that as a plus. And most of the business software the air force needs is available on PCs running Linux. But there is one major downside to this. China has adopted Linux as their standard operating system (for government and schools). This means Chinese software engineers will be more familiar with Linux than with Microsoft software, and thus better able to hack Linux systems.

The number of serious bugs found in Microsoft software is staggering. At the end of 2001, the number of known security flaws were (software used to run the internet, or in connection with the internet, and the number of major flaws for each):

Microsoft Outlook and Outlook Express: 20 (although these are two separate programs, some of the flaws were found in both)

Microsoft Internet Information Server: 44 (not only were there more flaws than in Apache, but more serious ones as well)

Microsoft Internet Explorer: 47 (the most widely used Web browser, and the most dangerous to use)

Microsoft Windows 2000: 79 (up until then, averaged about three new vulnerabilities a month since its release)

Microsoft Windows 98: 25 (an older operating system now, and still dangerous to use)

Apache: 29 (the most widely used, and safest, Web server software)

Debian Linux: 28

Macintosh Operating System: 2 (the older version of Macintosh software, and the safest operating system out there)

Mac Operating System X: 10 (the newly released Macintosh operating system)

At this point in time, the newly released Windows XP operating system, touted as the safest Microsoft operating system ever, was instead turning out to be as buggy as Windows 2000.

In addition, there were the popular (for businesses) online-database software systems (like Oracle). This software was set up differently for each site, but some 12 percent of all online databases were hacked in 2001.

As far as anyone knows, however, there aren't that many malicious (black-hat) hackers to take advantage of all this software vulnerability. White-hat hackers and sysadmins are much relieved because of this lack of exploitation. But at the same time, the white-hat hackers in particular are well aware of what kind of damage can be done. One way to look at it is that the best of the black-hat hackers would rather use these security flaws to make money. This means the flaws are being exploited quietly to steal information or money. Causing a lot of damage simply draws attention from the law, and a skilled black hat doesn't want that kind of attention. But at the same time, the military cyberwarriors are probably carefully studying these flaws for use in wartime situations. So don't feel too good, because the large number of vulnerabilities that are not being exploited right away can give us all headaches later.

Also consider that most of the reported Internet attacks in 2001 were caused by just three viruses. And it's quite likely that these three viruses were released by three individuals. That's a lot of damage (billions of dollars to clean up the mess) for three e-mail messages. There were also thousands of individual attacks on unprotected PCs and servers to place zombie programs for DDOS attacks or more similar antisocial behavior. The most serious attacks, against commercial sites for the purpose of theft, probably numbered in the hundreds. A lot of the "attacks," indeed the majority, were automated. There just aren't that many people out there with the skills to work their way into a protected site, and risk getting caught, for the sake of having a few thrills or making some money.

Most of the scams on the Internet don't involve programming wizards tinkering with defective software, but plain old-fashioned crooks working a new venue. With the increasing number of flaws appearing in Internet software, the risks to all of us increase.

Fortunately, the people with the most to lose, especially the commercial sites, are every bit as energetic at defending their sites as the black-hat hackers are at attacking them. The majority of computers with the serious (Microsoft) flaws are used by ordinary people. The combination of powerful PCs in the hands of millions of home users, plus the spread of fast connections, gives the black hats and cyberwarriors an easy-to-use new battlefield. If a cyberwar does break out, and you have one of these PCs, expect to be part of the "collateral damage."

The Dark Side's Superhighway

Military attacks, like water, take the path of least resistance. An example of this is one of the more obvious forms of cyberwarfare on the Internet: the DDOS attack. First seen in 1999, by the end of 2001, there were more than 500 DDOS attacks a day on Web sites and devices connected to the Net (like printers). The DDOS has become the favorite toy of the script kiddies, as it allows them to sneak into unprotected PCs, leave the zombie programs needed to launch the DDOS attack, then pick some Web site they don't like and activate their zombies to launch the DDOS attack and, in effect, shut down the site. The zombies can also be used to meddle around on the site they reside in. Commercial sites and antivirus software companies were quick to address the problem. But this only worked for people who were aware that they had a problem, knew there was a fix, and had the time and incentive to protect their servers from zombies. But just as zombie-driven DDOS attacks appeared on the scene, so did millions of home-PC users with cable modem and DSL connections. These were the perfect hiding places for zombies. While the script kiddies kept score by how many zombies they could plant and how difficult a site it was to get into, the home PCs with always-on and fast connections become the perfect target. The commercial and university sites were fairly well protected. While it was safe enough to launch the DDOS attack, it was getting more dangerous to plant the zombies. Commercial sites were increasingly equipped with intrusion detectors and people on call who could track down the intruder. The feds were prosecuting. This zombie and DDOS stuff was no fun if you got caught.

But home users with cable modems were most likely clueless about what was going on inside their PC. These home users weren't going to catch you, and probably wouldn't even notice the zombie at work until they got home to find their Internet connection gone and a phone message from the cable company to call the tech-support line about "disinfecting your computer." Even if a lot of home cable-modem users got a firewall and antivirus software, that was easier to deal with than a visit from the FBI.

Perhaps more ominously, the home PCs have become a prime launching site for cyberwar attacks. An enemy nation could practice the rapid deployment of military-grade zombies on thousands of home PCs, PCs with high-capacity access to the Net. Talk about "the enemy within." Such a force could shut down military and government sites for days, or weeks with DDOS (and similar) attacks, even if the U.S. cut its Internet connections to the rest of the world. All the attacker would have to do is program the military zombies to shift to "plan B" if they didn't receive any instructions from back home within a certain time. Chasing down all the military zombies could take months, as most of them would be on PCs used by people not well versed in technical matters. Because of the low-security of most home PCs, the military zombies could launch virus attacks to install themselves in more home computers. As long as one of them was still active, the attacks could begin again.

The militarized DDOS zombie is the perfect military weapon: relentless, effective, self-replicating, hard to detect, and cheap. And vulnerability to attacks from this quarter won't disappear for a few years. Indeed, they will never disappear completely, but everyone has been scrambling since 1999 to develop better forms of protection. That's easy to do compared to eliminating the attacker.

Another bit of science fiction come to life. Welcome to the twenty-first century.

Spare a Few Viruses?

In 2001, the Department of Defense was angered when it was discovered that U.S. software companies were giving China copies of deadly computer viruses that had not been "in the wild" much. Of the 71,000 computer viruses discovered over the last two decades, many of the most lethal ones were never released onto a network (put "in the wild"). Some of these super-viruses were only in the wild for a short time before they disappeared (because they were programmed to self-destruct, or because of a design flaw that prevented their spread). The handful of companies that make antivirus software maintain libraries of as many viruses as they can. For someone building an arsenal of military-grade computer viruses, these virus libraries would be a valuable resource.

Given the Chinese government's published attitudes toward cyberwar and the United States (the Chinese want to use the former on the latter), this particular export raised pulse rates in the Pentagon. However, like anything involving China and computers, all was not what it appeared to be. China wanted copies of those viruses so that it could test the antivirus software it was buying. The American firms figured they were just performing a courtesy, as they were pretty sure that they were not the only ones who possessed these particular 300 viruses. That might have been all there was to it. After all, the year before the Chinese had passed a law providing severe punishment for anyone releasing computer viruses. China has been having growing problems with computer viruses throughout the 1990s. Chinese hackers were releasing viruses designed to do more damage on PCs found in China. At the same time, there were a number of innovative new viruses released in 2001 that were traced back to China. One could make a case that China wanted access to those American virus libraries for sinister reasons.

At the end of 2001, there were over 71,000 computer viruses identified as "in the wild" (found on a computer other than the one they were created on). Ten years earlier, there only about a thousand known computer viruses. In December 2001 alone, 1,256 new viruses were discovered. Now most of the existing viruses are either obsolete (the hardware and software they were designed to attack no longer exist, or are very rarely connected to the Internet) or relatively harmless. Some were designed to be harmless, others were poorly put together and simply don't function as intended. Moreover, many "new" viruses are just variations of older ones. And, a few viruses tend to do most of the damage. In December 2001, over 90 percent of the reported virus infections were by one virus: Badtrans-B (a variant of the original Badtrans). This one spread as an attachment to e-mail when it was delivered to systems using Microsoft Outlook.

You can buy, or get for free on the Internet, "how to" kits for building computer viruses. Creating them has become a compelling, some say addicting, hobby for many programmers and network engineers. Normally, new ideas are freely exchanged, or at least posted in places where others will pick up and spread the word. Apparently there are also some reclusive, and quite good, virus designers who only communicate through their work, as well. The fear is that one of them, or the Chinese military, will develop a "doomsday virus" that will bring down the entire Internet. That is theoretically possible, for a while at least, if you hit the specialized computers (called routers) that control the behind-the-scenes work on the Internet.

Like most unknown terrors, this one has a smidgen of truth attached to it. And like most doomsday weapons, the best defense is to have some of your own. While this worked with nuclear weapons (the ultimate "doomsday" weapon), an Internet weapon of that caliber will only work if the other side knows you have it. But if you let them know you have it, you have to explain it for it to be credible. However, if you explain your doomsday Internet virus, countermeasures can be devised that will downgrade it from "doomsday" to, say, "damn nuisance" status.

China is probably not looking to build a doomsday virus, just more lethal viruses, and that's bad enough.

Microsoft the Patriot

The lack of security software on home PCs made it easier for all Internet criminals to operate. These vulnerable machines were also perfect for cyberwarriors to launch military attacks from. The only way to protect commercial and military servers is to upgrade operating systems on home PCs. This is not as difficult as it appears, for the major weakness is the operating system and the lack of firewall and antivirus software. Microsoft got religion in the late 1990s regarding the weak security in its software. But its efforts to improve quality have failed miserably. The vast majority of security breaches on the Internet, and attacks on users over the Internet, are because of flaws in Microsoft software. In early 2002, Microsoft announced that it was making the security features on its software a major goal. This was encouraging, as the company has demonstrated an ability to successfully shift its focus in the past.

The pressure on Microsoft was intense, and not just from the public denunciations and press releases from organizations announcing the abandonment of Microsoft software. So there was a commercial aspect to the new direction for Microsoft. But there was also the briefings from Department of Defense and other government computer-security officials about how the shabby state of Microsoft software was endangering national security. Moreover, the Department of Defense accounts for billions of dollars of business for Microsoft each year. September 11, 2001, probably also played a role in this. If the Department of Defense were really pushed, they could point out that terrorists are being aided in any Internet attacks by inexcusable security flaws in Microsoft software.

Microsoft can fix a lot of the security flaws using the periodic updates it issues for its software. This could include adding firewall and antivirus features and special software to deal with the always-on cable modem/DSL users. The latest Microsoft operating system, Windows XP, has a firewall built in. But a lot more is needed to provide effective protection, especially finding and removing many of the security flaws before new software is released. A lot could be done in a year or so if the problem were addressed directly. And Microsoft knows what it's up against. One reason for the many security flaws in Microsoft software is the effort to make it usable by the many PC users who see the microcomputer as another appliance. Apple has long been ahead of Microsoft in the "ease of use" department, and Bill Gates has long proclaimed that the ideal PC was "one that my mother can use." Apple has fewer security problems, partly because there a lot more Microsoft-powered PCs out there, and partly because Apple computers have always integrated networking software into its operating system more than Microsoft has, and has done it with more of an eye toward security.

If there is a major cyberwar in the next few years, the numerous flaws in Microsoft software will be spotlighted as a major contributor to whatever damage is done to the United States. That's not the kind of legacy any company wants to leave behind it, especially since we can see it coming.

CHAPTER 11

Surviving Cyberwar

If you don't want to be a victim of cyberwar, here are things you can do and things to watch out for. There are also some important things you should know about the companies that create the software that runs the Internet.

Malicious Microsoft

The Microsoft Corporation is often portrayed as the one company that bears most of the responsibility for the security problems users have with the Internet. This is largely true, if only because Microsoft is the largest supplier of software for Internet users and many Internet providers. Some of the problems, it should be noted, were unavoidable. For example, whoever created the operating system used on most home computers would end up having a new product that would be closely scrutinized by hackers for weaknesses. Undoubtedly, there would be weaknesses, because a mass-market operating system would have to deal with an ever-increasing demand for new hardware and software compatibility. Microsoft operating systems grabbed 90 percent of the PC market partially because Microsoft made an effort to support most old software and hardware and all the new stuff. This made the operating systems bloated and extremely complex. Lots of things can go wrong in a situation like that. Pressure to ship new versions of the operating system would mean that fixing compatibility problems would be more important than Internet security. Moreover, Microsoft's operating systems were designed before the Internet, or heavy use of PC modems, came along. So a lot of bad habits that were not so serious without the Internet, became positively fatal with the Net. The best example of this is the "buffer overflow" problem. Basically, this is a programming error that doesn't always show up unless the program gets just the right combination of instructions and data. The result is a program crash. Back before the Internet, programmers fixed buffer-overflow problems when they discovered them and didn't test new software exhaustively to find them. But when a program working with the Internet (a browser or server software) has buffer-overflow problems, this bug can be deliberately exploited by a hacker to slip a program into a Web site or PC. And the new program can then be used to allow a malicious programmer to take over a server or PC. Microsoft programmers who developed Microsoft's Internet software didn't give a lot of attention to the buffer-overflow problem, seeing it as just one of many ways things could go wrong in a program. Programmers who had worked on data communications software for their entire careers did pay attention, and were much more energetic in stomping out buffer-overflow problems. This is one reason why Microsoft's IIS server program is much easier to attack than the Unix-based Apache server software. Apache is not only twice as stable as IIS in operation, but has less than one-tenth the number of bugs that threaten Internet security.

Microsoft not only produced a lot of flawed Internet server software, but changed the terms of their software licenses to "encourage" customers to use nothing but Microsoft software. This discouraged firms that used Microsoft software for internal needs from at least using the safer Apache server software for their Web server.

One reason Apache is better server software, aside from fewer bugs, is the way Apache software is set up by the user. When a user installs Microsoft's IIS Web server, all options are turned on. Even on a Web server, there are a lot of features not everyone needs. And some of these features, even if not used, are another way for hackers to get in. When you install Apache, nearly all features are turned off. If you want some of the extra features, you not only have to turn them on, but that procedure makes sure you either know what it does, or have an incentive to find out.

But it got worse. Microsoft's server software was also vulnerable because it was aimed at the small- and medium-size user. These are the very organizations that are least likely to have people who can spot the software problems before they trigger some kind of disaster delivered via the Internet. These organizations also comprise the largest segment of the Internet (in terms of separate companies). Microsoft software-design philosophy is to make installation and use of its software as simple as possible. Thus, while there are many unneeded features, even if they are all turned on, they usually don't get in the way of one another. This is very clever, but pretty much ignores the hacker vulnerability problem. When fingers began to point at Microsoft, the reaction there was one of "Who? Us?" The programmers at Microsoft have given the impression that they haven't truly examined Internet security, or taken the problems of Internet security seriously enough.

Most Internet users aren't going to have a lot of trouble with flawed server software anyway. No, you are going to get hurt (if you haven't already) from using Microsoft's Outlook program. The most widely used e-mail program on the planet, Outlook is also the reason for most people getting hit by computer viruses. The problem is "featureitis." This is that Microsoft habit of adding more and more features to their programs, even if the great majority of users will never have need of these features. But in order to justify coming out with new versions of the Excel spreadsheet, or the Word word-processing program, more features are added: there is a corporation to run and employees and shareholders to consider as well. This in itself would not be a major problem, as most of the hardly used features are hidden away and most users never notice them.

But "scripting support" was one feature that opened up all manner of malicious opportunities for hackers. "Scripting" is nothing more than a system that allows a programmer, or user, to write out a list of commands in a file and have them automatically executed. Scripting is an old feature. The batch (.BAT) files from the 1980s were script files and were very popular with early PC users. Even before that, scripting languages were essential for the smooth running of the earliest mainframe systems. Microsoft noted the popularity of scripting and expanded its use. With the introduction of Visual Basic in the 1990s, and its integration with other applications in 1993 (first Excel, then Word), scripting was available within these programs and, essentially, anywhere within a Windows-equipped PC. When Windows 98 was introduced, it automatically installed scripting support for all Microsoft applications. It didn't take mean-spirited programmers long to figure out what splendid opportunities for mayhem this presented. The first e-mail viruses using scripts in Word or Excel files appeared in 1997. This led to such nasty experiences as the Melissa and I Love You viruses. It went downhill from there, despite the fact that the vast majority of PC users had no need for this much scripting "support."

Microsoft wasn't the only culprit here. Sun Microsystems developed the Java scripting language in 1995 for use on Web browsers. Even Microsoft adopted it, although Microsoft soon added its own ideas with its ActiveX scripting. ActiveX allowed viruses to be downloaded from Web sites without user knowledge. This allowed viruses to be imbedded in e-mail messages that were viewed on e-mail readers that could handle HTML (Web page–like) e-mail. The first one of these was the Kak virus, which appeared in late 1999. If you opened e-mail, and your scripting was turned on, Kak went to work and made changes to your system. First, it attached itself to all outgoing mail, then once a month it flashed a message and shut down Windows.

Microsoft managed to make it worse. Another feature in Outlook is the ability to plant a program within an e-mail message even if scripting is not turned on. When Microsoft was alerted to this problem in 2001, their advice was not to begin an e-mail message with "begin" (the magic word that made Outlook assume that everything that followed was an encoded attachment).

The pressure to shape up finally had its effect at Microsoft in 2002. Microsoft declared that security was going to be its number-one priority for the foreseeable future. This may be simply recognition of another growing market. In 2001, sales of security software hit $3.6 billion and will hit over $5 billion by 2003. Companies that provide network-protection services (consulting and online services) went from $720 million in 2000 to over a billion dollars in 2002 and is expected to double by 2005. One side effect of this is that the Microsoft programmers will be so busy dealing with security issues that they will have less time to add more unneeded features. But there will have to be some action by Microsoft first, and that will take awhile. Microsoft's attitude toward bugs in its software is, traditionally, that if the number of these flaws can be kept below a certain level, programmers could continue adding features and shipping new products. For Microsoft, this is a good business practice. The PC-software industry, from the beginning (in the late 1970s), was run by a lot of amateurs and entrepreneurs. Publishers and customers became accustomed to looking forward to what was new while learning to live with any glitches. Most PC users had never encountered a computer before they bought Windows, much less owned and used one. We all learned to tolerate the available product because there wasn't anything better. But, today, the Internet-software security bugs do have a very noticeable effect on PC users. Just ask anyone whose PC got hit with a computer virus.

It is possible to produce bug-free (or very close to it) software. This is done all the time for industrial and military applications. You do hear about it when bugs show up in this kind of software, but because such events are so rare, the stuff is largely bug free. The Japanese also tend to make bug-free software. It costs more to create, though, and the work isn't as much "fun" for the programmers. It takes a lot of discipline and tight management to produce bug-free software. Microsoft isn't, obviously, the only source of flawed Internet software. But Microsoft is the biggest source, and that makes Microsoft the likely place to begin when trying to clean up this situation.

To reduce its bug count, Microsoft would have to make some serious changes in the way its programmers operate. It can be done, but it can't be done immediately. Microsoft took the pledge in early 2002. Before the end of 2002, you could see the tightening in some Microsoft products. In a few years, you might see Microsoft setting new standards for bug-free PC software. It isn't easy, it is possible, and if it doesn't happen, the Internet is in a lot of trouble.

The Invisible Internet

When things go wrong for you on the Internet, or because of the Internet, it may not be something that's on your PC that's causing the problem. Or even something on Web sites you are visiting. Increasingly, the problem may be with hackers doing damage to the "invisible Internet." For years it was thought that the routers, DNS servers, and backbone software that invisibly (to users, anyway) kept everything on the Net moving efficiently were safe. But in early 2002 it was discovered that for ten years there had been a serious flaw (known as the "SNMP vulnerability") in router software that made it possible for someone with the right skills to shut down routers, or gain control over them. Black-hat hackers have often discussed taking down an entire country's Internet. This is their idea of a prank. India and China are often mentioned. Both of these countries have relatively small Internet infrastructures, plus, there are cultural issues (hackers can be as nationalistic and insecure as any other group).

A lot of American programmers are a bit miffed at the many lower-paid (but highly skilled) Indian programmers "taking American jobs." Indian programmers who immigrate to the United States often end up in senior positions (or starting their own companies) by dint of hard work and superior skills. This upsets some of the locals, so the idea of taking down the Indian Internet is a popular daydream.

These recently discovered router vulnerabilities bring such fantasies closer to reality. China doesn't send nearly as many programmers to the United States, but the programmers back in China are nationalistic and there are regular skirmishes between American and Chinese hackers. Taking down the Chinese Internet, if only for a few days, is seen as the ultimate "can you top this" Internet hack. For cyberwarriors, the ability to knock out, or take control of, selected portions of the Internet has real military value. Before the early 2002 SNMP problems were discovered, it was already recognized that the routers and DNS servers were vulnerable. But the SNMP problem provides the malicious hacker with a more precise weapon. By exploiting the SNMP vulnerability (by changing the software running the router), hackers could stop or divert large chunks of Internet traffic. Not for long, as the owners of those routers could eventually fix the problem. But the impact of such an attack garners the kind of media attention that hackers live for. This is more of a military peril than most other Internet vulnerabilities. The ability to shut down the Internet in a nation or region, if only for hours or days, also degrades the victim's military and police forces. There are other known or suspected flaws in the Invisible Internet, and these will remain a problem for some time to come. It's something to worry about, and a lot of the people that run the Internet are losing sleep over this.

Playing Defense

There are a lot of things the professionals do to keep key military and business sites safe that can be adopted by users lacking big budgets.

The hardest of these techniques is setting up your PC, or small, home or business network so there is no single point of failure. This means that you'll be able to take a hack attack, which might get part of your system, but which won't take it down entirely. While hard to do for a single PC, professionals with sites using many PCs deliberately set up their systems so that even a severe attack will take down only part of it. This is why cyberattacks require so much scanning and probing before war even breaks out. The big military and commercial sites are usually networks of networks. While you won't notice this if you just go to a big site to buy something, put something up for auction, or play a game, you will note that major attacks on these sites often don't shut the site down. No, a major DDOS or virus attack will usually just slow down access to a major site. And that's because the site was designed to take a major hit and keep on going. Oddly enough, the major military sites are not as well equipped, mainly because the Department of Defense hasn't got as much money and high-priced talent to make their sites less vulnerable. For a single PC, there's not much you can do with this technique since all the attacks are going to hit your one and only PC. But it's good to know of the concept, as home networks are becoming more common and more home users will find the "no single point of failure" concept useful.

There are other techniques used by the major Internet players that all of us can use. For example, be careful where you put data you don't want someone to steal. You can encrypt key data files or folders, and not store the passwords on the PC where the data is.

Perhaps the most critical failure of home-PC users (and many small businesses) is their poor track record with regard to backing up data. If a hacker makes a serious attack on your system, data will be destroyed or damaged. The only way to cope with this is to have backups of what's on your hard drive. Most home-PC users, and many small business owners, don't bother with backups. Since all hard drives fail eventually, this seems like an absurd situation. But people have persistently resisted getting into the backup habit because most have upgraded to new computers before the old ones could fail. Their files are moved from the old PC's hard drive to the new PC. There have not been enough disaster stories of home users losing all their hard-drive contents to scare a lot of people into doing regular backups. Moreover, there are companies that will, for a hefty fee, recover data from most hard drives that otherwise appear dead.

But the lesson is, if you're going to be vulnerable to a cyberwar attack, you had better have regular backups of your data. In the last few years, as more people installed CD-RW drives, they have begun to use them for just that purpose. But the fact remains, neither failure-prone hard drives nor damaging hack attacks exist in sufficient quantity to get a lot of people interested in backups. The professionals not only have regular backups (often literally up to the minute), but maintain them in generations. That is, there's a separate backup copy of files for today, yesterday, and often for several days (weeks or months). This would result in maybe a dozen copies of the same files. But if you get hit with a damaging virus, and don't discover the damage for a few days, you can and must go back a few generations to find a good copy of your data.

Another major advantage professional military and commercial sites have is access to computer-security experts. In an emergency, a little sage advice can go a long way. This is one of the major bonuses of a successful attack on communications systems. Bring the telephone system of a nation down, and your enemy is going to take longer to recover because their experts won't be able to phone in solutions. For the home user, the best you can do is bookmark security and software publisher sites that regularly cover Internet security (www.cert.org is a good place to start, but there are others that may suit your taste better).

Well protected sites also follow a list of basic dos and don'ts. Most don'ts apply to home PCs (like not allowing anonymous FTP—users uploading files to your server), but some do (like using a firewall program if you have a cable modem or DSL connection). Anonymous FTP is an old, Internet feature that continues to cause problems. Basically, it allows anyone to send a file to your server. But someone with the right skills and tools can use that ability to get into your server with more than just a file. Not all anonymous FTP setups are vulnerable to this, but many are and security conscious sysadmins just do without anonymous FTP. Besides, there are other ways to send files back and forth on the Internet. Not as fast as FTP, but easier to use, is HTTP, which is used on most Web sites.

Another useful habit for major sites is to log everything. Now most PC users have no idea what that means, but if you are using operating systems like Windows 2000 or XP, you have several logging programs going on. These logging operations only record key tasks the operating system is doing, and the logs are there for service technicians (or the operating system itself) to use when fixing something on your system. If you dig into the Help files, you can find out where these log files are and view them. Pretty dry reading, although perhaps surprising in that they record operation failures that were detected and fixed and which you never knew about. So welcome to the twenty-first century. The major sites have already gotten there and log just about everything. These logs often provide the first clue that the site has been hacked. Indeed, hackers will often want to get access to the logs to erase the signs that they were ever there.

Another tool of the professionals that is becoming more common with those of us with only a single PC to deal with is staying current with patches. Sysadmins have also been patching their operating-system software more diligently to eliminate ("patch up") flaws that hackers can exploit to get into the system. That's something quite new in the computer business, for until the 1990s, sysadmins would only patch their operating systems if they had to. This wasn't because of laziness, but due to the fact that patches tended to change more than what was broken. After the patch was applied, you might find that the patch had created new bugs, or changed how the system worked. Change meant more work for sysadmins and more uncertainty for the users.

But that changed after the World Wide Web came along and Web use exploded. This explosion meant that more PCs were exposed to the Web, and vulnerable PCs and servers could be hacked. The PCs that acted as servers were the most vulnerable, and the most valuable to hackers (servers often contained credit card information). But by the late 1990s, hackers were going after individual Internet users. Now it became important for nearly every PC user to keep their patches up to date. A few years ago, most PC users didn't know what a patch to their software was, and if you tried to explain it to them, you'd see anger or fear, or maybe both. Well, the anger toward, and fear of, PC operating systems is real, but so is knowledge of and willingness to regularly install patches to PC software. Because hackers can automatically spread virus programs via e-mail (and Microsoft's very vulnerable Outlook program) to a much larger number of victims, more people know about the terrible consequences of "not having the latest patches."

Microsoft quickly realized that even the easy availability of, and need for, patches would not get a lot of people to keep their software current. Now normally, this would not be a big deal. Plenty of people have used five- or ten-year-old, unpatched software with no problems. But with cyberwarriors looking to use vulnerable, unpatched home computers to store attack zombies and such, it became a matter of national security to reduce the number of unpatched systems. So Microsoft came out with "automatic patching" in their 2001 release of Windows XP. There were some bugs with this, of course, but it eventually reduced the number of places the enemy zombies could hide out.

The most common vulnerability of networked computers has always been the passwords. The bad guys would either guess them, or steal them. The guessing part was made easier when crackers created dictionary programs. These would keep trying to log in using a list of the most common passwords and, if none of those worked, would proceed to, literally, work its way through a dictionary of words, then words and numbers. This sort of thing can actually be easily defeated with a login software that recognizes a "dictionary attack" (which requires a lot of failed login attempts for one user as different passwords are tried) and suspends that user until the situation can be investigated. This kind of login software isn't common, so dictionary attacks still work. However, a password containing an equal number of letters and numbers will keep a dictionary attack going for so long that the attack will probably be discovered before it can succeed.

For secure systems, there are other ways to deal with the password security problems. For example, you can have a call-back system. You log in, and are then disconnected while the system you are trying to get into calls back to only one phone number. This was popular before the Internet, but even on the Internet it will work. Other hyper-secure approaches are one-time passwords (you get a list of passwords and just go down the list, using one password after another in sequence) and two- , or three-part logins. In other words, you need a different password for each level. There are many more techniques that have been developed, but the basic problem, stolen passwords, remains. The solution for that, biometrics, is starting to appear. A biometric "password" would be something like your thumbprint or voice. These can be stolen or gotten around as well, but with greater difficulty. Needless to say, every cyberwar organization has a password section, which spends all its efforts figuring out how go get around enemy password systems, and defending their own.

Internet security is a major industry, and the nation with the largest chunk of this industry (the United States) technically has the largest potential to get past any security. Indeed, many Internet security experts in foreign nations assume Internet security products coming from the United States will have secret backdoors to allow Department of Defense cyberwarriors to get through in wartime, or even peacetime in the name of economic espionage. Such backdoors are often little more than a special password that always works and can never be changed. No one will admit that these backdoors exist. But backdoors have shown up in the past. And efforts by the FBI to get laws passed forcing encryption systems to have a backdoor for the feds didn't change anyone's mind. On the positive side, this paranoia about secret backdoors will sometimes cause foreign governments to use inferior Internet security software. But not always, as there are many foreign companies that produce good programs

America's major disadvantage when it comes to Internet security is the sheer size of its Internet presence. Most of the Internet is in the United States, as are most of the Internet users. This is changing, as more of the world gets on the Internet, but there will always be more Internet sites and users in the United States than anywhere else. There's more to defend, and because there is more for enemies to attack, there are greater opportunities to do damage. The Department of Defense has decided to use quantity as well as quality in building its Internet defenses. Layers of defenses are used. These have proved to be the most difficult to penetrate when "tiger teams" of friendly hackers were turned loose to try and get through.

The very size of America's Internet resources makes it virtually impossible to shut down the Internet in the United States. Such is not the case in many other countries like India, where a large-scale attack could blow that nation off the Internet for days, weeks, or months.

As with other forms of warfare, when it comes to the Internet, the best defense is a good offense. As many hacking competitions have shown, there is no system that cannot be penetrated. The hacking competitions offer cash rewards to anyone who can penetrate a new Internet-security product within a certain time. The details of these competitions make sober reading. Some very bright, skilled, and persistent people have demonstrated in these competitions just how possible it is to get into the most seemingly secure system. Thus one has to keep in mind another bit of battlefield wisdom, "It's not a matter of who's better, but who's worse." The side with the worst cyberwarriors will lose.

Sneaky Spiders

Search engines, those very useful sites that enable us to explore cyberspace, have proved to be another Internet flaw. Which just goes to show you that Internet vulnerabilities can show up in the most unexpected places.

Using programs called "spiders," they search the Web and note what is found. They then put this information in a database. Search engine users search that database when they use the search engine. For years, the spiders did little but check to see if a Web site was live and note what was there for the search engine database. The Internet, however, is all about innovation and progress. In 2001, for example, search engines began checking all files on Web sites (not just the HTML, or Web page, files). This was all to the good, as Adobe, spreadsheet, PowerPoint, and many other file types were checked and indexed. You could now find useful information contained in these files.

Unfortunately, some of these files were not normally reachable by Web surfers and contained information Web surfers were not supposed to see. The spiders, however, could reach them, and put their Web address went into the search-engine index. Once you had the Web address, you could look at these files. Combine this with Webmasters who put password or credit card files in a place where the spider could spot them and, well, we have a problem. This was first noted when search engine users reported that they did a search on "password" and found files that contained, well, user passwords. The only way you can protect against this was to bring this problem to the attention of any site on which you have passwords and credit card information. The major sites were the first to become aware of the problem and fix it. As discussed, this is usually the case because the larger sites have staffs of professional Web site administrators to keep things tight. The sites at most risk are those like small businesses and schools that maintain their own Web sites on their own servers. Places like these don't have someone to keep a sharp eye on technical matters. This is where password or credit card (or personnel records) files are likely to be left where a spider can find them.

This spiders issue is not a unique situation. The Internet is so vast and full of different types of software that no one really knows what is vulnerable to what. The best one can do is to stay alert and be prepared to act fast. On the Web, you're either quick, or you're dead. This incident also points out that there are a lot of dangerous situations just waiting for the right set of circumstances for them to happen.

Adware

Internet users have long been accustomed to getting everything for free on the Net. That's why there are banners and advertisements all over the Web. But it doesn't work as well on the Internet as it does on radio and TV—and advertising companies know that. So a technological solution was developed to enable Web companies to pay for and maintain their sites. It's called "targeted advertising" and it's the process of identifying Web users by their interests and sending them ads for products they are most likely to buy.

What this led to was the use of what came to be called "adware" or, for the less charitable, "spyware." AdWare was downloaded with free programs like games or file-sharing systems. Once installed on your system, your Web-surfing activity was reported back to a central site where your preferences were matched to advertiser profiles of their likely customers. So if you hit a lot of automotive sites, you would see more ads about buying cars. Although the spyware didn't collect anything more personal than surfing preferences, and didn't actually know your identity, a lot of people were annoyed (although a lot more didn't really care). Spyware was also supposed to be "opt-in" (used voluntarily), but many users don't read the fine print when they download a free program for use with some online service. The major problem with spyware is that it acts like many hacker's zombie programs. For that reason alone, many Web users regularly scour their computers for spyware, and often find it has snuck in. Even after the spyware is removed, it's not unusual to find, when searching a month later, that more of it has gotten in. Kind of scary, and don't expect this stuff to disappear. After all, how many PC users really know what programs are on their computer?

Ancient Hardware

One advantage the U.S. military (and government officials) have when dealing with black-hat hackers is the ancient PCs and software many troops and bureaucrats are stuck with. While most civilian firms replace their PCs every two to four years, the military and government sometimes hang on to theirs for ten years or more. This is not as bad as it sounds. For one thing, when it comes to many basic tasks (like word processing, spreadsheets, or small databases), ten-year-old PCs can still get the job done. Since military and government organizations never get as many PCs as they need, they hang on to the old ones rather than have none at all. However, it take some ingenuity, and a visit to computer flea markets, to find spare parts for these ancient machines. But you will still find a lot of them in the back rooms of military bases and government offices. Until 2000, the FBI was still using a lot of late 1980s 386-class PCs (possessing about 2 percent of the computing power of today's PCs). The major problem with these older PCs is that they cannot run the more recent operating systems and modern Web browsers. PCs that old cannot, without great difficulty, access the Internet (the older communications software is not compatible with today's Internet and the more recent browsers cannot run on something like the FBI's old 386s). It is still possible to rig up some e-mail access with the computers, and interestingly, the major advantage is that these ancient machines are much less vulnerable to malicious viruses and worms snaking about the Internet. The older PCs literally cannot run the modern Internet viruses because they just don't have the more-recent capabilities required.

One military aspect of this is that many less-affluent nations have older PC equipment. There has always been a brisk market for older computer equipment in parts of South America, Africa, and Asia. Many of the armies, and rebel groups, in these areas have this ancient equipment, and the immunity to modern hacking tools that obsolete PCs bequeaths. Older is sometimes better, and cyberwarriors better be ready for it.

New Solutions

For all the fear of Internet terrorism, few, if any, people have been killed via the Internet. At least not yet. Anything so huge, that extends into so many homes and workplaces and consumes so much of people's lives, however, was bound to inspire some fear. In reality, most of the downside items on the Internet are annoyances, not disasters. Losing all your business data to a virus (and a lack of backups) is a disaster. Putting up with all the script kiddies wandering around, fear of viruses, endless software patches, and hassling with antivirus software and backups is an annoyance. But it's getting to be a major annoyance, and the fear that terrorists could turn the annoyances into disasters is actually forcing serious attempts to change the situation.

One reason Microsoft publicly announced a new attitude toward software bugs and security vulnerabilities (there could be a lot fewer of them) was because legislators were making noises about laws to hold software publishers liable for the damage caused by flaws in their software. This is not a new idea, but until 2001 (because of a sharp increase in Internet vulnerabilities and the war on terrorism), the software publishers had been able to keep it at bay. There were some attempts at making software publishers liable during the 1980s as an increasing number of PC users ran into a lot of infected software. Through a combination of special pleading ("hey, it's only PCs, we're all small companies"), a more pro-business attitude climate and promises to do better, they staved off the threat. In the last decade, software publishers have actually gotten better terms for themselves, often under the guise of helping limit software piracy. It's a pretty sweet situation for the publishers of PC software. A lot of that software isn't very good, but the legal system enthusiastically discourages any class-action suits against the publishers. However, with all the Internet problems, many of them traced directly to Microsoft products, the liability laws are being reconsidered. This scares the software publishers a lot, and it should. All those lawsuits would be expensive, and even if a lot of them were baseless, the negative publicity would hurt as well. So it's quite likely that the publishers will actually improve their quality control this time around.

There are, however, some negatives associated with creating better software. One law the publishers would actually like passed covers how software flaws, especially Internet related ones, are reported. According to the proposed laws, anyone finding a bug would be required, by law, to report it promptly to a designated federal agency or the publisher.

Publication of the bug, especially on the Internet, would be a crime. The basic idea behind keeping the bugs secret is to prevent the bad guys from exploiting them before the publisher can develop a fix and distribute it. The flip side of this is that most people believe that secret bugs will allow the publishers to ignore some of them and take their time fixing the rest. To most computer users, believing a software publisher who says "trust me," does not, well, compute.

Software publishers can see the threat of major cyberwar attacks made possible by flaws in their software, and the furious backlash that could result. Fear is a great motivator, and when it comes to cyberwar, there's a lot to be afraid of.

Important Things to Do

If you've been hit by a virus, like "I Love You," "Melissa," "Code Red," or "Nimda," then you have already been a casualty of a cyberwar skirmish at least once. You have probably been a casualty more often than that, for if you were online and noted that the Internet seemed "sluggish," it's quite possible that was because someone in your neighborhood was getting hit with a major DDOS attack. That will slow down portions of the nearby Internet. There are other ways to get hurt on the Internet. Had a credit card number stolen from a Web site you patronize? That's another common misadventure Internet users have to deal with.

It's not paranoia if you are afraid this could get worse. Cyberwar doesn't require one to build a lot of weapons. All you need is a few hundred people willing to do the dirty work, and a library of nasty tricks no one has seen before. A major cyberwar, "The Big One" could knock you off the Internet for days or weeks, and might even trash everything on your hard drive.

So how to protect yourself? There are ways to do it.

Pay attention, now. And while you're doing that, bookmark www.cert.org, the one Web site that will always have the latest information on Web security. The CERT (Computer Emergency Response Team) site is one of several that can be used as a one-stop location for what is going on in Internet security.

Below are the specific remedies. The items are ranked in order of importance. This is done to point out that, while there are a lot of ways for a hacker to get at your PC, the reality is that hacker attacks are rare. The most common hacker problems are those viruses that spread automatically because of flaws in Microsoft software (especially the scripting used in their Outlook e-mail program). Of the eleven items listed below, the first three will give you the greatest amount of protection. So pick the level of security you are most comfortable with.

1. If you are using Microsoft software, especially the Outlook (or Outlook Express) e-mail program, turn off the scripting. This in itself is not easy, especially with all those different Microsoft operating systems. To find out how to do this for whatever version of Outlook you have, go to www.microsoft.com and search there for "disable scripting" (without the quotes). Up will pop a document on how to do it for your PC.

2. Don't to anything with a file attachment if you don't know what it is, were not expecting it, or received it from someone you don't know. Even if you get one those "funny thing" (pictures, programs, or documents) files that people like to pass around, wait a day or two before opening it. Let someone else get hit and raise the alarm. If you have macro execution turned off for Word and Excel files, you can open these documents safely. But it's better to be consistent. If you don't know where a file came from, find out. And if you can't, then delete it. No great loss.

3. If you use Microsoft Office, and want to avoid macro viruses, turn off the macro execution. If you use Word97, you do this by using the mouse to click Tools/Options/General and check "Macro virus protection." In Word 2000 it's done differently. Click on Tools/Macro/Security and choose High. That, in effect, turns off macro execution. If you have another version of Word, go to www.microsoft.com and look for "disable macros." The same procedures are used for the Excel spreadsheet program. Although not as deadly or widespread as e-mail viruses, the macro viruses (executed when you open the document) have been around since 1995 (for Word, 1996 for Excel).

4. Be careful when you download files. If at all possible, only download material from reputable sites. There are still a lot of infected (with viruses and other destructive routines) program files out there on the Internet. "Reputable sites" are ones belonging to major companies or people you know. What makes a reputable site safe are the people who are running the site. They will run all downloadable programs and files past an antivirus program before making it available. A lot of smaller sites don't do this, and that's one reason viruses stay in circulation.

5. A lot of vulnerabilities to viruses and such are fixed with updates to your operating system and other software. As flaws are found in this software, the publishers prepare free programs you can download and run to "patch" your software. Your operating system and major, software programs have information in their Help systems about where to get the updates. Many recent versions of software will also use an available Internet connection to automatically update themselves. AOL's user software has been doing this for years.

6. Another useful bit of security software is an antivirus program. This is usually loaded when you turn your computer on. These just look for viruses (and other malicious software) and eliminates them when found. Installing the antivirus software to run on your PC full-time will sometimes destabilize your system and create problems when you are downloading material from the Web or trying to install new software. Keep in mind, however, that if you don't have a firewall, and are using Microsoft software, there are flaws in that software that can allow hackers to get into your PC without using an e-mail virus or document macro. Actually, if you are careful where you get files or e-mail attachments on the Internet, or what you put onto your PC, you can just run the antivirus program on your system around once a month just to be safe. When you run the antivirus software, it will also check to make sure it has the latest database of known viruses. All you have to do is be online. So check out the antivirus information. For solutions, go to any search engine and enter "antivirus software" (include the quote marks) and you will be shown the latest defensive software. It's a rapidly changing field, so it's safest to let a search engine take you to the latest versions of the available antivirus software.

7. Check to make sure you have turned off file sharing. This option (on Microsoft operating systems) is found either under Network Properties or under Properties and is called Sharing for your storage device or File and Print Sharing. You don't need file sharing if you are not on a local network. Home PCs often have file sharing turned on (by accident, usually when someone was playing around with the settings on the computer) and the only use of file sharing in this situation is if a hacker gets into your PC.

8. It's not a bad idea to dispense with Outlook (at least for e-mail, the calendar/scheduler ain't half bad). There's Eudora (www. eudora.com), which has been dealing with e-mail longer, and

more safely, than Outlook. Eudora (and many similar products) will easily replace Outlook. If you are an AOL user, you are already safer. Unlike for Outlook, very few computer viruses are written to attack users of the AOL e-mail program. Although AOL has over 30 million users, there are over ten times that many people using other ISPs to get on the Net, and most of these people have Microsoft software. Moreover, the AOL and Eudora (and other non-Microsoft e-mail programs) are written with more attention to security. So malicious hackers have two reasons to target Outlook users: Microsoft produces more vulnerable software, and there's a lot more of it out there.

9. Passwords have always been the biggest computer-security problem, and the biggest vulnerability on (or off) the Internet. You should change your passwords often and use ones that are difficult for hacker tools to figure out. This means a hard-to-remember combination of at least eight letters and numbers. As a practical matter, most people won't put up with hard-to-remember passwords if they have a choice. Which is why in many organizations where you don't have a choice, you see a lot of Post-it notes with passwords written down taped to computer screens. Help is on the way in the form of biometrics, a technique that uses things like fingerprints, face shape, or even your "fist" (how you pound the keyboard) to identify you. But in the meantime, "think different" when it comes to inventing passwords.

10. Don't always use the "save password" option for programs or Web sites. While this option saves you time in the future (you don't have to enter your password again), it is possible for hackers to read these passwords from files stored in hidden folders on your hard drive. So passwords to things like your bank or brokerage accounts should not be saved on the hard drive, although it's probably not necessary for things like getting into Web sites. It won't cost you any money if someone grabs the passwords for some news or entertainment Web site.

11. Don't store credit card information or online bank account or brokerage information on your computer. This means entering your password manually when you go to your banking or brokerage site. If you keep a list of credit card information on your computer, don't leave it on your hard drive; instead, copy it to a floppy disk and keep that somewhere else. If passwords are stored on bank or brokerage computers, that's a different matter. The large financial institutions have much better Internet security

than the average home does. If anyone cracks into your home PC, they will be looking for passwords and credit card information If you must store this kind of information on your computer, use encrypted folders to store it in. Microsoft operating systems like NT, 2000, and XP all support this, and there are programs available for operating systems that don't have the encryption built in. If someone cracks into your system, they could get around your encryption, but it does provide an extra layer of protection. To find software to encrypt folders on your hard drive, go to a search engine (like google.com) and enter "encrypted folders" (with the quotes) and up will come the latest products available. Some may be free, the others will be inexpensive.

For Cable Modem or DSL Users

If you have a fast, always-on connection (cable modem or DSL), you need a firewall program. Without a firewall, you are a sitting duck for hackers. When you used a telephone modem, you were protected from a lot of hackers because you got a new Internet (IP) address each time you logged in. But with always-on connections, you usually get your own, permanent address from your access (cable or phone company) provider. This makes it easier for a hacker to find you again. But more important for the hacker, you have a very fast connection. This allows more damage to be done to others using several attack methods. Since your PC is always on the Internet, you are more likely to be spotted by hackers scanning the Net for places to park their weapons or as way stations for more ambitious hacks. A firewall program will not stop a really determined hacker, although it can slow down any hack attempts on your system. A firewall also acts (literally) like a burglar-alarm system. That means that it will often cause most hackers to move on to a less well-protected target. The only major operating system to have one built-in is Windows XP. You can find firewall programs in most software stores. Online, go to a search engine and type in "firewall programs" and you'll see several available, as well as user discussions about how to use them. There are several good firewalls available for free (only for home use). At first, firewalls are a bit confusing and sometimes troublesome to use. You get asked to accept or refuse contact from a lot of sources you have never heard of. It all makes sense if you are an Internet expert, but is a bit perplexing for most people. Fortunately, you can just say no to those firewall questions about letting connections in or out, and just sort it out by trial and error. Such is the price of security. By the end of the decade, most of the usability problems with firewalls will probably be solved. Competition does that, and remember that this will eventually (maybe in five to ten years) tighten up security on the Internet quite a bit. A lot of upcoming Internet software pays a great deal more attention to security. But in the meantime, you may be at considerable risk. In the spirit of full disclosure, it should be pointed out that only a small fraction of fast-connection PC users would be used for a cyberwar attack. Only a few thousand PCs, at most, would be needed for such an operation. That's less than one fast-connection PC in a thousand. But the attacker might decide that there is military value in destroying data on most fast-connection PCs in the United States. This could be done with a few custom viruses.

Unix/Linux Users

The following is for Unix or Linux users. If you aren't one, you can skip this item. Unix or Linux users also get hacked, but not as much as Microsoft systems. Even so, there are things you can do to minimize your vulnerability. For example, don't use "root" for anything that doesn't have to be in root. In particular, don't run shells like X Windows or apps like IRC in root. These programs are easier for hackers to get into, and once they do, they have root access and, therefore, the ability to do some real damage. Also be sure to stay patched, turn off all services you don't need, and keep backups current. These warnings apply most specifically to Linux users. Unix has long been the operating system for the professionals. But Linux is now hitting a broader market. While Linux and Unix are safer than Microsoft operating systems, there are still dangers.

Remember, no matter how good the operating system, any server or PC can be penetrated if the attacker is capable and persistent enough. Script kiddies and black-hat hackers will tend to avoid any PC that appears to have some protection. But in most cases, a successful attack results in some kids finding a place to park more zombies, his pornography collection, stolen movie videos, or pilfered credit card information. There's also a chance your hacked PC will be taken over by some foreign cybersoldier or Middle Eastern cyberterrorist looking for a place from which to launch cyberwar attacks. So put up a little resistance and they will go away and find an easier place to work. It's like the joke about what to do if you and a friend encounter an angry bear. Bears can run faster than any human. But to escape in this situation, you don't have to run faster than the bear, only faster than your friend.

Don't Worry, Be Happy

If you do all you reasonably can to keep your PC safe, there's no point in getting upset if something nasty hits you anyway. For whatever gets to you under those circumstances is probably hitting a lot of other people and Web sites. That, at least, puts a lot of others under a great pressure to do something (that you have probably already done). One of the fundamental truths about the Internet is that it is relatively easy to defend yourself. But because most people don't take the technology very seriously, and there's no reason they shouldn't, many more people are very vulnerable to Internet attacks. PC and software manufacturers have long realized that they could not sell a large amount of hardware and software unless the PC was about as easy to use as a toaster oven. Okay, that may be overstating it. But VCR manufacturers learned over the years that their "easy-to-use" programming features baffled most users. PC makers took that to heart; witness the success of the Macintosh and Windows "point and click" concept for using computers. Unfortunately, no one was able to catch the Internet during its development stages and impose some sturdy security. One of the great debates among Internet developers is the need for reform for the way the Internet is run and the software it runs on. What we are likely to see is the emergence of a new Internet, one that will deal with things like spam, security, and protection from vandals who unleash viruses for no better reason than to see what kind of mayhem it will create. Help is on the way, and you can afford to wait if you take a few precautions (as listed above).

APPENDICES

U.S. Air Force and Cyberwar

In 2001 the U.S. Air Force complained that after a decade of defense cuts there was a serious problem with, as the air force puts it, an aging fleet of aircraft that must be replaced. This itself is a contentious issue as the air force is designing and building aircraft to compete with opponents that no longer exist. Nevertheless, the air force wanted a minimum of $20 billion extra per year to deal with projected shortfalls of $7 billion (or more) a year starting in 2002. What caused the shortfall was the air force's desire to pursue nontraditional forms of warfare, in particular Information War. This includes Internet-based warfare, something the air force has been active in throughout the 1990s. Indeed, so successful has the air force been in its Information War efforts that it has lost the most-skilled cyberwarriors to more lucrative civilian careers. Well, the air force doesn't lose these ace Information Warriors completely, they can, and often do, hire them back as civilian contractors (at several times what it cost to pay them when they were air force officers and NCOs).

The Afghanistan War and the war on terror solved the air force's budget problems. But while a lot of that new money may buy things they don't really need, the money spent on cyberwarfare is being put to good use. Keep in mind that in 2002, the United States government spent $44.9 billion on computers, software, and networks. Half of that was spent by the Department of Defense. And nearly half of that was spent, or controlled by, the air force. And the best way to explain how they did that is to read it in the air force's own words.

STATEMENT OF: Lieutenant General John L. Woodward, Jr., USAF Deputy Chief of Staff, Communications and Information, United States Air Force, Information Assurance, before the House Armed Services Committee transcript, May 17, 2001

Mr. Chairman, distinguished members of the committee, thank you for your continued interest in this nationally important issue. This is the Air Force's fourth opportunity to provide testimony on this important subject. Through the support of Congress, our journey over the last four years has continued to strengthen our network protection posture. As an aerospace force, information and decision superiority remain critical to Air Force's global vigilance, reach, and power. As our Air Force Chief of Staff, Gen. Ryan states, "Our information systems and networks go to war with us—and because they are part of the fight—we must treat them as weapon systems."

In 1997, the Air Force began its work to create a strong network protection posture as it transformed its doctrine to establish Information Superiority as a critical warfighter-enabling tool. At that time, we had plans in place to provide every Air Force base with an intrusion detection system. Although we began to field firewalls, they were the exception. In addition to prototyping base network-control centers, we developed a Defense in Depth security concept, known as Barrier Reef, and our Air Force Computer Emergency Response Team (AFCERT) was starting its fourth year of operation.

In 1998, with Congressional funding support, we completed an aggressive program to install an initial suite of network management capabilities and base information protection (NMS/BIP) tools at 109 bases. We also installed firewalls, scanning tools, and network management tools at our main bases. We were in full swing with our concept of "Operationalizing and Professionalizing the Networks," in other words, we were treating networks like the weapon systems they had become. To maximize the effectiveness of our deployable networks and ensure the skills to manage them are widely available, the tools fielded with our Theater Deployable Communications suites (our go-to-war communications package) mirror the core tools installed at our fixed bases.

By 1999, the AFCERT became the Air Force component to the Joint Task Force for Computer Network Defense and we published our initial Information Operations Doctrine. Every Air Force base had a Network Control Center with an initial network protection tool set and we began establishing Network Operations and Security Centers at our Major Commands. Following Operation DESERT FOX we shored up our cyber-defenses as intrusion attempts into our base networks continued to grow.

By the year 2000, intrusion detection systems were protecting every Air Force base, actively scanning our networks for malicious activity and vulnerabilities. We upgraded our information protection tool sets and we operationally tasked our Network Control Centers to report their readiness, like every major weapon system, through the Status of Resources and Training System. We are running a world-class weapon system, our network, but the threats to it are real and dangerous. Operation ALLIED FORCE tested our mettle and we withstood what many refer to as the first "cyberwar" effort.

In my testimony today, I will focus my remarks on our operational Information Assurance successes, the network environment we work in, and the Air Force way ahead with Information Assurance.

OPERATIONAL SUCCESSES

The Air Force has adopted and directed an exciting concept called One Air Force—One Network. This concept revolves around an enterprise, or corporate networking environment, and capitalizes on industry-best practices. The Air Force is leveraging the power of the Net and is putting that power in every airman's hand. In fact, we continue to leverage information superiority for combat success even though our communications networks are repeatedly subjected to probing, barrages of e-mail, and the "virus of the week" program. However, mission operations continue unaffected. Let me illustrate with a few examples:

- Our integrated information enterprise captured over 315 million suspicious connection attempts last year on our AF sensor grid, which resulted in one unauthorized connection by an outsider for every 20 million suspicious connection attempts. In all, no mission impacts occurred. This is information assurance.
- The Air Force recently raised our Information Condition (INFOCON) to a higher state of readiness because of the advertised hacker activity after the EP-3 incident. We have successfully combated increased hacking incidents against our mission capability.
- Critical to the success of any Expeditionary Aerospace Force is the previously mentioned Theater Deployable Communications (TDC). To date, we fielded over thirty-three lightweight multi-band satellite terminals providing long-haul reachback capability. Our integrated communications access package that provides deployed base communications infostructure similar to the fixed bases was certified for joint interoperability.
- The reachback concept continues to work well for our Global Reach and Power missions. Our information systems, consisting of both commercial off-the-shelf and military communications equipment, enabled reliable, timely reachback to the continental United States for intelligence, logistics and people support that otherwise would have had to deploy forward to Joint Task Force—South West Asia.
- Our response to viruses has also improved. In the recent past, the

"ILOVEYOU" and the "Melissa" viruses infected e-mails were opened by many users. Today, as a result of training, awareness, policy, and procedures, virus infected e-mails like "Naked Wife" and "Anna Kournikova" were not opened.

Despite our successes, we can't underestimate the dangers facing us in the information age. Just because we've had little trouble defending ourselves does not mean we are safe from cyberattack. The cyberattacks we continue to experience are real and dangerous. In the final analysis, our information assurance posture has ensured cyberattacks are nothing more than a nuisance with little impact on combat operations, but we must continue to learn and improve to remain ahead of the threat.

INFORMATION ENTERPRISE ENVIRONMENT AND AIR FORCE POSTURING

Powerful and sophisticated threats continue to change, thus challenging our ability to maintain an information superiority posture. We work to prevail over these challenges through a Defense in Depth strategy that integrates the capabilities of people, operations, and technology. This strategy ensures we deliver accurate information to the warfighter anytime, anyplace. Our philosophy is simply that security is everyone's business and that we treat every computer incident as a potential attack until proven otherwise. To that end, we are aggressively pursuing awareness and training programs.

- To emphasize that Information Assurance is the responsibility of every Air Force member, the Air Force Chief of Staff initiated a year-long IA awareness and implementation campaign that began in January 2001. As an Air Force–wide campaign, each Major Command and Air Force agency sponsors a month and develops the specific program for that month for the entire Air Force. The campaign is designed to win battles and win wars by ensuring all users are aware of and executing their IA responsibilities.
- Commanders are involved at all levels to maintain awareness over threats to and attacks against our networks. We've established firm guidelines in conjunction with DoD, for implementing Information Conditions (INFOCONs) that assure commanders are correctly postured day-to-day as well as being prepared for network attacks at any time. In addition, the Air Force modifies its operational reporting process and now requires mandatory reports for all network intrusion incidents.
- The AF participates fully in DoD's Information Assurance Vulnerability Alert process and further complements it with our AF Time

Compliance Network Order system. Our effort ensures vulnerabilities are identified and the risks mitigated through network patches, and a commensurate command and control reporting system that is in place at all levels and is auditable.

- The Air Force's centralized computer emergency response organization is the 33rd Information Operations Squadron (a.k.a., the Air Force Computer Emergency Response Team). At the Forward Edge of the Cyber Battle Area, our frontline warriors are the communications professionals in the Major Commands' Network Operations and Security Centers and base level Network Control Centers. Together they monitor Air Force networks in real-time to identify malicious activity. The 33rd IOS will downward-direct defensive actions and initiate up-channel reporting to the Joint Task Force-Computer Network Operations. They are also responsible (in conjunction with the DoD CERT) for identifying network vulnerabilities and directing their mitigation and follow-up compliance reporting. Our network professionals assure day-to-day mission communications while countering malicious activity.

- We test our IA security policy and procedures through compliance inspection activities. Compliance testing is done through policy directed, mission-based inspections similar to our Operational Readiness Inspections and Nuclear Surety Inspections that exercise our installations' ability to survive-to-operate in an operational environment. The Air Force Inspector General also focuses on specific IA management activities through the use of Special Inspection Items. The Air Force Information Warfare Center also conducts several technically based IA assessments to include: Red Teaming, Computer Security Engineering Assessments, Multi Disciplinary Vulnerability Assessments, and Information Assurance Assessment and Assistance Program Assessments. Red Teams regularly probe our networks, augmenting scans performed by the AFCERT and our network control facilities. We obtain independent validation through Air Force Audit Agency and Inspector General inspections.

- We continually exercise and test our networks to ensure user information is available at the right time and in the right format. Scenario events are crafted to allow people to practice using our processes and tools in a realistic environment. We recently participated in CJCS Exercise POSITIVE FORCE 2001, which included the largest Computer Network Defense exercise to date—the players included nearly every CINC, all Services, and many Agencies. Additionally, annual exercises such as the Joint User Interoperability Communications Exercise (JUICE) allow us to specifically test deployable communication configurations and their interfaces to the Global Information Grid. Besides providing great training opportunities, these types of events allow us to refine our equipment configurations, monitor the applicability of tool sets, and evaluate our reporting procedures.

- As a complementary function, the Air Force deploys several Scope Network support teams to Air Force bases to fine-tune base-level networks. These highly skilled, focused teams will completely baseline the Air Force network's performance by visiting every Air Force installation this year. Their enterprise approach will assure standardization, security configuration, and standard Air Force–wide network performance. Scope Network's mission is to optimize and tune networks to ensure the network and firewalls are properly configured. Scope Net teams also provide hands-on measurement, analysis, training, and mentoring to keep Defense in Depth at its strongest possible capability. Information content experts complement these two functions by detecting and directing the efficiencies of information assets.

We face a considerable challenge, as does industry, on the people front to recruit, train, and retain qualified network technicians able to build, run, and sustain the information technologies that enable us to be so effective. While there are no simple and quick solutions to the people challenge, we continue to operate at a high state of readiness. Let me give you some examples:

- Just as aircraft operators and maintainers must be certified before working on an aircraft, network operators and maintainers must be certified before working on a network. A Mission-Essential Task List was developed to ensure strict enforcement of network "mission" qualifications and that only mission-ready people deploy. This improves our support for combat operations. When called, these licensed professionals deploy in Information Warfare flights consisting of an integrated Information Operation team to include a deployed Network Operations Security Center.
- We recognize that, not only is training our key IA people important, but we must also find ways to incentivize people to stay in the Service. A Gartner Group study determined that retention comes from both monetary and psychological compensation. Monetary compensation for our military members comes through Selective Reenlistment Bonuses for 17 of our 21 enlisted career fields (including the highest available bonus for 3 critical career fields). Air Force leadership is pursuing a critical skills retention bonus, and a thrift savings plan that matches funds for critical skills. For our civilian people, OPM implemented a special salary rate basis for Information Technology workers. Psychological compensation is provided via

several initiatives that target training, professional development, and personnel actions. They include Aerospace Communications-and-Information Expertise (ACE) officer accession and development strategy, the Operationalizing and Professionalizing the Network (OPTN) program includes officer continuing education, the Keesler Air Force Base Center of Excellence, investing in basic and advanced communications technical training, supplemental courses, network training centers, and structured on-the-job (OJT) training, the SCOPE Champion senior civilian development initiative, and self-service information available on the Air Force portal.

These efforts inwardly focus on what we're doing to enhance our people strengths. We must also maintain our focus on mitigating the external threats to our networks. Individual hackers and hacker groups have proliferated over the last year and we must always remain vigilant against the potential of these attacks every day. Good networks, good procedures, good training, and good protection tools are the bedrock of our defense.

As I said earlier, viruses remain a potential threat. In the recent past, "I LOVEYOU" and "Melissa"-virus infected e-mails were opened by many and it resulted in significant numbers of our e-mail servers being isolated from the network to either prevent infection or to clean the systems due to infection. Today, as a result of training, awareness, policy, and procedures, virus infected e-mails like "Naked Wife" and "Anna Kournikova" were inoculated and not opened. As computer systems users received suspect e-mails, they took appropriate actions not taken before. However, these examples provide a stark reminder that we CANNOT ever let our guard down.

Let me point out what we are doing or have done to mitigate threats to our information systems:

- network lock downs
- known vulnerabilities closed
- standardized base information protection and firewall configurations
- installed automated antivirus software and altering all units when a new virus appears
- using intrusion detection systems
- standardizing Internet scanning tools
- network consolidation actions and building 9 Network Operations and Security Centers

We also developed and fielded a suite of defensive tools for our deployed Network Control Centers and Network Operations and Security Centers.

Way Ahead—Roadmap

We've accomplished a lot over the past year, but we must continue to raise the bar. Just as Congress saw the need for stronger information system security by passing the Government Information Security Reform within the FY2001 Defense Authorization Act, the Air Force is and will continue to push for greater security. Several key initiatives are highlighted below.

- Technology/Architectures. The Air Force continues to upgrade the information technology components at all operating locations. Our Combat Information Transport System (CITS), Network Management System, and Base Information Protection Program is entering its third phase, as described in the beginning of this testimony. In the first two phases, the Air Force provided the hardware needed to protect our base network boundaries, including firewalls, intrusion detection systems, standardized network management systems at active duty and reserve AF bases, and virtual private networks to geographically separated units. Phase three provides tool sets needed to manage and protect the Air Force Enterprise through Major Commands' Network Operations and Security Centers and the Air Force Network Operations Center.
- In conjunction with the fielding of these tool sets, we are creating an Air Force Intranet to limit our exposure to the Internet. We are reducing our gateways from 109 base enclaves to 9 Network Operations and Security Centers. In addition, we are establishing a common-user virtual private network to secure and protect all network traffic among Air Force sites. We are also establishing community-of-interest virtual private networks to protect specific functional users.
- We benchmarked corporate Info Tech concepts with industry IT leaders and are now on the fast-track to implement an Air Force Enterprise as part of the Global Information Grid. We are moving from a system of stand-alone information systems supporting individual functional communities to "network-centric" operations using Web-enabled applications supporting multiple users.
- Public Key Infrastructure (PKI). Another technology we are incorporating into our Defense in Depth strategy is the use of a common, integrated, interoperable DoD Public Key Infrastructure to enable security services at multiple levels of assurance.
- Common Access Card (CAC). We are adopting smart card technology throughout the USAF. The CAC will replace the standard identification card for military, civilian, and eligible contractors. This smart card will be used to enable physical access to buildings and controlled spaces and will be used to gain access to the Department's computer network capabilities.

- Biometrics. Thanks to Congressionally provided monies, the AF has moved out smartly to implement biometrics initiatives in support of DoD efforts. Our strategy is to evaluate technologies to support the Information Assurance Roadmap along with Force Protection, Medical Readiness, Nuclear Surety, and Weapons Systems Protection. We established a formal partnership with the Army's Biometrics Management Office and their Biometrics Fusion Center. We are developing our own pilot program at the Air Force Communications Agency.
- Cryptographic Modernization Roadmap. Air Force supports the National Security Agency and OSD effort to modernize our cryptographic capabilities. We have partnered with our operational and acquisition communities to identify our most critical requirements.
- Presidential Decision Directive 63 (Critical Infrastructure Protection). The Air Force is marching lockstep with the broad federal and DoD efforts to protect our critical infrastructures. We have functional community representatives for each critical sector developing their Defense Infrastructure Sector Assurance Plans. Additionally, we are working with DoD and looking for ways to improve on-going functional assessment processes toward an integrated vulnerability assessment approach.
- Leadership and Organizational Initiatives.
- Information Operations General Officer Steering Group (IO GOSG). In March 2000, a cross-functional senior Air Force steering group reviewed how we organize, train, equip, and sustain IO forces; provided guidance and direction to ensure successful integration of the significant investments we made and were projected to make. The next IO GOSG is scheduled for June 2001. That meeting will address a wide range of issues to include: depiction of our tactical, operational and strategic information, network protection, and architecture defense, and finalization of Air Force Doctrine 2-5.
- Information Assurance Steering Group. The Air Force also established a cross-functional IA Steering Group to review, develop, coordinate, and recommend IA positions. The steering group is composed of senior-level officers and key civilians from throughout the Air Force. Representatives from across the research and development, acquisition, policy, and operations communities meet to review Air Force IA strategy, policy, architectures, technology, programs, and associated funding requirements. The steering group's intent is to provide a clear and consistent IA policy, mitigate duplication of efforts, and coordinate organizational efforts to ensure that the Air Force has the resources to implement its IA strategy.
- Information Operations Numbered Air Force (IO NAF). On 1 February 2001, the Air Force realigned our IO warfighting forces under

existing Numbered Air Force (NAF) command and control structure. Our Air Intelligence Agency (which was previously a Field Operating Agency subordinate to the HQ USAF, Deputy Chief of Staff for Operations) was realigned under the Air Combat Command's 8th AF strengthening the Air Force's command and control capabilities for Information Assurance and Information Operations.

- Air Force Network Operations and Security Center (AFNOSC). The USAF is developing an AFNOSC to fully integrate network security and operations functions under a single commander with tactical control to direct enterprise-level actions. This unified capability should result in an integrated, common operational picture with a rapid response and surge capacity and a high level of survivability for continuity of operations. The AFNOSC will be the "tip of the spear" for all USAF network management, information assurance, and computer network defense.
- Military Communications Electronics Board (MCEB). Communications among the Services and Agencies is critical to warfighter success. We participate in the MCEB functionally oriented panels. The functions included are C4I and Data Systems Interoperability, Frequency Management, IA, Military Communications Procedures, and Publications, Standards, Networks Operations, and Interoperability Testing. The MCEB coordinates on operational guidance and direction to the CINCs, Services, and Agencies.

The Air Force is focused on the right issues and building the programs that provide the best information service and information protection possible. Our Air Force Posture Statement highlights the importance of Information Superiority and Information Assurance and our programs demonstrate our commitment to that goal. We need support for all levels for our Information Assurance and base infostructure programs. Our Information Technology Exhibit will support the Air Force effort to leverage networked information systems that guarantee our Information Superiority. Information Assurance is my highest priority, and the Air Force is committing resources to provide it, but we could still do more. We're ready to put any additional resources to work, whether it is funding additional Combat Information Transport System capabilities, accelerating implementation of the base infostructure, securing all Internet connections including our telephone switches, or for training and retaining people for the future.

We need to explore avenues to successfully investigate and prosecute computer intrusion, computer vandalism, and computer crimes. The foundation of our Information Technology laws owes its legacy to telecommunications law and specifically links back to the Communications Act of 1934. It was good and appropriate for its time. However, the cyber world is moving at light speed and we need laws that deal with today's reality. The ability to track down or search for hackers who vandalize Web pages or organized hacking groups that infiltrate information systems and extract sensitive information CANNOT hinge upon outdated criminal or civil legal processes. The law needs to catch up with the realities of cybercrime and investigative needs by "out of box thinking" such as use of verbal search requests and dedicated IT-trained approval magistrates. It is our understanding that the Department of Justice is considering legislation to address these issues, and any such effort warrants your fullest attention. We also need to send a clear and hard-hitting public message—you violate the computer network laws, we will hunt you down and hold you accountable.

As presented earlier, any and all additional compensation opportunities for our communications and information warriors—our intellectual capital—is welcomed and encouraged. We will use this, for example, for critical skills training and to fund additional communications officer and enlisted continuation education.

Our Nation and our Air Force can be very proud of our communications and information warriors. Throughout the spectrum of conflict and in the competency of Information Superiority and Decision Superiority, the U.S. military has no peer. The United States Air Force is organized to win, prepared for the now and the future, and committed to supporting our nation's security needs—anytime, anywhere.

NIPC (National Infrastructure Protection Center)

For those who like to attack the Internet, one of their major assets is the inability of governments to get their acts together. Case in point is the slowness with which the FBI became aware of cyberwar and developed the capability to deal with it. One of those capabilities was yet another organization, NIPC (National Infrastructure Protection Center). The NIPC was created in early 1998. As Michael A. Vatis, Director, National Infrastructure Protection Center, put it in testimony before Congress shortly after the NIPC was established:

Let me address briefly why the NIPC is located at the FBI. First, as you know, the FBI has had existing programs and authorities to investigate computer crimes and to prevent and investigate acts of espionage and terrorism. These programs and authorities naturally support and mesh with the infrastructure-protection mission. Second, in the case of most cyberattacks, neither the identity nor the objective of the perpetrator is known. This means it is often impossible to determine at the outset if an intrusion is an act of vandalism, computer crime, terrorism, foreign intelligence activity, or some form of strategic attack. The only way to determine the source, nature, and scope of the incident is to investigate. And the authority to investigate such matters—and to obtain the necessary court orders or subpoenas—normally resides with law enforcement. This does not mean that, once the perpetrator is identified and the scope of the attack known, the response is limited to law enforcement.

It simply means that in cases in which the only information we have is that an illegal intrusion has occurred, but we don't know the answers to "who, what, why, or how?" the initial response normally must come from law enforcement. But the FBI clearly must coordinate with, and have the support of, other agencies that may have relevant information or may need to be part of the response. For instance, if it is learned that an intrusion is part of a strategic, military attack, clearly the Defense Department and other agencies with national security responsibilities could be called on to respond.

MISSION AND COMPOSITION

The NIPC incorporates and expands the mission and personnel of the FBI's CITAC. The NIPC's mission is to detect, deter, warn of, respond to, and investigate unlawful acts involving computer intrusions and unlawful acts, both physical and cyber, that threaten or target our critical infrastructures. This means we do not simply investigate and respond to attacks after they occur, but we try to learn about them and prevent them beforehand. This is a large and very difficult task. It requires the collection and analysis of information gathered from all available sources (including law enforcement investigations, intelligence sources, data provided by industry, and open sources) and the dissemination of our analyses and warnings of possible attacks to potential victims, whether in the government or private sector. To accomplish this mission, the NIPC relies on the assistance of, and information gathered by, the FBI's 56 Field Offices; other Federal agencies; state and local law enforcement agencies; and perhaps most important, the private sector.

The Defense Department is important to our mission because its reliance on information technologies makes it a prime target for our adversaries and because it holds much of the government's expertise in defending against cyberattacks. Our intelligence agencies have a critical role because of their responsibility for gathering information about threats from abroad. And other civilian agencies with regulatory Jurisdiction or protective responsibility under PDD-63 for critical infrastructures—such as the Departments of Treasury, Energy, and Transportation—have similarly significant roles.

But infrastructure protection is not just a mission for the Federal government. State governments must be involved because they own and operate some of the critical infrastructures and because their agencies are often the first responders in the event of a crisis.

Finally, this mission requires the intensive involvement of the private sector. Private industry owns and operates most of the infrastructures, so it must be involved in helping us defend them. And it also has the greatest expertise in identifying and solving the technical problems.

In recognition of the vital roles all of these entities must play, I want to emphasize that the NIPC is founded on the notion of a partnership. We are building this partnership first through inclusive representation. Our intent is that the Center be staffed with professionals from other Federal agencies, from state and local law enforcement, and from private industry. This will foster the sharing of information and expertise, and improve coordination among all the actors in the event of a crisis. In addition, the Center will augment the physical presence of these representatives by establishing electronic connectivity to the many different entities in government and the private sector who might have—or need—information about threats to our infrastructures.

Equally important is the need to build a two-way street for the flow of information and incident data between the government and the private sector. The government, with unique access to national intelligence and law enforcement information, can develop a threat picture that no entity in the private sector could develop on its own. We need to share this with the industry. At the same time, we need to learn from industry about the intrusion attempts and vulnerabilities that it is experiencing. This will help us paint the vulnerability and threat picture more completely, and will give us a head start on preventing or containing a nascent attack. This is a new concept for all of us, particularly for the agencies that go to great lengths to protect sensitive sources and methods. But I believe this two-way dialogue is the only way to deal with our common concern about protecting our infrastructures. We believe it is possible to share the necessary information about threats and vulnerabilities without jeopardizing sources and methods, and without compromising companies' proprietary data. And we are currently designing rules and mechanisms to accomplish this.

Let me say at this point something about what we are not. We are not the Nation's super–systems administrator or security officer, responsible for securing everyone's infrastructures or systems against intruders or advising on the latest security software or patches to fix vulnerabilities. That role clearly must be filled by systems administrators in each company, by chief information officers in government agencies, and by industry groups and other entities (such as computer emergency response teams) with expertise in reducing vulnerabilities and restoring service. Rather, our role is to help prevent intrusions and attacks by gathering information about threats from sources that are uniquely available to the Government (such as from law enforcement and intelligence sources), combining it with information voluntarily provided by the private sector or obtained from open sources, conducting analysis, and disseminating our analyses and warnings to all relevant consumers. And, if an attack does occur, our role is to serve as the Federal government's focal point for crisis response and investigation. That is the mission the Center has been assigned. This job is big and difficult enough, and this is where we must keep our focus.

How the NIPC Is Organized

To accomplish its goals, the NIPC is organized into three sections:

- The Computer Investigations and Operations Section (CIOS) is the operational and response arm of the Center. It program manages computer intrusion investigations conducted by FBI Field Offices throughout the country, provides subject matter experts, equipment, and technical support to cyberinvestigators in federal, state, and local government agencies involved in critical infrastructure protection; and provides a cyberemergency response capability to help resolve a cyberincident.
- The Analysis and Warning Section (AWS) serves as the indications and warning arm of the NIPC, providing analytical support during computer intrusion investigations and long-term analyses of vulnerability and threat trends. When appropriate, it distributes tactical warnings and analyses to all the relevant partners, informing them of potential vulnerabilities and threats and long-term trends. It also reviews numerous government and private sector databases, media, and other sources daily to gather information that may be relevant to any aspect of our mission, including the gathering of indications of a possible attack.
- The Training, Administration, and Outreach Section (TAOS) coordinates the training and education of cyberinvestigators within the FBI Field Offices, state and local law enforcement agencies, and private sector organizations. It also coordinates our outreach to private sector companies, state and local governments, other government agencies, and the FBI Field Offices. In addition, this section manages our collection and cataloguing of information concerning "key assets" across the country. Finally, it provides the entire Center with administrative support, handling matters involving personnel, budget, contractors, and equipment.

A NIPC document provided more details about the theory behind what many other government agencies saw as overly ambitious empire building.

National Infrastructure Protection Center (NIPC): The NIPC will include FBI, USSS, and other investigators experienced in computer crimes and infrastructure protection, as well as representatives detailed from the Department of Defense, the Intelligence Community, and Lead Agencies. It will be linked electronically to the rest of the Federal Government, including other warning and operations centers, as well as any private sector sharing and analysis centers. Its mission will include providing timely warnings of intentional threats, comprehensive analyses, and law enforcement investigation and response.

All executive departments and agencies shall cooperate with the NIPC and provide such assistance, information, and advice that the NIPC may request, to the extent permitted by law. All executive departments shall also share with the NIPC information about threats and warning of attacks and about actual attacks on critical government and private sector infrastructures, to the extent permitted by law. The NIPC will include elements responsible for warning, analysis, computer investigation, coordinating emergency response, training, outreach, and development and application of technical tools. In addition, it will establish its own relations directly with others in the private sector and with any information sharing and analysis entity that the private sector may create, such as the Information Sharing and Analysis Center described below.

The NIPC, in conjunction with the information originating agency, will sanitize law enforcement and intelligence information for inclusion into analyses and reports that it will provide, in appropriate form, to relevant federal, state and local agencies; the relevant owners and operators of critical infrastructures; and to any private sector information sharing and analysis entity. Before disseminating national security or other information that originated from the intelligence community, the NIPC will coordinate fully with the intelligence community through existing procedures. Whether as sanitized or unsanitized reports, the NIPC will issue attack warnings or alerts to increases in threat condition to any private sector information sharing and analysis entity and to the owners and operators. These warnings may also include guidance regarding additional protection measures to be taken by owners and operators. Except in extreme emergencies, the NIPC shall coordinate with the National Coordinator before issuing public warnings of imminent attacks by international terrorists, foreign states, or other malevolent foreign powers.

The NIPC will provide a national focal point for gathering information on threats to the infrastructures. Additionally, the NIPC will provide the principal means of facilitating and coordinating the Federal Government's response to an incident, mitigating attacks, investigating threats, and monitoring reconstitution efforts. Depending on the nature and level of a foreign threat/attack, protocols established between special-function agencies (DOJ/DOD/CIA), and the ultimate decision of the President, the NIPC may be placed in a direct support role to either DOD or the Intelligence Community.

Information Sharing and Analysis Center (ISAC): The National Coordinator, working with Sector Coordinators, Sector Liaison Officials, and the National Economic Council, shall consult with owners and operators of the critical infrastructures to strongly encourage the creation of a private-sector information sharing and analysis center. The actual design and functions of the center and its relation to the NIPC will be determined by the private sector, in consultation with and with assistance from the Federal Government. Within 180 days of this directive, the National Coordinator, with the assistance of the CICG, including the National Economic Council, shall identify possible methods of providing federal assistance to facilitate the startup of an ISAC.

Such a center could serve as the mechanism for gathering, analyzing, appropriately sanitizing, and disseminating private-sector information to both industry and the NIPC. The center could also gather, analyze, and disseminate information from the NIPC for further distribution to the private sector. While crucial to a successful government-industry partnership, this mechanism for sharing important information about vulnerabilities, threats, intrusions, and anomalies is not to interfere with direct information exchanges between companies and the government. As ultimately designed by private-sector representatives, the ISAC may emulate particular aspects of such institutions as the Centers for Disease Control and Prevention that have proved highly effective, particularly its extensive interchanges with the private and nonfederal sectors.

Under such a model, the ISAC would possess a large degree of technical focus and expertise and nonregulatory and non–law enforcement missions. It would establish baseline statistics and patterns on the various infrastructures, become a clearinghouse for information within and among the various sectors, and provide a library for historical data to be used by the private sector and, as deemed appropriate by the ISAC, by the government. Critical to the success of such an institution would be its timeliness, accessibility, coordination, flexibility, utility, and acceptability.

GLOSSARY

Technobabble terms used in this book:

Apache is an Open Source Movement (that is, free) software program (also known as "server software") for running Web sites on a host computer. The majority of Web sites you see out there are run via Apache.

ARPANET stands for Advanced Research Projects Agency Network. This was what the Internet was called in the 1970s and '80s when it was still a Department of Defense research project.

Baud is the unit of data moved per second over a phone line via a modem. Roughly speaking, eight baud equals one letter or numeral. So a 300-baud modem (from the 1970s) can move about thirty-seven characters a second. Most modems today operate at 56,000 (or 56k) baud.

Buffer Overflow Exploitation is a technique whereby you send a certain type of data to a Web server and trigger a software flaw (which is common in many Microsoft products) that allows you to sneak in a virus or zombie program and, in effect, get inside the server despite defenses. There are many other types of bugs that can be exploited in this fashion. When these flaws are discovered, the publisher tends to quickly provide a fix. But sometimes it takes awhile, and in the meantime damage can be done. A major fear among cyberwarriors is that the enemy will find one of these flaws first, and that they will keep quiet about it. If no one else stumbles across the flaw, the people who know about it have the makings of a powerful cyberweapon.

Bulletin Board System (BBS) is a computer program that allows users to connect to the BBS via their modems (today this is done via the Internet) and read and write messages from and to all the people using that BBS. The Internet version of a BBS is Usenet, which has thousands of separate forums (for different topics).

CERT—Computer Emergency Response Team, an organization originally founded by the U.S. Department of Defense in 1988 to quickly analyze mischief, or major disasters, on the Internet. CERT operates out of Carnegie Mellon University. CERT still serves as the major international clearinghouse for problems on the Internet.

CIC—combat information center. Invented during World War II when a lot of electronic sensors (radar and sonar) appeared and it seemed a good idea to send all this information to one large room (on a ship or in a bunker) where it could be sorted out, and put on maps and displays so senior commanders could take it all in and make decisions. Today's CICs are a roomsful of computer displays. The CIC later became a staple of science-fiction descriptions of what the "bridge of a starship" should look like.

Crackers are hackers who are up to no good. These malicious Internet vandals are also called black-hat hackers. This is to differentiate them from the good hackers, also known as white-hat hackers. The Internet was basically built by a lot of hackers (programmers who "hack away" at a software problem until they get it right. That solution would be known as "a good hack").

CRT is cathode ray tube. That's your computer monitor. CRTs of a different sort are used in televisions.

Cyberpolice (or cybercops)—People in law enforcement (plus a number of Internet professionals who volunteer to help out) who have the skills to track down criminals operating on the Internet. In the 1990s, most of these were self-taught (cops who worked with computers as a hobby), but now there is a big rush to train a lot of law enforcement people to handle Internet crime.

Cyberwarrior is any military or government Internet specialist who knows how to make attacks using communications networks (like the Internet) and defend friendly networks from such attacks. Since World War II, this sort of thing has been called "electronic warfare." When the Internet is involved, civilian volunteers are often brought in for this work as well.

Data Mining is a new technology in which huge amounts of data, like purchases of products by millions of individuals over years, are used as statistical tools to find useful relationships. For example, what kinds of products do people buy before and during certain events (going on vacation or around holidays) and for different income levels. Data mining reveals patterns of purchasing previously unknown and enables more effective marketing. This approach to marketing has been around for over a century, but with data mining it's a lot faster and accurate.

Database is a computer file, often a very large one, with lists of information (names, addresses, and other stuff for all customers, employees, or whatever). Users of the database employ special software to find information in the database and update that data.

DDOS Attack—distributed denial of service attack, using several computers to send massive amounts of data to a Web site. Web sites can only handle a limited number of users at once. Normally, this is not a problem, but if you purposely try and grab all of a Web site's capacity, as in a DDOS attack, no one else can use the Web site.

Decision Cycle—is the time it takes to recognize new information, figure out what it means, make a decision, and act on it. In military terms, the fighter pilot, or infantry unit commander, with the shorter decision cycle will usually win. Decision cycles also play a role in designing software and fighting Internet crime. Speed counts.

Decryption is breaking codes (encryption) used to keep information secret. Before the twentieth century, this meant deciphering what amounted to puzzles, as encryption back then was based on things like substitution (using certain numbers or even symbols for letters). But in the last hundred years, machines were developed to use more complex codes, and computers were developed during World War II to more quickly try all the possible "substitutions" to crack the codes. Basically, decryption means either just using many powerful computers to try all substitution combinations until you can read the code, or (and this is what scares users of encryption the most) using special routines (algorithms) that find shortcuts in the substitution routines.

Encryption is using codes to make your e-mail or data difficult (or impossible) for someone else to use. Encryption has been around for thousands of years, and still uses the same basic principle of substituting what you wrote with other letters or numerals. Anyone with the decryption key (showing what must be substituted in the coded material to turn it back into something recognizable) can read the encrypted data. Computers changed the encryption business. One of the first, modern computers was invented during World War II to decrypt German codes. Since then, computers have been used to encrypt and decrypt (applying the key) coded messages. It is theoretically possible to use a computer to decrypt a coded message without using the key, but this takes a lot of computer time. Depending on how powerful the encryption code is, such "brute force decryption" is, for all practical purposes, impossible.

Fiber Optic is a type of cable for carrying data over long distances. Unlike the older wire (copper) cable that moves data with electrical signals, fiber optic uses light flashed through these bundles of hollow cables. Much more data can be moved more cheaply with fiber-optic cable.

FTP is file transfer protocol, which is a computer program that allows Internet users to get files (data or programs) from another computer.

Geek Magnet—Any organization, or activity, that attracts a lot of people with computer and Internet skills. Microsoft Corporation is a geek magnet, as are some types of software (like the Linux operating system).

Hacking is using your technical skills to work on a software program or the Internet. Usually the intention is to improve the way the software works, but evil hackers just want to destroy.

Honey Pot—A server set up on the Internet whose only purpose is to attract hackers. Once hackers find the Honey Pot server, and this usually happens within hours of the server going online, the intrusion detectors and tracking tools the Honey Pot is equipped with record everything the hackers do as they attempt to hack their way in. In this way, white-hat hackers (the good guys) find out what the black-hat hackers (the bad guys) are up to. There is a network of Honey Pot servers, called HoneyNet, where people share information on hackers with one another and law enforcement agencies. Most of the Honey Pots are run by volunteers, often paying the server expenses out of their own pockets.

IP Address is the "Internet protocol address" that every computer connected to the Internet must have so that it can instantly communicate with any other computer on the Internet. Think of it as your Internet "phone number."

ISP is Internet service provider. These are the companies, like AOL or EarthLink, that provide consumers with access to the Internet. Actually, what the ISPs do is pay a lot of money to telephone companies that build and maintain the Internet "backbone" of high-capacity long-distance lines that carry most of the Internet traffic (e-mail, Web page requests, file downloads and, well, you get the idea).

LAN is local area network, an inexpensive system of software and cables that connects many PCs in an office. The LAN itself is often connected to the Internet so all the LAN users can surf the Net.

Linux is a free operating system developed by the programmers of the Open Source Movement. Linux is rapidly becoming a popular operating system for businesses and schools. Although not as easy to install or maintain as commercial products (like Microsoft Windows), the software itself is free.

Mainframe Computers are what the largest, most expensive, complex, and powerful computers, short of supercomputers, are called. These machines usually take care of most of the computing needs of a large organization. Note that the first mainframes of the 1960s have less than 1 percent of the speed and storage capability of today's cheapest ($500) PC.

NIPC is the National Infrastructure Protection Center, founded by the FBI to assist in running down Internet criminals.

NIPRNET is the Department of Defense's unclassified Internet that only has a few connections to the regular Internet that the rest of us use.

Nodes are one (or more) servers (see definition below) that serve up the information for a Web site.

NSA—The U.S. National Security Agency. A top-secret organization (during the Cold War, the government wouldn't even admit it existed) that develops secret codes (encryption) to keep American secret communications secret. The NSA also works on how to crack enemy codes (decryption). The growing use of encryption on the Internet has attracted a lot of attention from the NSA.

OPSEC—The military term for Operational Security. OPSEC is the term given to all the things you do to keep the enemy from getting into your bases, buildings, or Internet servers.

PAO—Short for public affairs officer. These are the people who deal with the media. Every military force has them, for the media more and more has become a powerful weapon.

Password Guessing Tool—A program (often refered to as a "password dictionary") that uses a large (sometimes over a million entries) file of known or typical passwords to gain illegal entry into a password-protected Web site or server. All you need is a user name. These tools are not as useful as they used to be because more and more sites are shutting out a user name if too many incorrect passwords (three to ten, for example) are entered one after another. The site then tells the user to try again in five minutes or so. This is okay for a real user, but long enough to make password guessing ineffective. It would take days to grind through hundreds of thousands of possible passwords. Without the delay, the guessing tool could be in within minutes or, at most, an hour or so.

Psyops—Is short for psychological operations. This is playing mind games with the enemy. The crudest form is dropping leaflets on enemy troops explaining why they really ought to surrender. At its more sophisticated, psyops sets up radio stations that the enemy thinks are on their side, but are broadcasting demoralizing information.

Red Attack (or Red Team or Tiger Team) is a group of friendly Internet experts who will hack your system to see how good your defenses are. This can be expensive (starts at $5,000 and quickly runs to six figures), depending on how big your system is.

Remailer—Otherwise known as an "anonymous remailer service." This is a Web site that offers anonymity for your e-mail. You send e-mail to the remailer and it gives you an anonymous return address. In some cases, the remailer retains information that can, if forced by court order, reveal the true identity of those using a remailer. Other remailers destroy all evidence of the true identity of their users. Police and antiterrorism agencies are not happy with remailers, but they can be set up anywhere and would be very difficult to stamp out completely.

Script Kiddies—Generally young men, often teenagers, out for illicit Internet thrills via easy-to-use hacking tools available on the Internet. More of a nuisance than a threat, but from this, some go on to serious, and often criminal, hacking.

Security Software—These are programs that make your personal computer less liable to be damaged by attacks over the Internet (viruses, in particular). The most common security software is antivirus software (which monitors your PC for the presence of viruses and eliminates them when found) and firewall software (which keeps bad stuff from getting into your PC in the first place).

Server—A computer from which Web sites operate. A server is often just a PC, like the one you use at home, but with special software and a very fast connection directly to the Internet. Basically, any PC can be turned into a server with the right software and a direct connection (which is quite expensive—several hundred bucks a month and up) to the Internet.

SIPRNET is the Department of Defense's classified (secret) Internet that sends everything using encryption (coded) and is not connected to the Internet the rest of us use.

Smart Bombs—Regular old bombs (metal casings filled with explosives and dropped from aircraft) with guidance kits strapped on. These kits contain little fins powered by batteries and directed by a guidance system. Dumb bombs are not very accurate, landing around one hundred meters of where you are aiming. Smart bombs land within ten meters.

Sniffers are hacker tools that just collect information entering and leaving a computer (usually a server). The information is then sent to whoever planted the sniffer. Sniffers are good for picking up passwords and user IDs.

SysAdmin is short for system administrator. This is the person responsible for keeping a Web site, LAN (local area network in an office), or server going. It's a tricky job, as there are a lot of things that can go wrong, and the software that runs the server, Web site, or LAN must be constantly updated to keep everything running, and to keep the system secure from intruders. There are never enough good sysadmins available, and this produces a lot of Web sites that are very vulnerable to hacker attack.

TCP/IP is the set of standards for any computer to communicate over the Internet. Any computer with software that adhered to the TCP/IP standards could be connected to the Internet. This was a radical idea at the time (the 1970s), but was needed to put the "inter" in the Internet.

Trojan horses are programs masquerading as another, legitimate, program. Someone would modify a program that, for example, told you what day of the week it was for any date in the last two hundred years. The modification would add routines that did something cute, or nasty. Before the Internet came along, Trojan horses were an annoying form of vandalism you had to watch out for. There were many variations, but the basic idea behind Trojan horses was to get a program you didn't know about, or want, onto your PC. Trojan horses were first used as pranks, and performed harmless practical jokes (like having bugs crawl across your screen). But during the 1980s, the Trojan horses turned nasty; some destroyed data and programs. Some Trojan horses, once you ran them, would spread by modifying another program with the Trojan horse routines. At about the same time the Trojan horse creators began rapidly spreading their infected software via the BBS systems. Before that, most people were not online; most of the software was exchanged via floppy disk. Once BBSs became popular, distribution became faster, and Trojan horses got onto the (then new) hard drives. Out of all this came the antivirus software industry. Even now, however, most PC users still don't bother with antivirus software.

Vampires are worms or viruses whose sole purpose is to run so intensively that the infected computer can't do anything else. The results are like what happens when too many programs are run at once on your PC: it becomes very sluggish. A vampire running on a Web server will insure that most people trying to reach Web sites on that server will time out (drop connection due to no reply) because the vampire has slowed the server so much.

Virus is a computer program that, once it gets on your PC, will try and spread itself to other PCs via your e-mail address list and do any number of other things on your computer. Depending on the particular virus (over 70,000 have been identified to date), there may be no damage, or it may destroy all the data on your hard drive.

Wireless Internet Devices—They look like slightly oversize cell phones, but they are attached to the Internet instead of the phone system and use e-mail instead of voice messages.

Worms are viruses that don't attach themselves to other programs. For example, a logic bomb is a program that is hidden on a computer system and activates when certain conditions are met. At that point, the logic bomb goes off and does something. Usually something very bad. Logic bombs are generally inserted by a programmer that has legal access to the computer in question. Managers are always worried that an unhappy (and recently fired) programmer will leave a logic bomb that will go off if the departed programmer is no longer around to tell the logic bomb to keep waiting. When the logic bomb does go off, it does something unhelpful, like deleting payroll records or doing more subtle damage to business records. Those who create the logic bombs often get caught, and, in recent years, more of these wayward lads are being sent to prison.

Zombie is a program hackers slip into poorly protected computers (either a server running a Web site or a PC with a cable modem or DSL connection). There are dozens of different zombie programs, but what they all have in common is the ability to communicate with the hacker who put them there and seize some control over the computer they are planted in. Antivirus programs can spot, and remove, zombie programs.

INDEX